THE VICTORIA HISTORY OF ESSEX

NEWPORT

Anthony Tuck and others

VICTORIA
COUNTY
HISTORY

First published 2015

A Victoria County History publication

© The University of London, 2015

ISBN 978 1 909646 05 6

Cover image: View of the centre of Newport looking west from the hills to the east. © W.D.J. Evans.

Back cover image: The shell hood above the entrance to Crown House, Bridge End, Newport. © W.D.J. Evans.

Typeset in Minion pro by Emily Morrell

CONTENTS

IN MEMORIAM

Imogen Mollet and Joy Pugh,
who contributed so much to the study of Newport's history

LIST OF ILLUSTRATIONS

Unless otherwise stated the illustrations in this volume come from the collections of *Newport News* (NN) or the Newport Local History Group (NLHG). With thanks to both for permission to publish.

Figure

LIST OF MAPS

FOREWORD

I AM DEEPLY HONOURED to be asked to write this foreword, my qualifications for doing so being limited to the fact that I came to live in Newport in 1965 and have been the Managing Editor of our village magazine, *Newport News*, since I started it in 1974.

The Victoria County History of Essex has already covered parts of the east and south-west of the county, including those parishes which are now part of Greater London. This, however, is its first venture into north-west Essex, and the third to be published in the series of VCH 'shorts' dealing with just one parish.

Over the past 50 years Newport's population has virtually doubled to its present 2,400, with much further expansion envisaged. This reflects the village's position on a main London to Cambridge route, both for road and rail, its excellent primary school and long established secondary school, Joyce Frankland Academy, which dates from 1588. We also have a doctors' surgery, two public houses, a small supermarket and a lively community spirit. We are therefore a living village with a future as well as a past.

That past has been vividly brought to life under the talented team of researchers and writers which Anthony Tuck has gathered together. He is a retired Professor of Medieval History at Bristol University, whilst Bernard Nurse was formerly Librarian at the Society of Antiquaries – he was also one of the three authors of the award-winning *A Village in Time: the history of Newport, Essex,* which came out in 1995 and helped to inspire some of this volume.

Gillian Williamson was joint editor of *Littlebury, a Parish History,* whilst David Evans is the Village Recorder for Newport. Ben Cowell is the National Trust's Regional Director for the East of England, and James Bettley is the author of the revised edition of the Essex volume of Pevsner's *Buildings of England*. All six of the above have a solid record of published material behind them.

The combined input of this talented team has resulted in a scholarly, meticulous and informative history of the village of Newport which both the general reader and the academic can profitably consult and enjoy.

John Gordon MBE

ACKNOWLEDGEMENTS

THIS HISTORY OF THE PARISH of Newport in Essex has been written by five past or present members of the Newport Local History Group: Anthony Tuck (convenor of the VCH Group), Ben Cowell, David Evans, Bernard Nurse and Gillian Williamson. James Bettley, author of the revised edition of Pevsner's *Buildings of England: Essex* has contributed the material on the buildings of Newport, and we are grateful to Shirley Durgan for assisting with research on the economic history of Newport.

We have incurred numerous other debts of gratitude in the preparation of this volume. The Marc Fitch Fund generously gave the project a grant towards research expenses, fees and other costs, and *Newport News* also gave a grant towards the cost of licensing images for publication. We are grateful to the Managing Editor, John Gordon, for this and also for writing the Foreword to this volume.

At Newport, we owe a particular debt of gratitude to Angela Archer, former Editor of *Newport News*, for reading the whole of the book in draft and offering numerous suggestions and corrections. We also appreciate the kindness of several residents of Newport who made the deeds of their houses available for consultation, and we are grateful to the owners of the six houses in the village which were selected for dating by dendrochronology for their ready co-operation with that project. Christine Griffin, clerk to Newport Parish Council, kindly made the records of the Parish Council available to us. We are also grateful to Barney Miller of Design Mill, Newport, for cartographic work.

The dendrochronological analysis was carried out by Martin Bridge, of University College London, and funded by grants from the Vernacular Architecture Group, the Essex Society for Archaeology and History, the Stansted Airport Community Trust, and *Newport News*. We are grateful to all these bodies and to Dr Bridge. The dating project was separate from the VCH and will be published in full elsewhere, but the results are summarised here in Dr Bettley's section on the secular buildings of Newport.

Further afield, we have received help from the staff of numerous libraries, archives and county record offices, but in particular from Allyson Lewis and her colleagues at the Essex Record Office and Zofia Everett at the Archive Access Point in Saffron Walden Public Library. Tessa Murdoch at the Victoria and Albert Museum gave us useful information about her family, the Meyers of Shortgrove. Mrs Sally Campbell made private papers relating to the Smith family available to us, and Professor Henry French (Exeter University) allowed us to see the data from his study of the Essex Hearth Tax Returns. We are grateful to all of them.

Throughout the progress of the project we have benefited from the wise advice and helpful criticism of Christopher Thornton, the VCH Essex County Editor, who initiated us into the methods and style of the VCH. We owe him a great debt of thanks. We are also very grateful to the VCH Essex Trust for agreeing to underwrite the cost of publication of the volume.

At VCH Central Office we have had much help and guidance from Adam Chapman, Jessica Davies and Matt Bristow, and, at an earlier stage of the project, from the former Executive Editor of the VCH, Elizabeth Williamson. They have made working with the VCH Central Office a pleasure. We are also grateful to a former Director of the VCH, Professor John Beckett, who encouraged us to undertake the project in the first place and who kindly agreed to read the whole work in draft when it was completed.

Many owners of documents, whether in private hands or deposited in public collections, have allowed us to cite their material, and they are acknowledged in the relevant footnotes in the text.

INTRODUCTION

LANDSCAPE, POPULATION AND SETTLEMENT

Landscape and Geology

THE PARISH OF Newport lies in the valley of the river Cam about three miles south west of Saffron Walden and about nine miles north of Bishop's Stortford (Herts.). The village lies at the north end of the Stort–Cam gap, the high ground which divides the river systems flowing towards the Thames estuary (the Lea and the Stort) from the river Cam, which drains via the Great Ouse into The Wash. It is situated about three miles north of the source of the river Cam, and the surrounding area thus forms part of the North Sea drainage province. The village is on a significant landscape boundary, between the North Sea and the Thames/Channel drainage areas.[1]

During the Anglian glaciation about 450,000 years ago, ice sheets covered the chalk beds in north-west Essex that had been laid down during the Cretaceous period, and as the ice retreated boulder clay was deposited over the layers of chalk. The boulder clay layer was thin, and in some places, especially in the south of the parish, the chalk is exposed.[2] In the river valley itself the soil is mainly alluvium, poorly drained in places, giving rise to marshy land and ponds, and it is liable to flooding. Elsewhere in the parish the clay soil overlying the chalk proved ideal for crop growing, especially wheat, with the chalk being quarried for lime to improve the soil.[3]

The parish extends for about two and a half miles (4 km) from north to south, and about two miles (3.2 km) from east to west. The hamlet of Birchanger lay within its boundary on the west side of the river and north of Bury (or Wicken) Water; in 1086 it consisted of one hide only, and the name gradually fell out of use. On both the western and the eastern edges of the parish the land rises to about 350 ft (107 m.), while the river valley itself slopes gently from about 220 ft (67 m.) at the southern end of the parish to about 175 ft (53 m.) at Shortgrove Park in the north. The village thus lies in a shallow bowl. Two streams, Bury Water to the west and Debden Water to the east, drain the surrounding higher ground into the Cam. In 2012 the area of the parish was 2090 a. (846 ha.), and with a population of over 2,000 it has become one of the more densely populated parishes in north-west Essex.

Until the mid 20th century Newport was mainly an agricultural community, with arable farming being more important than stock rearing. Large common fields developed

1   T. Williamson, *The Origins of Hertfordshire* (Hatfield, 2010), 18–19.
2   H.J. Osborne White, *The Geology of the Country near Saffron Walden* (London, 1932), 62–73.
3   A.J. Thomasson, *Soils of the Saffron Walden District* (Harpenden, 1969), 13–17 and map.

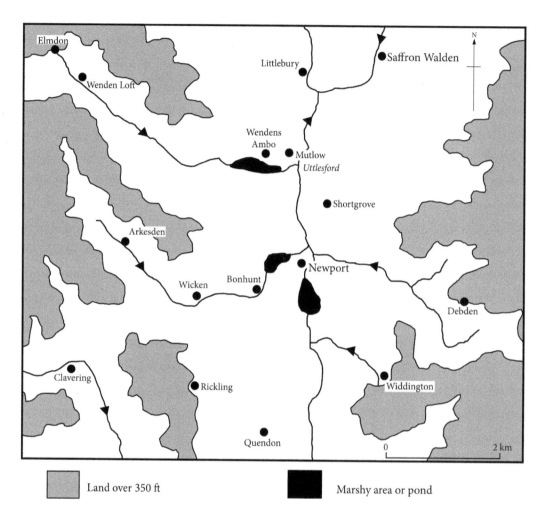

Map 1   *Newport and surrounding area showing settlements known to exist by 1066.*

in the parish during the medieval period, and general inclosure did not take place until 1861.[4] Its economy, however, was never wholly agricultural. Commercial activity and craft industries always played a part, and for a time during the late 12th and early 13th centuries, and again in the second half of the 19th century, the village developed some urban characteristics. In the second half of the 20th century good communications encouraged its growth as a commuter village and agriculture has declined in importance.

Parish Boundaries

The intricate boundary between Newport and Widdington parishes, which probably originated in the 12th century, remained unaltered until the late 19th century.[5] In

4   Below, p.70.
5   Below, p. 3.

1877 there were five detached portions of Newport parish within Widdington, and 12 detached portions of Widdington within Newport.[6] The Divided Parishes Acts of 1876 and 1882, however, authorised the incorporation of detached parts of a parish within the parish which surrounded them.[7]

With the exception of one detached portion of Widdington parish, which amounted to about 157 a., none of the detached portions were of any great size; the five detached portions of Newport, for instance, amounted to no more than 22.51 a.[8] The Local Government Board's proposals for the revision of the boundaries, however, aroused considerable opposition.[9] Its first proposal was to amalgamate the two parishes; but the Poor Law Guardians in Widdington strongly objected. They argued that Widdington was a small rural parish, whereas Newport was 'a rising village and soon will be a town with high rates' and would probably need expenditure on sanitary improvements from which Widdington would not benefit. Representatives of both parishes suggested that a better solution would be to make Debden Water and the river Cam the boundary between the two. This was opposed by Charles Wade, the agent for W.C. Smith of Shortgrove. He argued that Newport would lose the railway station, the gas works, two villas (now Buriton House and Berwyn), the coal yard and a large maltings, all of which contributed to the rates, but in exchange Newport would gain 279 a. with only a gamekeeper's cottage. Consequently, the Newport Vestry recommended to the Local Government Board that no action should be taken.[10]

The outcome was a modest revision: seven detached portions of Widdington were incorporated in Newport, and one detached portion of Newport remained within Widdington.[11] In 1938 Essex County Council transferred those parts of Widdington parish, including the detached parts, which lay to the north and north–west of Debden Water to Newport.[12]

There was a further adjustment in 1960, when a substantial area south of Bromley Lane and east of the railway line was transferred from Widdington to Newport. Residents in that area argued that their natural ties were with Newport rather than with Widdington when it came to shopping, church-going, and social and recreational activities. Both parishes agreed, and after a local inquiry the Minister of Housing and Local Government made the necessary order in March 1960.[13] A minor alteration followed in 1983, by which the Chalk Pit was transferred to Newport from Widdington, and Newport lost a small number of houses at the north end of the parish to Wendens Ambo.[14]

---

6   *Ordnance Survey Book of Reference to the Plan of the Parish of Newport* (London, 1870), 4; *Widdington* (London, 1877), 4–6.

7   39 & 40 Vict. c.61; 45 & 46 Vict. c.58.

8   OS Books of Reference.

9   TNA, MH 12/3720.

10 NPC, Parish Boundaries File.

11 OS Maps 1:2500 Essex, Sheets VIII (16), IX (13) (1897).

12 NPC, Parish Boundaries File.

13 MHLG, Order H.L.G 8314 (1960).

14 NPC, Parish Boundaries File.

Population

There are no reliable figures for the size of the population of Newport before the 1801 census. From Domesday Book onwards, however, there is some evidence for the number of households in the parish. In 1066 in Newport, Birchanger and Shortgrove there were 34 villeins and bordars, and 13 slaves. By 1086 the number of slaves had fallen to seven, while there were 48 villeins and bordars.[15] Over the next 200 years the population probably doubled in size: the 1299 extent of Newport, compiled by Tilty Abbey, recorded 94 households.[16] In 1327 there were 28 individuals whose movable goods were assessed at 10s. or more, and taking into account the number of exemptions from tax a figure of 90–100 households is likely.[17] There is indirect evidence for a fall in population in the later 14th century, as a result of successive outbreaks of plague.[18]

By the 16th century the evidence is better. The number of individuals assessed for tax (with a low threshold) in 1524 was 105,[19] and in 1594 the number of households in Newport was 120.[20] The number of baptisms rose from an average of 15 annually between 1560 and 1567 to 18 in 1597.[21] In 1635 the number of communicants (probably persons over 16 years of age) was put at 350;[22] some 129 households were listed in the Hearth Tax return of 1663, 130 in the return for 1670, and in 1778 there were said to be about 120 houses in the parish.[23] These figures are broadly consistent with one another, and suggest a population of between 500 and 650 between 1500 and 1800. The 1801 census recorded 663 inhabitants, and in 1810 there were 148 families.[24]

In 1830 the vicar, Revd Monk, carried out a census of the parish which recorded 195 families in the village.[25] On the assumption that there were, on average, four or five persons per household Monk's figure is not inconsistent with the 1831 national census, which puts the total population at 914; the same as that in 1901.[26]

Newport's character as a thoroughfare village may help to explain the increase in the mobility of its population in the 19th century. According to the 1841 census, 66 per cent of the 813 persons resident were born in Newport, and 25 per cent elsewhere in Essex, suggesting substantial mobility within the immediate region. By 1881, out of a population of 992 only 48 per cent were born in Newport, 34 per cent elsewhere in Essex, and 11 per cent in adjacent counties. Only seven per cent (60 people) were born

15   DB, 971, 973, 991.

16   ERO, T/B 3.

17   J.C. Ward (ed.), *The Medieval Essex Community: the Lay Subsidy of 1327* (Chelmsford, 1983), 51.

18   Below, p. 65. The poll tax records for this part of Essex have been lost.

19   TNA, E 179/108/155, 171.

20   Ibid., C 2/Eliz/N5/57.

21   B. Nurse, 'Occupations in Parish Registers: The Evidence from Newport, Essex', *Local Population Studies*, 52 (1994), 40.

22   TNA, E 13/558.

23   ERO, T/A 169/1; H. French, 'Essex and the Hearth Tax in the Late Seventeenth Century', in C. Ferguson, C. Thornton and A. Wareham, eds, *Essex Hearth Tax Return Michaelmas 1670* (London, 2012), 54–64 and 410–11; LPL, FP Lowth 5, ff. 434–7.

24   *VCH Essex* II, 352 for population figures for Newport 1801–1901; LPL, FP Randolph 11/48; for 20th century see http://www.visionofbritain.org.uk.

25   *The Inhabitants of Newport, Essex, in 1830*, NLHG Collections (original in private hands).

26   *VCH Essex* II, 352.

elsewhere in the British Isles. By 1901 39 per cent of the total population (914) had been born in Newport, with 49 per cent born in Essex or the adjacent counties, and 12 per cent elsewhere.[27]

The number in all the censuses from 1841 who were recorded as born elsewhere is of greater significance than the figures themselves suggest. Middle-class professional people, clergy, doctors, school teachers, engineers and senior railway officials, who came from all over the country, gave the population a more varied, perhaps more quasi-urban, character than neighbouring villages. The 1901 census shows that four of the principal farms in the village were tenanted by men who came from the further parts of the British Isles. Jesse Heaton at Pallett's Farm came from Lancashire, William Roy at Hospital Farm and Thomas Tudhope at White Ditch Farm were Scots, while Thomas Henry at Pond Cross Farm came from Gerrans near Falmouth (Cornw.), specific examples of a general trend which has been linked to the agricultural depression of the late 19th century.[28] For much of the 20th century the population increased slowly but steadily, from 914 in 1901 to 1,262 in 1971. In the following decade, however, the population increased by 63 per cent, and as a result of the extensive housing development in the village in the 1970s it reached 1,994 by 1981 and 2,352 in 2011.[29]

Prehistoric Settlement

The earliest evidence of human remains in Newport comes from after the Anglian Ice Age. An implement found in the parish and shown at a meeting of the Essex Field Club in 1884 was thought to be Palaeolithic and between 250,000 and 100,000 years old.[30] About 1878 Mesolithic flints were found on a chalk terrace about a quarter of a mile south–east of Newport railway station, with a number of flakes and cores indicating a manufactory. More flints were later collected from the same site, which was above the largest pond in Newport, now the Common.[31] A little further from the railway station and nearer the chalk quarry, numerous worked flints, implements, flakes and animal bones from the Neolithic period (c.4000–2500 BC) have been discovered. About 1935, on the other side of the river, a collector found a neolithic pit dwelling. He obtained from the bottom of the pit one perfect arrow-head, one flake with a curved point, 11 flint saws, 14 scrapers, 13 worn flakes, 150 good flakes, 45 cores, 285 waste flint chips and some worn grooved pottery.[32]

---

27   NLHG Collections, photocopies of census returns for Newport 1841–1901; the expression "throughfare village" is used by French, 'Hearth Tax', 41.

28   Census return for 1901; for emigration to Essex from Scotland, see *The Agrarian History of England and Wales* VII 1850–1914 Part I, ed. E. J. T. Collins (Cambridge, 2000), 173–5, 776–8.

29   http://www.visionofbritain.org.uk; Below, p. 154–60.

30   *Essex Field Club Transactions,* IV (1884), 95; *Proceedings of the Prehistoric Society of East Anglia,* 2 (1914–15), 400.

31   *Cambridge Archaeological Society Reports,* 39 (1878–9), 95; Cambridge Museum of Archaeology, accession nos, 51, 528; Saffron Walden Museum, accession 18848.48 1–10, T64, 1939.12.

32   G. Morris, 'Some Neolithic Sites in the Upper Valley of the Essex Cam', *Essex Naturalist,* XX (1922–3), 64–5; S. Hazzledine Warren, 'Archaeology of the Submerged Landscape of the Essex Coast', *Proceedings of the Prehistoric Society,* new series 2 (1936), 193; idem., 'Some Geological and Prehistoric Records', *Essex Naturalist,* XXVII, part IX (1945), 276.

The use of different metals for making tools and weapons gradually followed. A mysterious object from Newport has been dated to the Bronze Age (*c.*2500–800 BC) but its purpose has never been established. It is made of red sandstone, 189 mm. long and slightly tapering; but the most unusual features are the five narrow equidistant grooves along the length which are believed to have been cut by a metal tool. The object was recovered in 1904 from the northern part of the parish near the boundary with Wendens Ambo in the field between the main road and the railway line. A Bronze Age burial urn was buried in the same hole, near where another urn had been found two years earlier. Suggestions have ranged from an implement for breaking flax to something of religious significance, but nobody really knows what it was used for.[33]

Roman Settlement

Extensive field walking on land north of Newport (around Littlebury) and west (around Arkesden) has revealed enough pottery to suggest that much of the land had been cleared and farmed from as early as the 3rd century BC.[34] This pattern is likely to have been repeated in the Newport area, with small, widely scattered settlements generally located just below the heavier soils but near to water. Excavations on the site of the Roman villa at Wendens Ambo about a mile north-west of the boundary with Newport showed how one settlement developed from a small self-contained farmstead around 300–200 BC to a substantial complex with a bath-house. In the 2nd and 3rd centuries AD, more wheat was grown, more cattle were grazed and a surplus produced which was exchanged for luxury goods, suggesting that the villa controlled a territory beyond its immediate area.[35]

Another excavation, on a site to the south-east of the parish in advance of the construction of a gas pipeline, revealed a sizeable Roman cremation cemetery and nearby a quantity of Roman tiles and bricks, suggesting an important building, perhaps another villa.[36] Other archaeological evidence from Newport is sparse. Archaeologists field-walking the route of the M11 motorway in 1974 found pieces of Romano–British pottery and Roman ditches.[37] A fine gold armlet was discovered in meadowland on the Shortgrove estate in 1761; it was then thought to have been medieval but later considered to have been Roman. A drawing was made at the time in the Society of Antiquaries' Minute Book, but what happened to the armlet afterwards is not known.[38]

33   R. Miller Christy, 'On a strange stone object from a Bronze Age Interment in Essex', *MAN*, 27 (1916), 38–42.

34   T. Williamson, 'The Development of Settlement in North-West Essex: the result of a recent field survey', *EAH*, 17 (1986), 120–32.

35   T. Williamson, 'Settlement, Hierarchy and Economy in North-West Essex', in *Villa Economies*, ed. K. Branigan and D. Miles (London, 1986), 73–82; I. Hodder, *The Archaeology of the M11* (London, 1982), 2: *Excavations at Wendens Ambo*.

36   D. Cater, 'An Important Roman Cemetery found near Newport', *NN*, 60 (2003), 20–1. The site has not yet (2014) been fully published.

37   I.G. Robertson, 'The Archaeology of the M11 Motorway in Essex, 1970–75', *Essex Journal*, 10 (1975), 88–9.

38   Society of Antiquaries of London, Minutes, *29 January 1761*, 290; *VCH Essex* III (1963), 163.

Early Saxon Settlement

There is evidence for the presence of people of Germanic origin in the Roman town of Great Chesterford about six miles (9.5 km) north of Newport and, to a limited extent, in the upper Cam valley from the mid to late 5th century. Their penetration may well have been peaceful, and some place name evidence, such as (Saffron) Walden, Bonhunt, Radwinter and Cumberton Bottom (in Little Chishill) suggests the survival of a Brittonic population.[39] Saxon objects have been discovered near Newport by metal detectorists, but unfortunately no record has been provided of precisely where they were found. A saucer brooch, said to date from the late 5th or early 6th century AD, was discovered in 1987 on the banks of the Bury (or Wicken) Water. It may have come from the Saxon settlement at Bonhunt.[40] Finds from this period were also discovered in 1848 at Mutlow in Wendens Ambo.[41]

The settlement at Bonhunt, about 600 yds (550m.) west of the Newport parish boundary, was discovered in the 1960s. Excavations were carried out between 1967 and 1973 in advance of motorway construction and again in 1992–3 as part of an assessment of the effects of widening the motorway. The site was clearly an important one, although the results have not (2014) been published, so it is hard to assess the relationship between Bonhunt and the origins of Newport.[42]

Casual occupation of the Bonhunt site goes back to the Mesolithic period, but the majority of finds and the only evidence of permanent large-scale settlement date from the Middle Saxon period c.650–850 AD. Only between a third and a half of the settlement has been investigated. However, there were at least 25 buildings: the largest, of 152 sq. yds (130 sq. m.), was partitioned and had a hearth. At one stage the buildings seem to have been planned and grouped around a courtyard. Most of the pottery was fine ware brought from Ipswich, and about 10 per cent came from the continent, mostly from France, possibly via London. An enormous collection of animal bones was found in one ditch, of which 36,000 have been identified, including those from pigs, cattle and sheep, as well as chickens, geese, ducks, ten doves and one peacock.

The quality of the pottery, the quantity of bones and the name 'Bonhunt' have given rise to the suggestion that the site may have been that of a hunting lodge belonging to the kings of Essex. On the other hand the name may be derived from the Latin loan-word *funta*: Bonhunt springs lie close to the site.[43] No other Anglo-Saxon site in East Anglia has produced such a high proportion of pig remains. A large number of the animals killed were mature adult animals of an age usually taken to market rather than young ones killed for the local population. The domestic birds were also mature and must have

39   J.T. Baker, *Cultural Transition in the Chilterns and Essex Region 350 AD to 650 AD* (Hatfield, 2006), 138–86.
40   J. Gordon, 'A Saxon Find', *NN*, 30 (1988), 101.
41   W.T. Jones, 'Early Saxon Cemeteries in Essex', in *Archaeology in Essex to AD 1500*, ed. D.G. Buckley, CBA Research Report 34 (London, 1980), 89.
42   The following paragraph is based on K. Wade, 'A Settlement Site at Bonhunt Farm, Wicken Bonhunt, Essex', in Buckley, *Archaeology in Essex to AD 1500* (CBA Research Report No. 34, 1980), 96–102; R. Bradley and B. Hooper, 'Trial Excavations on a Saxon site at Bonhunt, Essex', *Essex Journal*, 9 (1974), 38–56.
43   Wade, 'Settlement Site', 102; Baker, *Cultural Transition*, 173–5.

been kept for their eggs. Bonhunt could therefore have been more than a hunting lodge and possibly served as a royal centre for collecting food rents.[44]

The nearby place names Quendon (the valley of the women) and Rickling (the people of Ricola) also suggest that the district was a royal centre.[45] Ricola may have been the Kentish princess named by Bede as the wife of Sledda, king of Essex at the beginning of the 7th century.[46] It is possible, therefore, that the putative estate provided maintenance for the household of the queens of Essex. It may have included not just Quendon, Rickling and Bonhunt, but also Wenden Lofts, Wendens Ambo (formerly Great and Little Wenden), and the land which became Newport, thus forming an area which would have been comparable in extent with other royal estates which are better documented. From the early 9th century the kings of Essex acknowledged the overlordship of either the Mercian or West Saxon kings, who probably now came into possession of the Bonhunt estate and the right to tax, presumably in the form of food-renders.[47]

Origins of Newport

The settlement at Bonhunt seems to have been abandoned in the late 9th or early 10th century, perhaps during the period of Danish dominance in north and east Essex and East Anglia.[48] In 912, however, Edward the Elder (king of the West Saxons 899–924) began a series of campaigns aimed at bringing these Danish lands under his control, and he has some claim to be regarded as the founder of Newport.[49] By early 917 most of Essex was under his authority, and it is possible that he established a *burh* at what became Newport, on a major route northwards, as a forward base for his advance on Cambridge, where the Danish army submitted to him in the autumn of 917.[50] The *Aldewerke* at Shelford (Cambs) has been identified as the site of a private estate for the leader of the Danish army of Cambridge, and Domesday Book records that the manor of Great Shelford was attached to Newport as a berewick or outlying dependency, paying tax to the sheriff of Essex rather than the sheriff of Cambridgeshire.[51] Newport and Shelford taken together paid a revenue to the king equivalent to two nights' provisions to maintain the royal household, as did the manor of Writtle, another royal estate in Essex.[52] Such

---

44   P.J. Crabtree, 'Animal Exploitation in East Anglian Villages', in *Environment and Economy in Anglo-Saxon England*, ed. J. Rackham, CBA Research Report, 89 (London, 1994); c.f. R. Hodges, *Dark Age Economics* (2nd ed., London, 1989), 142.

45   P.H. Reaney, *The Place Names of Essex* (Cambridge, 1935), 532.

46   Bede, *Historia Ecclesiastica Gentis Anglorum*, ed. J.E. King (Loeb edn, Cambridge MA, 1962), II, 214–5.

47   B. Yorke, *Kings and Kingdoms of Early Anglo-Saxon England* (London, 1990), 57; C. Hart, 'The Ealdordom of Essex', in *An Essex Tribute: Essays Presented to Frederick G. Emmison* (London, 1987), 57–60.

48   Wade, 'Settlement Site', 102; S. Rippon, 'Essex c.700–1066' in *The Archaeology of Essex: Proceedings of the Writtle Conference*, ed. O. Bedwin (Chelmsford, 1996), esp. p. 121.

49   L. Abrams, 'Edward the Elder's Danelaw', in *Edward the Elder 899–924*, ed. N.J. Higham and D. Hill (London, 2011), 128–43.

50   C. Hart, *The Danelaw* (London, 1992), 12–16; David Hill, *An Atlas of Anglo-Saxon England* (Oxford, 1981), 56–7.

51   C. Hart, 'The *Aldewerke* and Minster at Shelford, Cambridgeshire', *Anglo-Saxon Studies in Archaeology and History*, 8 (1995), 43–68.

52   J.H. Round, 'Essex Domesday', *VCH Essex* I, (1903), 336–8.

payments were generally associated with ancient royal estates. There were other royal estates between Newport and Shelford, such as Great Chesterford, but the link between Shelford and Newport, perhaps as a result of Edward's grant, suggests the latter had an important role in the district. It seems to have taken on Bonhunt's role as a royal tax-collecting centre, and it may have become the administrative centre for the Hundred of Uttlesford. The Uttles Ford, across the river Cam, is on the boundary between Newport and Wenden parishes, and very close to the boundary with Saffron Walden parish.

There are other indications that Newport may have been established as a local centre in the late Saxon period. The geld assessment of the manor of Newport in the Domesday Book at eight and a half hides is very close to the size of the town fields, about 1200 a., attached to the southern fortified area or burh of Cambridge, also thought to have been established by Edward the Elder. Another early 10th-century creation, the town fields at Colchester, comprised about the same amount of arable land at Domesday. These have been explained as areas of land given to the inhabitants on the occasion of the foundation of a burh by the king.[53]

It also been suggested that Newport was the site of the *burh* or fortified centre called *Wigingamere* in the *Anglo-Saxon Chronicle*.[54] This interpretation was widely accepted for a time, but Linslade near Wing (Bucks) may be a more likely candidate. Even if Newport was not *Wigingamere* it may be that it was nonetheless a *burh*, and the progress of Edward the Elder's campaign makes a foundation date of 917 a serious possibility. The name Newport itself means new market and its position as a royal centre on a main road meant that trade would develop, and tolls would be levied. In Edward the Confessor's reign some coins are recorded as minted at 'Newport', but it is not clear whether this is Newport Essex or Newport Pagnell (Bucks.). The presence of a mint at Newport would, however, be consistent with its character as an important royal centre, and at that time it was a larger place than Newport Pagnell.[55]

Settlement Pattern

In contrast to many other villages in Essex, Newport has been characterised as a nucleated village, with houses and farms grouped along the main road and in a densely settled area between the church and the High Street.[56] It might be better called a thoroughfare village, however, for its most distinctive characteristic was its narrow, elongated nature, stretching for more than a mile along the main route from south to north: High Street, Belmont Hill and Bridge End as far as the Coach and Horses Inn. On the east side of the river Cam (much of which lay in Widdington parish until the 20th

53   J. Haslam, 'The Anglo-Saxon Burh at *Wigingamere*', *Landscape History* 10 (1988), 29–30.

54   Haslam, 'Anglo-Saxon Burh', 25–36.

55   Haslam, 'The Location of the Burh of *Wigingamere – a Reappraisal*', in *Names, Places and People. An Onomastic Miscellany in Memory of John MacNeal Dodgson*, ed. A.R. Rumble and A.D. Mills (Stamford, 1997), 111–30; J.M. Dodgson, *Wigingamere*, ibid., 383–9; M.A.S. Blackburn and others, 'A New Type of Edward the Confessor for the "Newport" Mint', *British Numismatic Journal*, 62 (1992), 125–6; D. Secker, 'A re-used Anglo-Saxon cross shaft fragment from St Mary's Church, Newport,' *EAH* 4th series (2013), 233.

56   French, *Hearth Tax*, 55; see also A. Burns, 'Beyond the "Red Vicar": Community and Christian Socialism in Thaxted', *History Workshop Journal*, 75 (2013), 101–46.

Figure 1 *Coach and Horses Inn, Cambridge Road. A 16th-century building with exposed timbers.*

century), rising ground discouraged extensive settlement, even in the late 20th and early 21st centuries. The western side is more open, but has seen only limited development beyond Frambury Lane and along Whiteditch Lane on the north-western side of the parish.

In the 13th and 14th centuries settlement was concentrated along the main thoroughfare and on Church Street, Elephant Green and the adjacent part of Wicken Road, next to the church and immediately west of the High Street.[57] That pattern had changed little by the late 18th century. The map made in 1786 for Percy Charles Wyndham shows a very similar pattern of development, but in the late 18th century a group of cottages was erected on the south side of Bury Water Lane.[58]

The coming of the railway in 1845 led to some industrial development around the station,[59] while in the later 19th century there was some housing development along Wicken Road west of Parsonage Farm. One of the promoters of these developments was Thomas Shirley. He was a man of modest origins who acquired the tenancy of Pond Cross Farm in 1851. He became a director of the gas works, churchwarden, overseer of the poor, governor of the Grammar School and member of the School Board. He built several houses in the village, including a pair of high-status villas in Wicken Road. He demonstrated his piety and philanthropy by placing a new stained glass window in the baptistery of the church to commemorate his golden wedding in 1889.[60]

After the First World War there was some very limited development of housing along London Road at the southern end of the village, and along Cambridge Road beyond

57   Below, pp. 59–60.
58   ERO, D/DU 205/19.
59   OS Map 1:2500 Essex sheet IX (16), 1877; Below, p. 75–7.
60   'Mr and Mrs Shirley's Golden Wedding', *NN*, 11 (1979), 93–101; below, p. 71.

the railway viaduct to the north. At the same time there was pressure to improve the living conditions of the working class. The 1919 Housing Act, which encouraged local authorities to build houses for rent, led to the building of a group of council houses along Frambury Lane in 1920.[61] Another four were built there in 1936, and after the Second World War a temporary building, also in Frambury Lane, which had been used as a Women's Land Army hostel and then as a POW camp, was converted into council bungalows.[62] Even by the beginning of the 21st century, however, there was little development east of the river.[63]

TRANSPORT AND COMMUNICATIONS

Newport is situated on an important road running through the centre of the village. The road formed part of the Hockerill Turnpike from 1744 until 1870, and was classified as the A11 London to Norwich trunk road in 1923; but in 1979, after the opening of the M11 through the west of the parish, it was downgraded as the B1383. Nonetheless, in 2014 it was still an important and busy highway. The main railway line from London Liverpool Street to Cambridge runs south to north through the village, and since its opening in 1845 it has had a major influence on the development of the parish.

The road network before the establishment of the Hockerill Turnpike

In prehistoric and Roman times a network of roads and tracks linked the numerous settlements and farmsteads. A long-distance prehistoric trackway from the Thames to the Fenland Basin ran along the valleys of the rivers Stort and Cam via Stansted and Cambridge, while another road, which may have been in use during the Roman period, ran from Radwinter to Newport and was called Elder Street at Debden. At Newport it would have followed either the present road from Ringer's Farm or the footpath towards the railway station. A Roman road has also been traced on the eastern side of the Cam from Little Chesterford to south of Audley End, which if continued would have gone through Shortgrove on the higher ground and joined the east-west route near Debden.[64]

　　The earliest map showing the roads around Newport, 1594, has a road running from Saffron Walden, via Newport, to Rickling, Berden, the Hadhams and Hunsdon to Ware.[65] From Ware goods would have been carried to London either down the river Lea, navigable from the 1570s, or by road through Hoddesdon and Edmonton. By 1637 there was a weekly carrier service from Saffron Walden to Bishopsgate Street in London, presumably by this route. The carrier arrived in London on a Wednesday and returned the following day.[66] Much of this road has been incorporated in the modern network, and the section from Newport to Rickling survives as a bridleway.

61　9 & 10 Geo. V c.35; *VIT*, 139, 144.

62　*VIT*, 160 and accompanying images.

63　Below, Map 5, p. 155.

64　S.R. Bassett, *Saffron Walden: excavations and research 1972–80*, CBA Research Report, 45 (London 1982).

65　J. Norden, *Speculi Britanniae Pars, An Historical and Chronological Description of the County of Essex, 1594*, ed. Sir Henry Ellis (Camden Society 9, 1840); ibid., *Hertfordshire, 1598* (reprinted Ware, 1903).

66　J. Taylor, *The Carriers Cosmographie* (London, 1637; reprinted Norwood NJ, 1974).

The 1594 map, and also one published in 1603, show another road running south from Newport and east of Quendon to Elsenham and Stansted, but not to Bishop's Stortford and southward. It is not shown on a map of 1678, which instead shows a road running south from Newport via Quendon, Stansted Mountfichet, Bishop's Stortford, Sawbridgeworth, Eastwick, Rye House, Hoddesdon and on to London.[67] This route too survives, and from Hoddesdon southwards is part of the A10 trunk road. Detailed information about the route Charles II took from London and Hoddesdon to Newmarket via either Royston or Newport was presented in the various accounts of the Rye House Plot, 1683.[68]

It was also possible to reach London from Newport via Harlow, Epping, and Woodford, but until the creation of the turnpike from Epping and Ongar to London via Woodford in 1768 the route via Hoddesdon remained the more important.[69]

The Hockerill Turnpike Trust and the Stort Navigation

The Essex and Herts Turnpike Trust (later known as the Hockerill Turnpike Trust) was formed in 1744 to manage the road from Thornwood Common north of Epping to Stump Cross on the Cambridgeshire border. The Middlesex and Essex Turnpike Roads Trust had been established in 1721,[70] and with the establishment of the Epping Highway Trust in 1768,[71] the management of the whole of the road from the Cambridgeshire border to London via Woodford (roughly the line of the modern A11) was in the hands of just three trusts. The toll bridge over Bury Water in Newport, first mentioned in 1450, which belonged to the owners of the Shortgrove estate was specifically excluded from the Trust's control under the initial Act.[72] All three turnpikes were treated as one, measured in miles from Shoreditch Church.[73] In 1775 Parson Woodforde travelled this way from London to Norwich, and observed that it was 'the best of roads I ever travelled.'[74]

The Hockerill Turnpike was not a new road. The Trust's responsibility was to manage and maintain the whole length of existing road from Thornwood Common to Stump Cross, and to raise tolls to defray expenditure on maintenance. Initially the Trust erected two toll gates, one at Ugley south of Quendon and the other at Spelbrook south of Bishop's Stortford. The Ugley gate was soon moved further south to Palmer's Water near Bishop's Stortford, and in 1767 a gate was erected at Great Chesterford where tolls were levied on long-distance traffic but not on local journeys.[75]

Carriers from the Newport area with goods bound for London could avoid the toll by taking the road via Little Hadham and Much Hadham to Ware and on to London by

---

67 Hans Wounteel's map (1603) is reproduced in F.H. Maund, *The Hockerill Highway* (Colchester, 1957), at p. 2; *Map of Essex* by John Ogilby and William Morgan 1678 (ERO Publications 24, Chelmsford 1975).

68 For example, *A True Account and Declaration of the Horrid Conspiracy against the late King, His Present Majesty, and the Government* (2nd edn, London, 1685), 51–2.

69 Maund, *Hockerill Highway*, 6–12.

70 Ibid., 1–5; 8 Geo. I c.30.

71 B. Winstone, *Minutes of the Epping and Ongar Highway Trust 1769–1870* (London, 1891), 54–83.

72 Below, p. 17.

73 HRO, TP 3/1, p. 45; T/P 3/3.

74 J. Beresford (ed.), *The Diary of a Country Parson* I, 1758–1781, 150–1 (Oxford, 1924).

75 HRO, TP 3/1, pp. 16, 217, 221.

river. However, the opening of the Stort Navigation in 1769[76] shifted the advantage in favour of the turnpike, despite its tolls. Barley from north-west Essex could now be taken by road to Bishop's Stortford, where it was turned into malt, and shipped down river to London.[77]

The Act establishing the Trust laid down that the section of road from Quendon to the northern end of Newport was to be improved before any other section, presumably because it was most in need of repair. This work was carried out immediately, making the road 30ft wide, and the section north of Newport was improved to the same width in 1766.[78] The Trust later carried out minor improvements, most of which required the purchase of adjacent land. In 1816, at Joseph Smith of Shortgrove's suggestion, a more substantial widening took place, entailing the purchase of some property: Benjamin Gurson, for example, was paid £15 compensation for the demolition of his cottage.[79]

In 1826, however, the Trustees proposed to build an entirely new road between the toll bridge and a point about 250 yds further north. It would by-pass the existing road (now Bridge End) on slightly higher ground, but it required extensive purchases of land, mainly from William C. Smith but also from ten other owners of smaller pieces of land along the proposed line. Smith refused to sell at a price that was acceptable to the Trustees, suggesting instead a new line to the east of the existing road (which would have been prone to flooding had it been adopted).[80] The deadlock was resolved only when the Trustees promoted a private Act of Parliament in 1829 which allowed the Trustees to build the new line of road on the alignment they had originally proposed. It opened in 1830. The costs of building the road itself and compensating Smith and other landowners came to £112 15s. 5d. and the expenses in obtaining the private Act amounted to £574 16s. 4d.[81]

Canals and Railways

The success of the Stort Navigation led to the development of a series of schemes to link Cambridge with Bishop's Stortford by canal. Three were prepared between 1779–80 and 1811, but in each case the promoters met strong opposition from the maltsters of Bishop's Stortford, who feared the development of a rival malting centre at Saffron Walden, and from Lord Braybrooke at Audley End, whose objections were aesthetic as well as practical.[82] However, the decisive issue was probably the failure of the promoters to raise the necessary capital.

Nonetheless, the improvement of communications from Cambridge via the Cam-Stort gap to London remained a live issue, and railway technology now began to shape promoters' approaches to the problem. In 1834 Nicholas Cundy surveyed a route for a locomotive-hauled railway from London to Cambridge via Bishop's Stortford and Newport, where it would run west of the turnpike.[83] In the following year the Northern

---

76   J. Cooper, *Bishop's Stortford: A History* (Chichester, 2005), 55–7.
77   Ibid.
78   17 Geo. II c.9; HRO, TP 3/1.
79   HRO, TP 3/2, pp. 410–13; it is not clear when the widening took place.
80   Ibid., TP 3/3.
81   HRO, TP 3/3.
82   Ibid., D/DBy O4.
83   TNA, RAIL 1075/369/15.

and Eastern Railway promoted a bill to authorise a railway from London to Cambridge and on to Lincoln and York. The company commissioned James Walker, President of the Institution of Civil Engineers, to survey possible routes, and the route which he eventually recommended was essentially the same as Cundy's: up the Lea and Stort valleys to Bishop's Stortford, then via Stansted and Elsenham and over the watershed to Newport. It would run under the turnpike at Quendon, and pass to the west of Newport church, avoiding both the plantation at Shortgrove and Audley End Park.[84]

In 1836 the Company received parliamentary authority to build the railway on this alignment, at an estimated cost of £870,000. The bill received royal assent in July 1836, but progress in building the line was slow,[85] and the initial optimism of the railway's promoters proved misplaced. In 1835 they had told the Commons committee examining the bill that they had every confidence that the carriage of malt would prove one of the most important items of traffic between London and Cambridge.[86] When the railway reached Bishop's Stortford in 1842, however, the Directors were told that many maltsters had been unwilling to break their long-established contracts with river shippers, and the coach owners had proved surprisingly resilient to rail competition.[87]

Nonetheless, in 1843 the Company sought to revive their powers to extend the line to Newport. They were persuaded to do so, paradoxically, by disappointing goods revenues from the line to Bishop's Stortford. They envisaged Newport as the railhead for a wide malt-producing area, with produce going direct to London by rail rather than transferring to river transport at Bishop's Stortford. They believed that about two thirds of the malt hitherto shipped down the Stort Navigation came from this area of north-west Essex. 'Until the Company reaches Newport,' the proprietors argued, 'it must compete with others. There it may command. It will have possession, at once, of the whole traffic, both passengers and goods, as long as its rates continue low enough and its management sufficiently good, to prevent opposition upon the road.'[88]

In May 1843 the Company received parliamentary authorisation to extend the line to Newport, and in January 1844 it amalgamated with the Eastern Counties Railway.[89] Later in 1844 this stronger company promoted the Newport Deviation Bill, which proposed, following a survey by Robert Stephenson, that the line should deviate from Cundy's and Walker's route and pass to the east of the turnpike, keeping very close to the river and thus reducing the cost.[90] The bill passed, and the line was built on its present alignment. The adoption of the Newport deviation meant that the Cambridge extension would have to cross the turnpike at the north end of the village to reach the higher ground to the north west. However, as early as 1841 the Turnpike Trust had decreed that no level crossing would be permitted on the turnpike.[91] This prohibition was incorporated in

84   Ibid., RAIL 541/6.
85   Ibid., RAIL 1111/34.
86   Ibid.
87   Ibid., RAIL 541/2.
88   *Railway Times*, 11 Feb. 1843.
89   TNA, RAIL 541/2; ERO, Q/RUA 28.
90   7 Vict. c.35; *Railway Times* 28 March and 10 Aug. 1844.
91   HRO, TP 3/3.

the 1844 Act,[92] and thus both legal and engineering considerations meant that in the following year the Company had to build a large and visually intrusive viaduct to carry the line over the turnpike when it was taken north from Newport.

The total cost of the Newport extension was £94,774;[93] but the Company also had to purchase land from various proprietors in Newport, at a total cost of £2,895. Anne Cranmer of Quendon Hall received £1,000, Henry Webb £850, and Joseph Living £300, but William Charles Smith of Shortgrove parted with very little land, receiving only £50 for about 17 a.[94] The presence of so many navvies in the parish while the line was being built gave rise to some concern on the part of the vicar, Edward Gould Monk.[95]

Great celebrations marked the opening of the line from Bishop's Stortford to Norwich on 29 July 1845, and an account of the first journey along the line appeared in the *Illustrated London News*. The train consisted of 13 double carriages and an open carriage carrying the band of the Coldstream Guards. It conveyed the directors of the Company, Lord Braybrooke, and many other eminent persons. As the train passed through Newport, the writer noted that 'the houses [presented] their white sides and fronts to the spectator, and [stood] out well from the green landscape.'[96]

Initially there were three trains a day in each direction, including one 'parliamentary' train which might have been affordable to those too poor to travel by the other, faster, services. The speed and relative comfort of rail travel, however, soon put the long-distance stage coaches out of business, and in August 1845 500 carriage horses were sent for sale.[97] In the following year some residents of Newport unsuccessfully petitioned the Company to provide a more frequent service from Newport to London.[98]

During the 1850s and 1860s the pattern of service and level of fares remained much the same, and even as late as 1920, with a somewhat more frequent service, most trains still took about one and three quarter hours. By 1938, however, as part of the general speeding-up of passenger trains in the 1930s, some journeys took only an hour and ten minutes, and daily commuting to London became a realistic possibility.[99] In terms of travel opportunities for residents of Newport, the opening of the line from Audley End to Saffron Walden in 1865 was probably more important, for it enabled people to live in Newport and work in Saffron Walden: the first stage in the development of Newport as a commuter village.

For businesses in Newport, however, freight traffic was more important than opportunities for passenger travel. Within a year of the line opening the Company had decided to build a goods depot at Newport, and one landowner, Stephen Robinson, reached agreement with the Company for the provision of a private siding on his land at the north end of the parish, though there is no evidence that it was actually built.[100]

---

92 7 & 8 Vict. c.62 sec. 147; this section also prescribed the dimensions for viaducts across both public and private roads.

93 ERO, Q/RUA 28.

94 TNA, RAIL 186/71 pp. 73, 78–9.

95 Ibid., RAIL 186/69 p. 55; below, p. 139.

96 *Illustrated London News*, 2 Aug. 1845.

97 B. Wilson, 'The Railway Comes to Newport', *NN*, 43 (1995), 23.

98 TNA, RAIL 186/38.

99 Ibid., RAIL 981/90; GER and LNER Public Timetables 1864, 1920, 1925, 1938–9 (in private collections).

100 TNA, RAIL 186/38; ERO, D/DU 1581.

Figure 2 *Railway staff at Newport Station, probably c.1920.*

By 1854 there was sufficient traffic for two goods trains a day to call at Newport.[101] Agricultural products could be shipped to London from Newport in less than four hours by freight train, and coal and building materials brought in. Both the Station Road maltings (from 1855) and the Newport Gas Company (from 1867) had their own private sidings.[102] Haulage of goods by road did not, however, succumb entirely to competition from the railway. As late as 1859 Samuel Lampkin's wagon left Newport for London every Thursday, returning on the Saturday, and William Chalk's wagon passed through Newport every Friday on its way from Linton (Cambs.) to London. Their customers were probably those for whom time was less important than cost. Thomas Trott, and later William Trott, however, offered a daily carriage service of goods by rail on one or other of the goods trains.[103]

The Dissolution of the Turnpike Trust

The railway caused immediate financial difficulties for the Turnpike Trust. In July 1845 the Trust's monthly income from tolls was £312 19s. 7d., but in August it fell to £186 10s. 0d. and in September to £175 4s. 8d.[104] By the end of the first year of the railway's operation income had fallen by almost two thirds, and over the next 25 years it rarely reached £1000 a year. The railway had captured most of the goods traffic to and from London.

In 1866 the Home Office asked the Trustees to enquire whether the parishes through which the road ran were in favour of the Trust's abolition. However, Newport, along with most other parishes, replied in favour of continuance, fearing that the abolition

101 TNA, RAIL 981/91.
102 Ibid., BT 31/1322/3435; OS Map 1:2500, Essex sheet XIV (1) (1877).
103 *White's Dir. Essex* (1848), 62; *Post Office Dir. Essex* (1859), 133.
104 HRO, TP 3/12.

of the Trust would increase the burden on the rates if the parishes had to pay for the maintenance of the road.[105] The opposition of the parishes merely delayed the inevitable, and in 1870 the Trust was dissolved. The cash balance in hand at the dissolution was distributed amongst the parishes, Newport receiving £56 18s. 11d. The toll bridge over Bury Water, however, survived and was taken over by Essex County Council in 1911.[106]

Road Transport

Although the opening of the railway brought about a rapid decline in long-distance stagecoach traffic, it created a demand for local transport from outlying villages to stations on the railway. As early as 1848 a horse-drawn omnibus service operated between Saffron Walden and Audley End station (then called Wenden).[107] These omnibuses were operated by private individuals, but in 1921 the National Omnibus and Transport Company introduced a motor bus service on four days a week between Bishop's Stortford and Saffron Walden via Newport. In 1929 the National Company was broken up into various smaller units, with Essex being served by the Eastern National Company, who ran a daily service on the same route. In the early 1930s H. Wilson, trading as Clavering and District Bus Services, developed a network of routes serving the villages north and west of Newport, as did the Cambridge-based Premier Travel. Eastern National took over Clavering and District in 1938, but the network of routes, including those of Premier Travel, continued into the 1960s.[108]

In offering travel opportunities to the less well off, and in particular to women, children and the elderly, the development of the bus network was probably of greater significance than the coming of the railway. Bus travel was cheaper and more flexible than the train, and for shopping, visits to friends and relatives, journeys to and from school and leisure travel – to the cinema, for example – the bus became essential to rural communities, even where, as in Newport, a railway service existed.

The rise in private car ownership, and the increasing cost of bus travel, brought about a decline in the rural bus network. The Sunday service through Newport ceased in 1977 and attempts by the parish council to persuade an alternative operator to take it on failed. By 2000 most evening services had ended as well.[109] However, in 2014 Newport still had an hourly bus service during the working day to Saffron Walden and Bishop's Stortford, and occasional services through the village to neighbouring places such as Clavering.[110]

The M11 Motorway

In the 1960s the government began to develop a programme of motorway construction, and as part of this programme a motorway to relieve the A10 and A11 roads from London to East Anglia was proposed. In 1965 a feasibility study envisaged a motorway

---

105 Ibid., TP 3/31.
106 Ibid., TP 3/4; section 6 of the Local Government Act 1888 (51 & 52 Vict. c.41) empowered county councils to take over private bridges.
107 *White's Dir. Essex* (1848), 648.
108 Eastern National Omnibus Company Public Timetables 1950–6 (in private collections); *Years Between*, 2 (Poole, 1984), 45, 169–70; Premier Travel Public Timetables 1946–70 (in private collections).
109 NPC Minute Book, 11.
110 ECC Bus Timetables, October 2010.

along the present route of the M11 but reaching no further north than Quendon, with an improved A11 trunk road taking traffic on to Cambridge and Norwich. The Ministry of Transport condemned this proposal as 'illogical', however, and recommended that the motorway should extend to Stump Cross, on the border between Essex and Cambridgeshire.[111] Unlike the railway, which ran up the Lea valley, the proposed motorway would follow the Roding valley to Epping, then east of the Stort valley from Harlow to Stansted Mountfichet, after which it would run roughly parallel to the railway as far as Quendon. From there it was to run under the A11 road, passing through part of the Quendon Hall estate and along the western edge of Newport parish, then west of the railway and the Audley End estate to Stump Cross.

The Ministry adopted this route as its preferred line in 1970,[112] and attention now turned to the positioning of interchanges. The Ministry's consultants had recommended an interchange between Quendon and Wendens Ambo, to 'meet the needs of traffic to and from Newport and Saffron Walden.' They suggested, however, that the number and location of the interchanges should depend on whether a proposed scheme for a new town in the neighbourhood of Stansted Mountfichet went ahead.[113] The Ministry's Divisional Engineer for Eastern England recommended that if a new town was not built at Stansted, then an interchange between the A120 and Stump Cross 'would be something of a luxury.'[114] Even so, as late as August 1967 the Ministry was still considering an interchange in the vicinity of Saffron Walden, but no final decision was taken even after the motorway opened to Stump Cross.[115] Ministry of Transport proposals for service areas in 1969 (near White Ditch Farm)[116] and in 1973 (near Wicken Road)[117] were abandoned, but an emergency access point was eventually built at the point where the motorway crossed Wicken Road (B1038) on the western edge of the parish.[118]

After some delay, the contract for the 15-mile (24km.) length of motorway from the A120 to Stump Cross was let in May 1977, and the motorway opened on 28 November 1979 (see fig. 3).[119] It cost £17.7 million, yet it was not entirely satisfactory. Although it relieved the A11 through the village of most long-distance lorry traffic, noise was an immediate problem, partly because the road had been built with a concrete surface.[120] Twenty-five years later a better surface was laid and acoustic barriers erected, but noise remained intrusive. Another important issue was access. Traffic from Newport and Saffron Walden had no easy access to the motorway, and Newport was not relieved of through traffic to the extent that residents had hoped at the planning stage. In 2014 the motorway remained a two-lane road north of Bishop's Stortford, despite proposals to widen it.[121]

111 TNA, MT 120/174, 16 Dec. 1965.
112 ERO, A10550; NPC, Minute Book 1961–71, 8 Sept. 1970.
113 TNA, MT 120/74. The scheme was eventually abandoned.
114 Ibid.
115 Below, p. 19 .
116 ERO, A9449 Box 1; NPC, Parish Meeting Minute Book 1945–89, 175.
117 Ibid., 179.
118 ERO, A10550.
119 From the table given in G. Charlesworth, *A History of British Motorways* (London, 1984), 109–10, table 7.3; *Saffron Walden Weekly News,* 29 Nov. 1979.
120 ERO, A9449 Box 1; NPC, Minute Book 1961–71, 133, 143, 204; 1971–91, 8 Sept. 1980.
121 NPC Files, Highways Agency: Motorway Widening Proposals, 1994.

Figure 3 *Opening of M11 Motorway, November 1979, with Rt. Hon. Kenneth Clarke, MP, junior Transport Minister, in the foreground.*

A survey of residents living along Newport High Street conducted in 1980 revealed that residents thought the opening of the motorway had made little difference to the volume of traffic through the village.[122] The campaign for an intersection near Newport continued: in 1978 the parish council had raised the possibility of an intersection north of Newport in the vicinity of Sparrows End, so that traffic from the south could reach Saffron Walden without travelling to Stump Cross. This proposal was revived in 1988, when the parish council wrote to the Department of Transport again suggesting an intersection near Newport. The Secretary of State replied that the Department had no plans for a new junction at any point on the section of motorway between the A120 and Stump Cross.[123]

Electrification of the Railway

The section of the line from London to Bishop's Stortford via the Southbury Loop was electrified in 1960 and the Lea Valley line in 1969, but it was another 18 years before electrification was extended to the line from Bishop's Stortford to Cambridge.[124] In 1980 British Rail proposed electrifying the section through Newport to Cambridge, but the

122 P. Davies, 'M11: Peace in our time', *NN*, 14 (1980), 105.
123 *NN*, 29 (1988), 33.
124 D.I. Gordon, *A Regional History of the Railways of Great Britain* V, The Eastern Counties (Newton Abbot, 2nd edn 1977), 237.

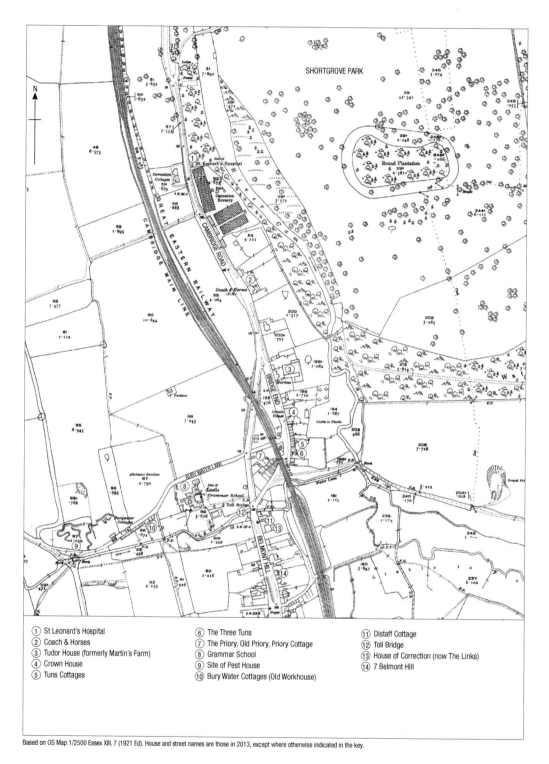

1. St Leonard's Hospital
2. Coach & Horses
3. Tudor House (formerly Martin's Farm)
4. Crown House
5. Tuns Cottages
6. The Three Tuns
7. The Priory, Old Priory, Priory Cottage
8. Grammar School
9. Site of Pest House
10. Bury Water Cottages (Old Workhouse)
11. Distaff Cottage
12. Toll Bridge
13. House of Correction (now The Links)
14. 7 Belmont Hill

Based on OS Map 1/2500 Essex XIII, 7 (1921 Ed). House and street names are those in 2013, except where otherwise indicated in the key.

Map 2   *Part of 1:2500 Ordnance Survey map of Newport (Essex sheets XIII 7 & 11), 1921.*

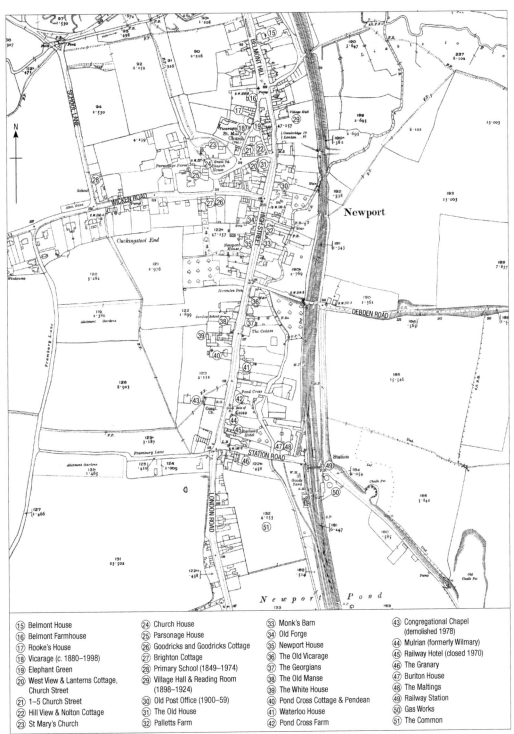

⑮ Belmont House	㉔ Church House	㉝ Monk's Barn	㊸ Congregational Chapel
⑯ Belmont Farmhouse	㉕ Parsonage House	㉞ Old Forge	(demolished 1978)
⑰ Rooke's House	㉖ Goodricks and Goodricks Cottage	㉟ Newport House	㊹ Mulrian (formerly Wilmary)
⑱ Vicarage (c. 1880–1998)	㉗ Brighton Cottage	㊱ The Old Vicarage	㊺ Railway Hotel (closed 1970)
⑲ Elephant Green	㉘ Primary School (1849–1974)	㊲ The Georgians	㊻ The Granary
⑳ West View & Lanterns Cottage,	㉙ Village Hall & Reading Room	㊳ The Old Manse	㊼ Buriton House
Church Street	(1898–1924)	㊴ The White House	㊽ The Maltings
㉑ 1–5 Church Street	㉚ Old Post Office (1900–59)	㊵ Pond Cross Cottage & Pendean	㊾ Railway Station
㉒ Hill View & Nolton Cottage	㉛ The Old House	㊶ Waterloo House	㊿ Gas Works
㉓ St Mary's Church	㉜ Palletts Farm	㊷ Pond Cross Farm	51 The Common

Based on OS Map 1/2500 Essex XIII II (eleven), 7 (1921 Ed). House and street names are those in 2013, except where otherwise indicated in the key.

scheme progressed slowly, and it was only on 16 January 1984 that the Minister for Transport announced to the House of Commons that the Government had approved the proposal to electrify the line from Bishop's Stortford to Cambridge, at a cost of about £10 million.[125] Work began in the spring of 1986, and the scheme was completed in May 1987.[126] Newport now had a regular, generally hourly, through service to London, with more frequent trains in the morning and evening peaks. The service remained slow: in 2014 most trains took just over one hour for the 40-mile journey from Newport to London Liverpool Street, but the regularity of the service and the peak-hour frequency have allowed Newport to develop as a commuter village for London, albeit at increasing cost, with a consequent effect on the value of property in the village.

SECULAR BUILDINGS

Newport contains a large number of historic buildings. These are to be found along the High Street and its continuation northwards, at the High Street end of Wicken Road, and in the cluster of little streets between the church and the High Street that was the site of the market place. Indeed, the majority of buildings in the core of the village are between one hundred and six hundred years old, and a significant proportion of them are timber-framed. A total of 27 buildings were recorded in 1916 by the Royal Commission on Historical Monuments, whose remit at that time extended up to 1714.[127] Seventy-three buildings in the same central area have been listed, six at grade II* and the rest at grade II.[128]

The oldest known house in Newport is the Old Vicarage, High Street (see fig. 4). It is a typical H-plan hall house, with a central hall and two projecting cross-wings. The cross-wings have exposed timbers and jettied upper storeys, with a carved bressumer on the south cross-wing. The north cross-wing, whose roof has a cambered tie-beam and kingpost, has been tree-ring dated 1386–96. The south cross-wing was added about a century later; timbers here indicate a felling date in the range 1492–1524. The hall was originally open to the roof; the floor was probably inserted in the 16th century. At the back of the house is an early 18th-century extension in red brick.[129]

At least four houses date from the 15th century, of which the most prominent are Monk's Barn, High Street, and Tudor House, Bridge End (see figs. 5 and 6). Monk's Barn has exposed timbers and brick nogging, and both wings are jettied. It is of Wealden type, that is to say with recessed central hall and flanking bays under a continuous roof, but it was built in two stages. The earliest part is the service wing at the south end. Its front wall was rebuilt when the two-bay hall and high-end cross-wing, under one roof, were built against it, replacing an earlier building; the exposed studding in this part is very closely spaced. The roof over the hall has a crown post and smoke-blackened timbers.

125 *Hansard*, 16 Jan. 1984, col. 3.
126 M. Donnelly, 'Newport Station goes Electric', *NN*, 26 (1986).
127 RCHM(E) Essex I (1916), 198–205.
128 http://list.english-heritage.org.uk, accessed 2 April 2014; *NN*, 23 (1985), 41–5; 24 (1985), 47–51, 25; 25 (1986), 51–4; 26 (1987), 53–7.
129 M. Jackson, 'The Old Vicarage', *NN*, 20 (1983), 83, 85, 87–9, 101; Oxford Dendrochronology Laboratory Report 2014/2, *The Tree-ring dating of The Old Vicarage, High Street, Newport, Essex* (2014).

Figure 4 *The Old Vicarage, High Street. Possibly the oldest house in the village. The north wing is late 14th century and the south wing early 16th century. It ceased to be the vicarage when Mr Tamplin (vicar 1876–1909) moved to an early 19th-century house on Elephant Green, close to the church.*

Figure 5 *Monk's Barn, High Street, photographed from the west. The south section is the earlier, and roof timbers in the north section have been dated to 1453. The original exposed timbers and brick nogging were plastered over at some point but uncovered again in the 19th century.*

Figure 6 *Tudor House (formerly Martin's Farm), Bridge End. Built in three phases from the 15th to the late 16th century, and used by Lady Meyer as her village health centre, c.1910–14.*

A common rafter from this roof has been tree-ring dated and was found to have been felled in 1453. This indicates construction that year or very soon afterwards, and means also that the brick nogging, if it is original, is the earliest example of brick nogging that can be dated. The other important feature of the house is the oriel window on the north cross-wing. The window itself has been renewed but the coving below it is original. It depicts the crowned Virgin and Child flanked by two angels, one playing an organ and the other a harp (see fig. 53).[130] Tudor House appears to incorporate the south cross-wing of a 15th-century hall house. This cross-wing now stands at the north end of a range that was built in the 16th century, in at least two phases, as shown by the variation in the bracing of the timber frame. The cross-wing is jettied and has exposed timbers, as does the upper storey of the later range, although the timbers were still entirely covered with plaster in 1938.[131] A single timber in the northern part of the 16th-century range has been tree-ring dated 1551–83. This section of the house has a very fine chimney-stack, with four circular shafts constructed of moulded bricks and with spurred caps. The four fireplaces have impressive brick surrounds with four-centred arched heads and, in one of the ground-floor rooms, carved spandrels and a frieze of dolphins' heads.[132]

Two other houses at Bridge End date from the late 15th century. The Three Tuns (see fig. 7) has a jettied front with exposed timbers, but was largely rebuilt following a fire

130 E. Purcell, 'Monk's Barn', *NN*, 19 (1983), 91–3; Oxford Dendrochronology Laboratory Report 2013/31, *The Tree-ring Dating of Monk's Barn, High Street, Newport, Essex*; John Walker, 'Monk's Barn, Newport: the dating of an Essex Wealden', *Essex Historic Buildings Group Newsletter* (April 2014), 10–11.
131 ERO, SALE B/1493.
132 RCHM(E), Essex IV, 203; *EAH*, 15 (1983), 159; unpublished notes for Vernacular Architecture Group Essex Conference, 1984; Oxford Dendrochronology Laboratory Report 2014/4, *The Tree-ring dating of Tudor House, Bridge End, Newport, Essex* (2014).

Figure 7 *The Three Tuns, formerly an inn, now a private dwelling house. Probably late 15th century, but damaged by fire in 1914.*

Figure 8 *Priory Cottage and The Old Priory, Bridge End. Formerly one house, built c.1497. Divided into three in the 19th century, and now two cottages.*

Figure 9 *7 Belmont Hill. Timber-framed house probably built in the 1490s. Formerly two cottages, now extended to the north.*

Figure 10 *Crown House, Bridge End. Built in at least three separate stages from the 15th to the 17th century. The front, with the shell porch, was remodelled with pargetting in 1692.*

in 1914.[133] Priory Cottage, The Old Priory and The Priory were formerly a single house dating from the late 15th century (see fig. 8); timbers from the Old Priory and Priory Cottage have been tree-ring dated, and one tree was found to have been felled in 1497. Much of the front is jettied, but the front of The Priory, at the south-west end of the row, was remodelled in the 18th or early 19th century, with sash windows. Priory Cottage, at the north-east end, has an original oriel window, and inside a room with remains of 17th-century painted decoration. It consists of a frieze about 13 in. deep, reminiscent of Tudor cresting. The wall below was originally covered with a design of foliage and flowers, boldly drawn in freehand and outlined in black with dark green leaves.[134] Another house of similar date is No. 7 Belmont Hill, with jettied front and close studding (see fig. 9). The house has very large moulded ceiling beams, one of which has been tree-ring dated 1498–9.[135]

Of Newport's 16th-century houses, the most famous is Crown House (see fig. 10), although it owes its fame to late 17th-century refronting. The house seems to have been built in a number of phases, the earliest part being the rear wing. The front was originally jettied, with a carved bressumer, and was not then symmetrical. The house was remodelled in 1692, according to the date on the doorway. The front was covered with pargetted panels decorated with a crown, garlands, swags, and large leafy branches. Over the central doorway is a large shell-hood made of lead and plastered. The house served as an inn in the 17th and 18th centuries.[136] The date 1694 is found in the much plainer plasterwork of Mulrian House, High Street, which in this case seems to refer to the construction of the house rather than alterations (see fig. 12). Waterloo House, a little to the north, appears early 19th century, but its timbers have been dated to *c*.1580–1620; it was probably originally a farmhouse, but has been used as a shop since about 1769. The north part was added in the 17th century and faced in white brick in the 19th. At the back is a long weather-boarded range extending to the east.[137]

Other houses of the 16th century include Tuns Cottages, the Coach and Horses, Cambridge Road, and the Old Forge, High Street, all with exposed timbers and jettied fronts. In Wicken Road, Goodricks and Goodricks Cottage were originally a single tenement with a long-wall jetty (see fig. 17). There are only two houses that are still thatched, both probably of the 17th century: Granta, Station Road, and Nos 1–5 Church Street (see fig. 11).

A few houses along the High Street have conspicuous red brick Georgian fronts. That of The Georgians, with its pilasters, distinctive two-storey canted bay windows, and square oriel over the entrance, conceals an older, probably 17th-century house (see fig. 13). Its present appearance dates from 1760. There is also a completely Georgian rear wing.[138] Belmont Farmhouse's simpler Georgian front, five bays wide with a parapet and

133 NMR, RCHM investigators' notes and photographs; J. Murray, 'Pubs from the Past', *NN*, 16 (1981), 83–7.

134 *Essex Review*, 32 (1923), 39; RCHM(E), Essex I, 185; Oxford Dendrochronology Laboratory Report 2013/28, *The Tree-ring dating of the Old Priory/Priory Cottage, Newport, Essex* (2013).

135 Oxford Dendrochronology Laboratory Report 2014/3, *The Tree-ring dating of 7 Belmont Hill, Newport, Essex* (2014).

136 Unpublished notes for Vernacular Architecture Group Essex Conference, 1984; *NN*, 60 (2003), 34–5.

137 F. William, 'The Georgians', *NN*, 23 (1985), 7–9; *VIT*, 47.

138 Ibid., 21 (1984), 75–9; 32 (1989), 6–10; *VIT*, 47, 66.

Figure 11 *Nos 1–5 Church Street, probably 17th century, with part-thatched and part-tiled roofs.*

Figure 12 *Mulrian, High Street, formerly known as Willmary, with date 1694 on plasterwork, probably the date of construction.*

Figure 13 *The Georgians, High Street. Brick façade c.1760, fronting earlier timber-framed house.*

flat hood over the door, was also added to a 17th-century timber-framed house (see fig. 14). The two-bay addition to the left was built in 1913.[139] Even more complex is Belmont House, Belmont Hill, which is predominantly Georgian, with deeds dating from 1724, but it is Tudor in its oldest parts and has later additions, mostly in white brick. It contains panelling variously said to have come from Newport and Saffron Walden churches.[140] Pallett's Farm, High Street, is wholly 18th century (see fig. 31), and has a mansard roof typical of the date (like the more modest Old Manse, c.1775,[141] or Rookes House, Elephant Green (see fig. 16)), but the pedimented doorcase adds a touch of distinction. By contrast The White House, next to the Old Manse, also with a mansard roof, has a much more vernacular appearance, being timber-framed and plastered. Yet it has an elaborate, if somewhat crudely executed doorway, with semicircular fanlight. Newport House, also in the High Street, is the most classically Georgian of all, with its five-bay, two-storey front of red brick, and dormers almost concealed by a parapet (see fig. 37). The pedimented doorcase is more elaborate than Pallett's Farm's, with attached columns and a triglyph frieze with geometric decoration on the metopes. At the opposite end of the scale, Nos 1–3 Bury Water Lane are modest timber-framed and plastered cottages, originally built in 1798 as a 'working room for the use of the poor in the adjoining buildings'.[142] The latter, Nos 4–6, are even more modest, being single-storey without even attics.

The Late Georgian Rookes House has already been mentioned. Of similar age, or a little later, is Brighton Cottage, Wicken Road, with its Regency Gothick detailing.

139 NMR, RCHM investigators' notes and photographs.

140 'Belmont House', *NN*, 40 (1993), 23–5.

141 T. and T. William-Powlett, 'The Old Manse', *NN*, 53 (2000), 77–8; 54 (2000), 35–6.

142 Plaque on rear wall; *VIT*, 76.

Figure 14 *Belmont Farmhouse, Belmont Hill. Georgian façade to a timber-framed house. Extended in 1913, when this photograph was taken.*

Figure 15 *Belmont Hill, looking north. The Toll House (left) built in the early 19th century controlled the toll bridge over Bury Water until the toll was finally abolished in 1911. On the front of the building is a copy of the notice of the toll charges. (The original is in Saffron Walden Museum.) Distaff Cottage, or The Distaff (opposite) was the home in the 19th century of Charles Norman, a Methodist lay preacher. Date of construction is unknown. The Links (right foreground) was built in 1775 as the House of Correction. Closed in 1841, it is now flats.*

Figure 16 *Rookes House, Elephant Green, an 18th-century house timber-framed beneath its Georgian brick skin.*

Figure 17 *Goodricks and Brighton Cottages, Wicken Road. Goodricks cottages are probably 16th-century, Brighton Cottage, early 19th century in 'Gothick' style.*

The Bell House, Elephant Green, is also early 19th century, built in a fashionable white brick with a shallow-pitched slate roof. The Revd George Tamplin made this house the vicarage shortly after being appointed in 1876; extensive alterations and additions were carried out for him by Frederic Chancellor, 1900–1, almost doubling the size of the house but preserving the original front.[143]

There are a few Victorian houses of note. The largest is Parsonage House, next to the church (see fig. 18). Its appearance, name and position suggest that it was built as the vicarage, although this is not the case. It is of red brick, and some windows have pointed arches. Its most distinctive feature is four pairs of tall chimneys, possibly modelled on those of the Tudor House.[144] Typical of the era in their use of decorative brickwork are West View and Lantern Cottage, Church Street (red brick with quoins and ornamental bands of white brick), the latter dated 1863. Considerably more picturesque are a pair of semi-detached cottages in the High Street, Pond Cross Cottage and Pendean (see fig. 19). With their jettied upper storey, exposed timbers and brick nogging, they clearly seem to be influenced by Monk's Barn. Pond Cross Farm House, on the opposite side of the High Street, was rebuilt in 1852 for Henry Webb of Quendon Hall.[145] It is of red brick, with

Figure 18 *Parsonage House, Wicken Road. Victorian farm house building, with Tudor-style chimney stack, built for W.C. Smith of Shortgrove. Despite its name it was never the vicarage.*

143 ERO, D/F 8/672; *VIT*, 104–5.
144 A. Turnbull, 'Parsonage House', *NN*, 38 (1992), 105; 45 (1996), 94, notes that moulds of the bricks of Tudor House's chimneys were made for W.C. Smith of Shortgrove and used for a number of houses in the neighbourhood.
145 *NN*, 25 (1986), 47.

Figure 19 *Pond Cross Cottage and Pendean, High Street. Picturesque mid-Victorian cottages, built for Henry Webb, c.1860.*

two single-storey canted bays. It has one cross-wing, gabled in the manner of an open pediment (see fig. 28). The barns north-east of the house date back to the 16th century and were converted to housing in 1986.[146]

The opening of the railway in 1845 resulted in a small amount of new building, principally in Station Road. The station house, of red brick with white-brick dressings, is of 1845, but the remaining station buildings were remodelled from 1879 under the direction of the Great Eastern Railway's architect W. N. Ashbee.[147] Work progressed slowly and the waiting rooms were not opened until 1889.[148] An extensive maltings was erected near the station in 1853–5, with two tile-clad conical kilns; the buildings were converted to other commercial uses in 1982 and 1987–9.[149] A pair of semi-detached villas was built in front of the maltings in 1856. On the south side of Station Road is another good example of an industrial building, known as The New Granary, and probably dating from the early years of the 20th century. It is of red brick with dressings and other decoration of dark blue engineering brick. The windows of both storeys have segmental heads and cast-iron glazing.

Most of Newport's 20th-century housing is to be found on the west side of the High Street behind the old frontage. One of the earliest, and largest, developments was Cherry Garden Lane (see map 5), by Federated Design and Building Group Ltd (chief architect, J. Benjamin). Planning permission was granted for 121 houses early in 1970

146 Ibid., 22 (1984), 8–13; 25 (1986), 39; L.P. Davies, 'Living in a Barn', 26 (1986), 83.
147 P. Kay, *Essex Railway Heritage* (Wivenhoe, Essex, 2006), 25, 44, 120.
148 J. Boutwood, 'Understanding your house', *NN*, 14 (1980), 35.
149 P. Barnard, 'New Life at the Station', *NN*, 18 (1982), 25–33; 31 (1989), 48–9; *VIT*, 170.

Figure 20 'Country Life' Cottages, built 1914, following a design competition in Country Life. The architect was H.W. Hobbiss and they were financed by William Foot Mitchell.

and the first houses were completed later that year. The varied layout of the housing and use of traditional materials led to its being selected as an example of good practice by the influential *Essex Design Guide*.[150] The most interesting individual building is the pair of cottages built between Church Street and Elephant Green by W. Foot Mitchell of Quendon Hall in 1914 (Hill View and Nolton Cottage). The walls are pargetted in the traditional Essex manner but the design is otherwise of its time, with a hipped slate roof that continues down at either end to enclose porches (see fig. 20). The design, by Holland W. Hobbiss, was the winning entry in its category of a competition organised by *Country Life*, of which Foot Mitchell was one of the judges.[151] Another example of modern pargetting can be seen on The Old House, High Street. The building is of the late 17th century, and had been used latterly as a shop. The pargetted frieze was executed in the traditional manner by Bill Sargent of Hessett, Suffolk, in 2010, following conversion to a private residence.[152]

In the early 21st century Larkfield, Debden Road, was built for Ian and Susan Vance to designs by David Mickhail Architects following a competition. Planning permission was granted in 2004 and it was completed in 2007. It is of two storeys, the rendered upper storey giving the impression of floating above the ground floor whose walls are largely of glass. In plan it is L-shaped, creating a sheltered courtyard on to which the main living rooms open. It was shortlisted for a RIBA award in 2008.[153]

150 ECC, *A Design Guide for Residential Areas* (Chelmsford, 1973), 24–5; *ERA*, 5 (May–June 1972), 14, 15, 19; *NN*, 60 (2003), 49–50; below, p. 154–60 for fuller details.
151 *Country Life* 35 (1914), 865; 37 (1915), 679; L. Weaver, *The "Country Life" Book of Cottages* (London, 1919), 64–6; L. Weaver, *Cottages: their Planning, Design and Materials* (London, 1926), 103–4; *NN*, 31 (1989), 96–7.
152 L.J. Gordon, 'A remarkable skill', *NN*, 74 (2010), 41.
153 *Building Design* no. 1614 (27 Feb. 2004), 6; *Building* 273 (15 Feb. 2008), 26–7; *Architecture Today* no. 186 (March 2008), 30–36; http://www.davidmikhail.com/projects.php/The-Vance-House-6/ (accessed 2 April 2014).

Figure 21 *W.C. Smith (1801–83), eldest son of Joseph and Margaret Smith. Date unknown but possibly 1860s. He inherited the Shortgrove estate in 1822.*

IN A LETTER TO THE SECRETARY of the Local Government Board in December 1886, Charles Wade, agent for the Shortgrove estate, wrote that 'the Quendon Hall estate…with the Shortgrove estate comprises nearly the whole of the parish of Newport.'[1] Thirteen years later, in September 1899, writing to the same body about a proposed sewerage scheme in Newport, Colonel Alfred Cranmer-Byng, the owner of the Quendon Hall estate, made much the same point. 'I am', he wrote, 'the greatest ratepayer and one of the largest landowners in the village.'[2]

These assertions were neither idle boasts nor exaggerations designed to draw attention to the burden of rates. Both the Newport tithe map and schedule of 1839–40 and the 1864 revised tithe award show that they were well-founded. Anne Cranmer (with her immediate relatives) and W.C. Smith, the owners of Quendon Hall and Shortgrove respectively, were by some distance the largest landowners in the parish in terms of acreage, and for much of the 19th century neither estate disposed of sufficient property to change the position substantially.[3] In the first half of the 20th century, however, both estates disposed of property on such a scale that by the latter part of the century their dominant position had been substantially eroded.

Shortgrove Estate and Manor

The history of the estate is very complex and it has passed through many hands, ranging from the noble to the notorious. Its core lay on the east bank of the Cam in the north-east of the parish of Newport. From the 11th century onwards it was based

1   TNA, MH 12/3722.
2   Ibid., MH 12/3727; *Return of Owners of Land*, (1871), Essex, 8, 41.
3   ERO, D/CT 252A,B; TNA, IR/12/243AA.

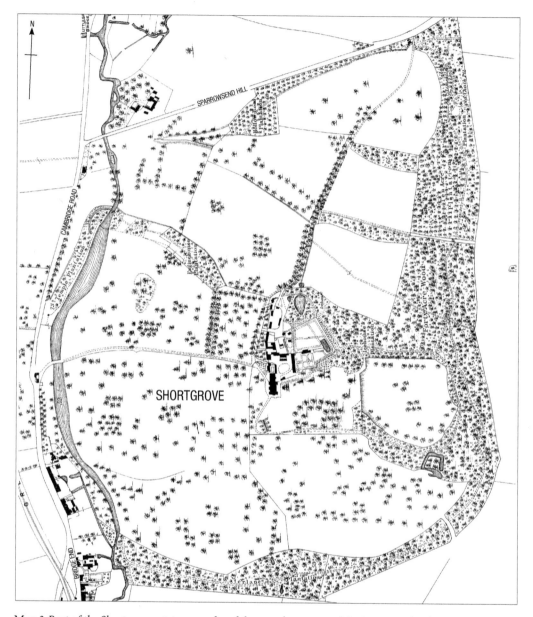

Map 3 *Part of the Shortgrove estate, reproduced from a plan prepared for Messrs Debenham, Tewson, Farmer and Bridgewater for the sale of the Shortgrove Estate in June 1889. The source is unknown, but may be the Ordnance Survey 1/2500 plan of 1877. The section reproduced shows the Hall at the junction of two long wooded drives overlooking the river Cam at the centre of a mature Capability Brown landscape. The pleasure grounds to the north-east of the house are a notable feature of the estate, while to the west are the lake, bridge, temple and deer park.*

on the manor of Shortgrove, and has passed through several cycles of expansion and contraction within Newport and into adjacent and distant parishes. It has had a long and close association with the parish of Widdington, notably with the estate of Widdington Veyses or Voyses.[4] The estate included many detached areas of Widdington parish, which were the consequence of intermingled strips in an open field system part of which was abolished when Shortgrove Park was formed in the 18th century.[5] Successive alterations to the parish boundaries of Newport and Widdington, notably in the years after the Second World War, have brought most of them into the present civil parish of Newport.[6] For most of its history the estate has been a mixed agricultural one, combining arable, pasture, dairy and woodland. In the 20th century it became a noted sporting estate, although agriculture continued to have an important role. After the Second World War the estate was gradually returned to intensive arable production, especially following the sale of the Hall and its subsequent destruction by fire.[7]

In 1066 the vill of Shortgrove was held by three Anglo-Saxon lords. Wulfwin and Grimkel held two hides as a manor, and another unnamed freeman held a further one hide and 30 a. In 1086 the land of Wulfwin and Grimkel formed part of the fee of Robert Gernon and his heirs, who also held Stansted Mountfichet.[8] The land of the unnamed freeman had been appropriated by Ingelric after 1066, but by 1086 it formed part of the fee of Eustace count of Boulogne and was described as a manor.[9] Ingelric was probably Ingelric the priest, one of the co-founders of the collegiate church of St Martin le Grand and a member of the household of count Eustace. He acquired lands and several churches in west Essex, which formed part of the endowment of his foundation.[10]

The count of Boulogne subinfeudated his manor of Shortgrove to Adelulf, a member of a younger branch of the de Merc family, *vicomtes* of Marck, a lordship which lay within the lands of the counts of Boulogne near Calais.[11] Sometime between 1189 and 1198 William de Warenne, who had inherited the Boulogne fee, ordered Adelulf's descendant Geoffrey de Merc to inform the bishop of London that henceforth he would render tithes to the college of St Martin le Grand, which already owned the church of Newport.[12] The tenurial arrangement in the vill of Shortgrove led to the manor of Shortgrove being in Newport parish, and the Gernon fee, which was later known, from the name of one of its tenants, as the manor of Widdington Veyses, being in Widdington parish. The complex boundary between Newport and Widdington parishes probably dates from this arrangement.[13]

4   Morant II, 566, 585–6.

5   O. Rackham, *The History of the Countryside* (London, 1986), 21.

6   Above, pp. 2–3.

7   Below, pp. 45–6.

8   DB, 1020.

9   Ibid., 990.

10   *The Religious Houses of London and Middlesex*, ed. C.M. Barron and M. Davies (London, 2007), 196–8, updating *VCH London* I (1903); P. Taylor, 'Ingelric, Count Eustace and the Foundation of St Martin-le-Grand', *Anglo-Norman Studies*, XXIV (Woodbridge, 2001), 215–38. Shortgrove is not included in the discussion of Ingelric's estates in this article, and the identification should be treated with caution.

11   DB, 990.

12   WAM, 962; Book 5, f. ix v.

13   Above, p. 2.

Between 1175 and 1180 a charter of Henry II confirmed the de Merc family's subinfeudation of their manor of Shortgrove to the Priory of St Bartholomew the Great in Smithfield,[14] and the Priory retained possession until the dissolution. In 1306 the Priory's rental noted that in the manor of Shortgrove the Prior and Convent paid to the parish church of Newport, in whose parish it was situated, 2s. for the lesser tithes arising from the manor.[15]

In 1540, after the dissolution of the religious houses, all the possessions of the Priory were granted for life to the last prior, Thomas Fuller;[16] but he died later the same year, and in 1544 Henry VIII granted the manor of Shortgrove and its appurtenances to Edward Elrington, a member of the royal household who also purchased other monastic lands, including Denny Abbey (Cambs.).[17] However, Elrington had great difficulty in gaining possession, since in 1534 Prior Fuller had granted it to John Wykham.[18] Shortly afterwards Wykham sold his interest to William and Thomas Hodge, who had entered the property. Elrington maintained that, in face of his grant from the Crown, the Hodges had no proper title to the property, and the matter ended up first in the Court of Requests and then in Star Chamber.[19] Elrington evidently won his case, for when he died in 1559 he was said to have been seised of the manor of Shortgrove, together with Widdington Veyses and Bonhunt.[20] The manor passed to his son Edward, who died in 1578 leaving as his heir his son, also called Edward, who was only seven years old. Elrington's widow, Dorothy, was left a life interest in the property.[21]

In September 1616 the third Edward Elrington sold the manor and its appurtenances to Richard Peacock for £48.[22] His son William Peacock inherited it in 1634, but over the next 20 years it changed hands three times: it passed to Elizabeth Dunbar in 1640–4, John Benson in 1646–8, and then in 1653–6 it was purchased by Giles Dent.[23] Dent was a London merchant, a member of the Salters' Company, and in 1653 an alderman of the City of London for Vintry Ward.[24] He also acquired the neighbouring Widdington Veyses estate, thus bringing under single ownership the complex intermingled strips of land some of which lay in Newport parish and some in Widdington.[25] He died in 1671, and his son, also Giles (d. 1712), inherited the manor and built the Hall, which survived until it was destroyed by fire in 1966.[26] Shortly before his death, probably in 1708–9, he sold the manor to Henry O'Brien, 7th earl of Thomond (1688–1741) who held land in both England and Ireland.[27]

14   *The Records of St Bartholomew's Priory*, ed. E.A. Webb (Oxford, 1921), II, appendix 1, 431.
15   Ibid., 431–2.
16   *L & P Henry VIII* 16 (1540–1), 715.
17   Ibid., 19 part 1 (1544), 278–9.
18   *Records of St Bartholomew*, II, 329.
19   TNA, REQ 2/17/111; STAC 4/10/25.
20   Ibid., C 142/118/52.
21   Ibid., C 142/180/47.
22   Ibid., CP 25/2/295.
23   D/DQ 14/135.
24   A.P. Beaven, *Aldermen of the City of London, Temp. Henry III–1912* (London, 1908 onwards); online version at http://www.british-history.ac.uk (accessed 16 Nov. 2013).
25   D/DQ 14/145.
26   Below, pp. 45–6.
27   ERO, D/ABW 81/62; D/P 15/8/4.

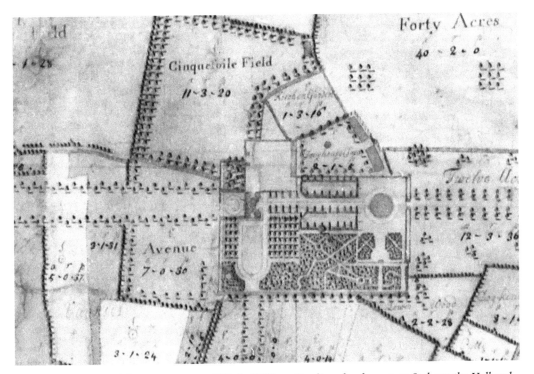

Map 4 Part of Map of Shortgrove estate, 1727, by William Gardiner, land surveyor. It shows the Hall and the grounds before they were remodelled by Matthew Brettingham and Capability Brown respectively.

While still a minor, Thomond had married Elizabeth Seymour, daughter of the 6th duke of Somerset and Elizabeth Percy, sole heir to the earl of Northumberland.[28] Henry Howard of neighbouring Audley End (later 6th earl of Suffolk) was his uncle and later his stepfather. Thomond served as MP for Arundel (1710–14),[29] and in 1714 he was created Viscount Tadcaster, in the English peerage, as a reward for his support for the Hanoverian succession. He also became a Privy Councillor for Ireland.[30]

Thomond greatly enlarged Dent's house, improved the gardens and by 1719 had purchased three manors in nearby Ickleton (Cambs.).[31] In 1727 he commissioned a survey of his estate, which now extended over about 600 a. including 12 detached parts of Widdington parish and five of Newport parish, together with land leased from the Suffolk estate and others.[32]

Thomond died in 1741 without issue and deeply in debt, owing to 'his feckless mismanagement and reckless expenditure'.[33] He willed his estate in trust for life to Murrough, Lord O'Brien, the son and heir of the earl of Inchiquin (a distant kinsman)

28   GEC, XII/I, 712–3.

29   *Hist. Parl.*, 1690–1715, V, 1–2.

30   GEC, XII/I, 712/3.

31   CRO, 51R 51/29/2B; *VCH Cambs* 6, 263–4.

32   ERO, T/M 298.

33   A.P.W. Malcomson, *The Pursuit of the Heiress: Aristocratic Marriage in Ireland 1740–1840* (Belfast, for the Ulster Historical Foundation, 2006), 86–8.

with remainder in default to his nephew Percy Wyndham, younger brother of the second earl of Egremont of Petworth House, in tail male conditional on his taking the name O'Brien.[34] Murrough O'Brien died an unmarried minor in 1741 shortly after Thomond himself. That, together with the difficulties of administering Thomond's encumbered estates, delayed a final settlement until 1772, though Percy Wyndham evidently had possession of the Shortgrove estate at least 20 years earlier, after he had changed his name to O'Brien.[35] In 1756 he was created baron Ibrackan and earl of Thomond (in the Irish Peerage).[36]

Wyndham was wealthy enough to invest heavily in improvements to the Shortgrove estate.[37] In 1760 he purchased Hospital Farm, (about 198 a.) valued at around £6,000,[38] together with the holdings of the earl of Bristol in the manor of Newport Pond formerly belonging to the earl of Suffolk.[39] These changes created a substantial estate with a large mansion having magnificent views set in splendid pleasure grounds and gardens. The lordships of the manors of Newport Pond and Shortgrove thus came into the hands of one owner.

Wyndham was an MP for 29 years, sitting for Taunton (1745–7), Minehead (1747–54 and 1761–8), Cockermouth (1754–61) and Winchelsea (1768–74). He generally supported Pitt and Grenville, without being very active in the House.[40] At Shortgrove he was mostly an absentee landlord, leaving his affairs largely in the hands of his steward, William Smith.[41] He died unmarried and intestate in 1774, and as a result the peerage became extinct.[42] His estate passed to his uncle George O'Brien, third earl of Egremont of Petworth House, Sussex, who also retained the large Irish estates.[43] In 1782, after delays caused by numerous claims and disputes, Egremont gave Shortgrove along with the manor of Newport Pond, property in Newport, Widdington and Wendens Ambo comprising about 800 a. freehold, and about 50 a. copyhold at Brook Walden, to his brother Percy Charles Wyndham (1757–1833).[44]

In 1786 Wyndham commissioned a map of Newport.[45] Though now in poor condition, it shows the Shortgrove Estate and the Brown/Brettingham alterations[46] including the lake, shelter belts, plantations and gardens. The complex pattern of small strips in the Veyses field is clear but the ownership of several fields cannot be deciphered. Wyndham was also an MP, sitting for Chichester in 1780–4 and Midhurst in 1790–6.[47]

34   TNA, PROB 11/712; WSRO, PHA, 1605; NRO, E(GB) 18.
35   PHA, 1139, 10957; NRO, E(GB) 22.
36   GEC, XII/I, 712–3.
37   PHA, 7428, K5/9.
38   PHA., K5/9.
39   ERO, T/B 142/7.
40   *Hist. Parl.*, 1715–54, II, 564; ibid., 1754–90, III, 667–8.
41   PHA, K5/9.
42   GEC, XII/I, 713.
43   Malcomson, *Pursuit of the Heiress*, 88.
44   PHA, K5/X16, 7874–5; ERO, Q/RPL 898, 891.
45   ERO, D/DU 205/19.
46   Below, p. 48.
47   ERO, D/DU 205/19; *Hist. Parl.*, 1754–90, III, 667.

In 1802 Wyndham sold his Shortgrove estate (about 895 a.) for £40,000 to Joseph Smith.[48] The Smiths were the first family since the Dents to make the Hall their principal residence. Joseph Smith, a graduate of Gonville and Caius College Cambridge,[49] had secured a position in the Treasury, becoming personal and confidential secretary to William Pitt the Younger, by whose patronage he obtained a number of lucrative posts.[50] He made an advantageous second marriage in 1798 to Margaret Cocks, a niece of Earl Somers, and an heiress in her own right (see fig. 22).[51] Margaret Smith was attracted to evangelical movements such as the Clapham Sect, and both she and her husband were described by the then vicar, Revd Bell, as 'rare instances of exemplary piety and unbounded but well directed charity.'[52]

Smith extended the estate, purchasing property in Newport in 1814.[53] He also acquired holdings in Wendens Ambo and Wicken Bonhunt, and it seems likely that other land was purchased at about the same time.[54] On his death in 1822 his entailed estate passed to his widow as trustee for their eldest son William Charles Smith (1801–83).[55] The estate proved to be heavily encumbered however, and the family was forced to retrench at home, though Margaret continued her benefactions to institutions outside Newport such as the Magdalene Hospital in London until her death in 1849.[56] The core estate was let on a long lease from around 1824 to Sir John St Aubyn Bt, FRS (1758–1839), an eminent natural scientist and a notable patron of the arts.[57] By 1834, however, Sir John's health had begun to fail and he moved to his London house. He made no material changes to the Hall and estate and the only reminders of his stay are various memorials to his grandchildren and personal servants at the parish church and a part of his collection of minerals, which he donated to the Saffron Walden Museum.[58]

Following the sale of Sir John's chattels at Shortgrove in 1834, the estate was returned by 1839 to William Charles Smith, who graduated from Gonville and Caius College Cambridge in 1822 and was admitted to Lincoln's Inn in the same year (see fig. 21).[59] In 1838–9 the Smith estate amounted to 951 a. in Newport and 335 a. in Widdington, approximately one half of which consisted of detached portions within the Park and fields in Shortgrove.[60] In Newport the estate comprised the Park and Home Farms and

48   TNA, CP 43/875 634 (Hilary term 42 Geo. III); ERO, Q/RPL 917, 918.

49   J. Venn, *Biographical History of Gonville and Caius College* (Cambridge, 1898), II, 1713–1897, 95.

50   P. Heriz-Smith, 'Joseph Smith and Shortgrove', *NN*, 35 (1991), 26–8; idem, 'The Smith Family of Shortgrove', *NN*, 34 (1990), 48–50.

51   Meyer Letters 1906–14, CLXXIX, referring to a remark by J.C.T. Heriz-Smith about the source of the family's wealth.

52   LPL, Randolph 11/48; ERO, TB/29.

53   G. White, 'Newport House in 1814', *NN*, 41 (1994), 86–7.

54   *The East Anglian* I, (1866), 220–9.

55   TNA, PROB 11/1675.

56   Smith Papers (in a private collection): (i) Q 23–27: letter to William Smith from Thomas Probert, solicitor; (ii) G 21–24: letter from Margaret Smith to Thomas Probert, dated 1825.

57   *ODNB* 48, 591–2; *NN*, 40 (1993), 107–8; *Pigot's Directory*, 1832. For an on-line exposition of the life and collections of St Aubyn see Plymouth City Museum & Art Gallery, St Aubyn Collection.

58   MISM, 4, 175, 417: *NN*, 40 (1993) 107–8, ibid., 71 (2009), 34–5; Saffron Walden Natural History Society, Register No. 1, 21 Aug. 1834, 140 specimens of minerals from Sir John St Aubyn of Shortgrove Hall.

59   CRO, 296/B190, 296/B473/5; Venn, *Alumni*, II, 573.

60   ERO, D/CT 252A; D/CT 398A.

Figure 22 *Margaret Cocks (1773–1847, married Joseph Smith of Shortgrove) and her niece, by Sir Joshua Reynolds, c.1790. Oil on canvas.*

other large farms including Hospital, Parsonage, Sparrows End and White Ditch farms, together with Monk's Barn, Newport House, the Priory cottages, Crown House, Martin's Farm (part of which is now known as Tudor House), the Coach and Horses inn and many more modest houses and shops. The construction of the railway in 1845 required the surrender of 17 a. of land.[61]

W.C. Smith added to his father's already substantial collection of silver, ceramics, glass, books and paintings. Two of the paintings from his collection form part of the Iveagh Bequest at Kenwood, London. One is the Sir Thomas Lawrence portrait of Pitt, probably commissioned by Joseph Smith, and the other a portrait of Margaret Cocks painted before her marriage.[62] W.C. Smith also continued the charitable and pious traditions of his parents, making large contributions to the church and raising funds for the rebuilding of the church tower, while he and his sister helped to defray the costs of building the National School.[63]

Smith died without issue, and under the terms of the entail made by Joseph Smith, the property then passed to W.C. Smith's nephew Joseph Charles Thomas Smith, who later assumed the surname Heriz-Smith.[64] He did not intend to live at the Hall, and in 1883 began to dispose of the estate. He held a successful four-day sale of its contents including

---

61   TNA, IR 29/12/243; IR 30/12/243; above, p.15..
62   Catalogue of Iveagh Bequest, Kenwood, 17, 24; private papers of Mrs S. Campbell.
63   Below, p. 98 and fig. 43.
64   TNA, PROB 11/1675; MISM Memorial no. 408.

Figure 23 *James Bailey, hotelier, company director, and MP. Owner of Shortgrove 1894–1903.*

furniture and wine.[65] This was followed by another successful sale at Sotheby's in May 1889 of a portion of W.C. Smith's library.[66] One month later he offered for sale the whole of his landed estate in lots, including Shortgrove Hall, the park, pleasure grounds etc. amounting in total to 3,123 a.[67] The estate failed to sell, however, and in May 1892, he promoted another auction at Shortgrove, this time of the remaining furniture and the collection of paintings.[68]

At some point after the unsuccessful sale in June 1889, Lord Cardross, later earl of Buchan, purchased the Hall itself and the parkland, together with some of the farms, mostly on the east bank of the Cam, and the lordship of the manor of Shortgrove. The sale took place sometime around 1892, probably by private treaty. Cardross made many improvements to the estate, but in 1894 he sold it to James Bailey for £30,000.[69] Bailey was a successful London hotelier who had sold his hotels when he acquired Shortgrove (see fig. 23). He was also a director of Harrods and other London retail companies and an active vestryman in Kensington.[70] In 1895 he was elected MP for Walworth (London). He lived on a lavish scale at Shortgrove, holding many weekend parties at the Hall, including one for 800 villagers.

Bailey's tenure too proved short-lived. In 1903 he sold the estate, which then amounted to *c.*930 a., for £60,000 to Carl Ferdinand Meyer (1851–1922).[71] Meyer was the second son of a Hamburg banker who had emigrated to London in 1872 with an introduction to the Rothschilds (see fig. 24). He was a major figure in international banking representing the Rothschild interest, especially in South Africa. He was a director of de Beers, the National Bank of Egypt, and the Hong Kong and Shanghai Banking Corporation. He was also a patron of the arts, especially the theatre and opera, and a racehorse owner. His services to the arts, notably a donation of £70,000 to a fund for the development of a National Theatre, were rewarded by his elevation in 1910 to a baronetcy with the title of first baronet of Shortgrove.[72]

65   CRO, 588/E111.
66   Ibid., 588/E112, 115.
67   ERO, D/DBI T46; SALE/B1574.
68   CRO, 588/E117.
69   ERO, SALE/A1055. Bailey was knighted in 1905.
70   *Survey of London* (London, for the LCC, 1900 onwards), 42: Kensington Square to Earl's Court (the Alexander Estate), 7; *NN*, 43 (1995), 83–7.
71   ERO, D/DU 775/1; TNA, HO 45/19685.
72   *ODNB* 37, 984.

Figure 24 *Portrait of Carl Meyer (1851–1922) by Hubert von Herkomer, 1908. Oil on canvas.*

Meyer's purchase of Shortgrove, along with Sir William Foot Mitchell's purchase of the Quendon Hall estate five years later[73] marks the arrival in Newport of the Edwardian plutocracy. Such men bought country estates for leisure and sport, and to express their new-found social status; and Meyer and his wife had been looking for a suitable house in north Essex for a year or two before they bought Shortgrove. They wanted a house that was fairly close to Newmarket, for Meyer was an enthusiastic race-goer, and which was suitable for entertaining, particularly shooting parties.[74] As Adèle Meyer, Carl's wife, put it shortly after the purchase of Shortgrove, 'we enrolled [among the] landed gentry.'[75]

Shooting parties were held regularly during Meyer's time at Shortgrove. In December 1904, for example, he noted that 'we had a splendid day's shooting again yesterday. 418

73   Below, pp. 54–5.
74   Meyer Letters, CXXXIII.
75   Tessa Murdoch and Anthony Meyer, 'Sargent's "Mrs. Carl Meyer at Home"', *The Catalogue of Art and Antiques*, Dec. 2004, 226–9.

pheasants. 15 hares, 11 wild duck.'[76] His parties were not always socially exclusive: in 1905 he wrote that 'the tenants…had an excellent day's shooting yesterday and killed over 120 head of game…The tenants, 7 in number, killed 50 cocks, 23 partridges, 36 hares.'[77] Meyer also enlarged his holdings, buying land on Cambridge Road in Newport and also part of the Debden estate, including Brick House Farm, which abutted on the Shortgrove estate boundary.[78]

Sir Carl was the object of anti-German feeling during the First World War, and in 1915 he was asked to resign his post with the Hong Kong and Shanghai Bank.[79] On his death in 1922, the estate, then extending to 1079 a., passed to his wife. She seems to have thought that the village showed little gratitude for what she had done to improve the welfare of mothers and children before the First World War, and in 1924 she offered the estate for sale by auction.[80]

It was purchased for £44,000 by Capt. F.J.O. Montagu M.C. (1878–1956), who had served with the Coldstream Guards in the South African and First World Wars. Like his immediate predecessors he valued the estate as much for its shooting as for the income it produced, especially during the post-war depression in land values.[81] He bought much of the rest of the Debden estate, mainly for the shooting, but he failed to find a tenant for Debden Hall, which was pulled down in 1936.[82] He retained Shortgrove until 1938 when he sold it for £38,000 to Thomas Place. The Shortgrove estate then included 1079 a. in Newport and Widdington and a total of 2286 a. overall.[83] Place, a property speculator, quickly sold the Hall, its park, pleasure grounds and adjacent farms, amounting to around 750 a., to C.H.A. Butler.[84] During the Second World War part of the estate was occupied by the military, including a US Army Field Hospital.[85] In 1963 the Hall and the adjacent gardens amounting to about 50 a. were sold to a development company. The Butlers moved to a new house on the estate, retaining the remainder of around 700 a., run in 2014 as an agricultural holding by C.H.A. Butler's son Arthur. In June 1966 the Hall was destroyed by fire.[86]

Shortgrove Hall

Shortgrove Hall was built in 1684 by Giles Dent, junior.[87] There had been an older house on a different site, probably within the homestead moat that remains about 400 yds south-east of the present house. Dent's house was built of red brick and was of modified H-plan, two storeys high. The entrance front was seven bays wide, the centre

76   Meyer Letters, CCXXII.
77   Meyer Letters, CCXXXVII.
78   ERO, D/DU 775/7, 9.
79   D. Kynaston, *City of London*, II (1995), 30.
80   NLHG Collections, Particulars and Conditions of Sale, July 1924; SPAB Archives, File on The Old Priory and Priory Cottage; below, pp. 84–7.
81   *Who's Who in Essex* (1938), 197; ERO, D/DU775/17.
82   V. Chapman, 'The Rise and Fall of Debden Hall', *NN*, 31 (1989), 12–15.
83   ERO, D/DU 775/22, SALE/B1493.
84   H. Butler, 'A History of Shortgrove', *NN*, 4 (1975), 47–8.
85   'The American Hospital at Shortgrove', *NN*, 70 (2008), 60–2.
86   Below, p. 46.
87   Dent's Monument in Newport Church; Morant, II, 586.

Figure 25 *Aerial view of Shortgrove Hall and immediate surroundings, taken in 1964, two years before it was gutted by fire.*

three bays being slightly recessed. The recess on the opposite (east) side was probably deeper (see map 4). There were three principal rooms on the ground floor, in addition to the entrance hall and separate staircase hall. The staircase had a balustrade of delicate wrought-iron scrolls.[88] The architect is not known, but Henry Winstanley of Littlebury has been suggested.[89]

Alterations to the house were made by Henry O'Brien, earl of Thomond, between 1712 and 1727. Three-bay pavilions were built at each corner, and a third storey was added. The east front, whose three-bay centre was framed by giant pilasters, was rebuilt further out a little later. By 1774 the house had 50 rooms.[90] The windows on the top floor have segmental heads characteristic of the early 18th century. A tetrastyle Tuscan portico was also added to the entrance front. The brick quoins and raised bands between the storeys were probably features of the 1684 house that were repeated on later additions. Percy Wyndham (later Percy Wyndham O'Brien, earl of Thomond) employed the architect Matthew Brettingham between 1757 and 1762, and Matthew Brettingham the younger was working at Shortgrove in 1767–9.[91]

88   RCHM (E), *Essex*, I (1916), 201–2 and investigators' notes at NMR; N. Pevsner, *Essex* (1954), 279. Pevsner thought that the house might have been built earlier in the 17th century, citing 'e.g. the secondary staircase', but it is equally likely that the staircase and other materials were reused from the old house.
89   Alison Barnes, pers. comm.
90   The corner pavilions are shown on an estate map of 1727 (ERO, T/M 298/1), but the west front appears to be in its original position: Inventory, PHA 6280; *NN*, 25 (1986), 48–9; see map 4.
91   H.M. Colvin, *Biographical Dictionary of British Architects 1600–1840* (New Haven and London, 2008), 156, 158; PHA, IC 5/9.

Figure 26 *Shortgrove Hall. The 13-bay brick-built house, with the smaller Giles Dent house of 1684 at its core. The Capability Brown ha-ha remains, but the house was destroyed by fire in 1966.*

Further alterations, probably made in the latter part of the 19th century, included a three-storey addition (with two-storey canted bay) between the two pavilions on the south side of the house, and a single-storey addition in the corresponding position on the north side. Beyond the latter was a two-storey, seven-bay wing, set slightly back, leading to a service court.[92] A single-storey ballroom was added to the south front after 1925. Shortly after the Second World War the north wing and service court were demolished and the house was generally modernised.[93]

Although the house was gutted by fire in 1966, the shell was not finally demolished until 1979.[94] In 1982 the site was sold with planning permission for a replacement house designed by Biscoe & Stanton. This would have been Georgian in style, five bays wide and two-and-a-half storeys high. It incorporated the ballroom, which had survived the fire.[95] In 1984 a new house was built, but on a smaller scale, designed by the owner, Paul Sharpe. Permission to build a castle-style house had been refused and in its place a modest neo-Georgian house was erected. It was of red brick, of three bays and two storeys. Plans to build additional wings were apparently not executed.[96] This was replaced in 2000–1 with a new house designed by Cowper Griffith Architects for James Scruby, who had purchased 17 a. of the grounds. It too is of red brick, and is two storeys high, with attics above a heavy cornice. The three-bay centre is recessed and there is a recessed portico with square columns. At the corners are one-bay pavilions, slightly higher than the centre. The windows are wide, and widely spaced. The house is situated on the footprint of the 1684 house, and reuses part of the original vaulted cellars, as well as a

92   RCHM(E), 201–2. The additions, and a further range to the north, are shown on the plan in the 1889 sale catalogue (ERO, SALE/B1574).
93   *NN,* 3 (1975), 47–8.
94   Ibid., 11 (1979), 7.
95   Sales particulars, NMR; *Country Life,* 169 (9 April 1981), 966.
96   *Saffron Walden Weekly News,* 9 Feb., 10 May, 27 Sept. 1984.

section of original walling. There is also a reused rainwater head with the initial and coronet of the earl of Thomond. A freestanding garage with pyramidal roof was built to the north of the house.[97]

A large stable yard stands to the north of Shortgrove Hall with a stable block on the east side. It is shown on the estate map of 1727,[98] and shares many of the stylistic features of the house as it then stood. It is of red brick, with brick quoins, and of two storeys. It is eleven bays wide; the outer bays and the wider central bay project slightly and carry stone busts. The central bay is wider, with an archway (now blocked), pediment, and timber clock-turret with an open domed bell-turret. The first-floor windows have segmental heads. In 1975–6 the block was converted to three houses by Michael Biscoe, of Biscoe & Stanton, in partnership with a builder, Paul Kerridge; they occupied two of the three houses themselves.[99]

North of the stable yard is a group of farm buildings, mainly of the late 18th and early 19th century. The earliest building is a late 18th-century dovecote in the centre of the farmyard. It is of red brick, square, with a pyramidal roof. A number of estate buildings were converted to residential use, c.2005–10.[100] Le Pavillon, north of the stable yard, was built from estate cottages enlarged and remodelled by Richard Tyler, 1962–3.[101]

Gardens were laid out by Henry O'Brien, earl of Thomond, between 1712 and 1727, in particular a walled garden on the east side of the stables. Morant noted that there were canals, or formal ponds, 'served with water thrown up from the river Cam below, by an engine contrived by Dr Desaguliers' (the natural philosopher and engineer J.T. Desaguliers).[102] In the mid 19th century this area was laid out as a rose garden and Italian garden by William Chater of Saffron Walden.[103]

The park, which in 1727 comprised small fields crossed by straight avenues running from the east and west fronts of the house, was landscaped by Capability Brown under contracts entered into in 1753 and 1754. Payments to Brown are recorded up to 1764 and landscaping work was still in progress in 1772.[104] As well as the planting of clumps of trees and more extensive belts of woodland, Brown's improvements included remodelling the approach to the house, and widening the Cam on the western edge of the park. The river was crossed by a stone bridge of three arches designed by the elder Matthew Brettingham (see fig. 27). He or his son also designed a classical temple, built in 1768 in a plantation on the west bank of the river north of the bridge. It was built of stone, on a half-H plan, with Tuscan columns and pediments at the ends of the wings. The mason was John Gilliam.[105] The gateway at the entrance to the park from Newport has piers of red brick with stone caps and urns, and elaborate wrought-iron gates and overthrow.

97   *EAH,* 32 (2001), 262; *NN,* 56 (2001), 33–5; http://www.cowpergriffith.co.uk (accessed 29 Mar. 2012).
98   ERO, T/M 298.
99   Ibid., D/DU 1122; *Country Life,* 169 (9 April 1981), 966.
100 *EAH,* 28 (2007), 182–3; Uttlesford District Council, planning applications.
101 A. Butler, 'Le Pavillon', *NN,* 61 (2004), 26–7.
102 Morant, II, 586. The gardens are shown on an estate map of 1727: ERO, T/M 298.
103 *Essex Gardens Trust Newsletter,* 9 (Autumn 2000), 4.
104 Ibid., 9, (Autumn 2000), 1–4; I. Mollet, 'Lancelot "Capability" Brown at Shortgrove', *NN,* 56 (2001), 22–3.
105 PHA, 7428; I. Mollet, 'The Temple at Shortgrove', *NN,* 57 (2002), 45–8. Part of it can be seen in the 1889 sale catalogue: ERO, SALE/B1574. Brettingham junior was involved, but perhaps only as his father's representative.

Figure 27 The Newport entrance to the Shortgrove estate showing the 19th-century gates, restored in 2000. The bridge is by Matthew Brettingham, who was working at Shortgrove between 1757 and 1762.

The gates seem to have been installed between 1889 and 1894, and the half-timbered lodge beside the entrance was built at about the same time. The urns and overthrow were added to the gateway in the early 20th century.[106] Only vestiges of the 18th-century landscape remain, notably Brettingham's bridge and Brown's ha-ha which still exists though the deer park is now a mix of pasture and arable land. Late in the 1940s the lake was drained to relieve flooding in Bridge End and the Temple was demolished in the early 1950s.[107]

The Manor of Newport Pond

The manor of Newport, or Newport Pond, was in the king's hands in 1086, and had been in the hands of Harold Godwinson before 1066.[108] It remained a royal manor until 1243, when Henry III granted it to his younger brother Richard earl of Cornwall (d. 1272) on his marriage to Sancha of Provence.[109] Although it was always an outlying part of the earldom and (from 1337) duchy of Cornwall (one of the so-called foreign manors), it remained part of the duchy until 1550, though regularly leased out.[110] The earls and dukes (and the crown when the duchy was in its hands) regarded the manor merely as

106 ERO, SALE/B1574 (1889); SALE/A1055 (1894).
107 English Heritage, UK database of Historic Parks & Gardens, Register GDI1736.
108 DB, 973.
109 *Cal. Chart.* 1226–57, p. 276; *Cal. Inq. p.m.*, Henry III, p. 274.
110 Below, p. 66, for example.

a source of income and patronage, and a means of discharging financial obligations to dependants and clients. There is no evidence that any of the lessees lived on the manor, and no evidence for the existence of a manorial hall.

In 1550 Edward VI granted the manor of Newport, along with many other lands, to Richard Fermour, a grocer formerly of London,[111] and it was thus permanently alienated from the duchy of Cornwall, in contravention of the terms of the great charter of the duchy (1337). Within two months Fermour had sold it for £460 to Sir Ralph Warren (c.1483–1553), a member of the Mercers' Company and one of the wealthiest men in London. He had been Lord Mayor in 1536, and owned much property in Essex, Cambridgeshire, Norfolk, Suffolk and Northamptonshire.[112] Warren may have used Hospital Farm, which he had also acquired, as a country residence.[113] His coat of arms was depicted on a window pane in the farm house, and part of the glass survives at St Mark's College, Audley End.[114]

Sir Ralph died three years later, in 1553, and by his will dated 30 June 1552 he devised the manor with the hamlet of Birchanger and the hospital of St Leonard within the manor to Joan his wife for her life, with remainder to Richard his son and the heirs of his body, and then to his daughter Joan and the heirs of her body. Soon after her husband's death his widow took possession of the manor and the other properties left to her without royal authorisation, and at some time in 1556 or 1557 (the document is undated) she obtained a royal pardon for her trespass, on payment of £36 16s. 8d. She then received licence to hold the property according to the terms of her husband's will.[115]

Joan remarried in 1558. Her second husband was Sir Thomas White, founder of St John's College Oxford, but they had no children and she died in 1573. Under the terms of her first husband's will, their son Richard Warren then inherited the manor of Newport Pond. He died childless in 1597. His sister Joan had married Sir Henry Williams of Hinchingbrooke (Hunts.), who took the name Cromwell from his mother's family. They had two sons, Oliver and Robert, and Robert's son, also Oliver (1599–1658), became Lord Protector of the Commonwealth in 1653. Oliver Cromwell senior evidently regarded himself as Richard Warren's heir, but this was disputed by Warren's widow Elizabeth.[116] The court found in Cromwell's favour, and although Elizabeth received the jointure to which she was in any case entitled, Cromwell inherited Warren's estates, including Newport Pond.

Cromwell's father Sir Henry, known as 'The Golden Knight', had been a spendthrift. Cromwell himself was never able to re-establish the family's finances, and he had to sell most of his property in Essex.[117] On 3 July 1606 he sold his manor of Newport to Thomas Lord Howard de Walden, earl of Suffolk, for £2,500.[118]

111 *Cal. Pat.* 1550–3, pp. 22–3.
112 *FFE*, V 1547–80, ed. Marc Fitch and Frederick Emmison (Oxford, Leopard's Head Press, 1991), 19; *ODNB* 57, 497–8.
113 Below, p. 143.
114 BL. Add. Ms. 33520, fo 28v; I. Mollet, 'Coats of Arms in Newport', *NN*, 52 (1999), 52–3.
115 *Cal. Pat.* 1555–7, pp. 449–50; his will is recited in his IPM: TNA, C 142/100, no. 30.
116 TNA, PROB 11/91; C 142/248, no. 42.
117 *FFE* VI, 1581–1603, 143, 145, 149, 153, 155, 163.
118 TNA, C 54/1839.

The lordship of the manor remained with the earls of Suffolk[119] until the partition of the Suffolk inheritance in 1753 between Elizabeth countess of Portsmouth (1691–1762) and George William Hervey earl of Bristol (1721–75). Newport Pond formed part of the earl of Bristol's share, but he held it for only seven years.[120] In 1760 he sold the manor to the owner of Shortgrove manor, Percy Wyndham O'Brien, earl of Thomond.[121]

The two manors in the parish of Newport were united in the hands of one owner and remained with the owners of the Shortgrove estate until J.C.T. Heriz-Smith sold Shortgrove c.1890.[122] Heriz-Smith retained the lordship of the manor of Newport Pond until 1920, when it was sold to Lieut. J. Ronald Long.[123] Long was an officer in the Coldstream Guards, who at the time of the purchase was living at Balby near Doncaster. He subsequently moved to Birmingham, where he was the master of a public assistance institution. He may have been an acquaintance of Captain Montagu, owner of Shortgrove Hall, who had also served in the Coldstream Guards, and whose family owned High Melton Hall near Doncaster.[124] Long held the title until 1955, when it was purchased at auction by William Foyle of Beeleigh Abbey, the proprietor of Foyle's bookshop in Charing Cross Road, London.[125] At Foyle's death in 1963 the lordship passed to his daughter Christina who died in 1999.[126] Shortly afterwards, the lordship of the manor of Newport Pond was bought by Brian Callan of Great Yarmouth, Norfolk.[127]

Tilty Abbey Estate

Tilty Abbey, a Cistercian house near Dunmow, acquired lands and tenements in Newport in the 13th and early 14th centuries. Some of these holdings were in the centre of the village near the church, but most lay in the northern part of the village, in the area now known as Bridge End.[128] Two deeds refer to their ownership of a tenement between the Newport to Walden road and Flemings Lane, which was probably an eastwards extension of Bury Water Lane. This is the site of what later became known as The Priory, The Old Priory and Priory Cottage.[129]

The Quendon Hall Estate in Newport

From the middle of the 18th century the owners of Quendon Hall in the neighbouring parish of Quendon began to acquire land and property in Newport and build up their own estate there. In 1741 Joseph Cranmer esquire, younger son of Joseph Cranmer of Mitcham, Surrey, bought Quendon Hall from the widow of the previous owner, John

---

119 GEC, XII/I, 475–8.
120 ERO, D/DBY T 10/5.
121 Ibid., T/B 142/7; PHA, K5/9, 21 January 1760.
122 Above, p. 40, 43.
123 Catalogue of auction sale by Messrs Strutt & Parker Lofts & Warner of lordships of manors, 7 Dec. 1955, 50.
124 ERO, T/B 142/7.
125 NLHG Collections, letter dated 14 July 1980 to J. Gordon from RCHM (England).
126 *ODNB* 20, 715–7; press release by Christie's, 13 July 2000.
127 Pers. inf. from the late Imogen Mollet.
128 ERO, T/B 3.
129 Above, p. 27.

Figure 28 *Pond Cross Farm House, High Street. Rebuilt on the site of an earlier farm house in 1852 for Henry Webb of Quendon Hall.*

Turner. His money had come from his elder brother Henry, who had died childless in 1737, and after making provision in his will for his widow Henry left the residue of his estate, consisting of both land and money, to Joseph, requesting him 'to turn my money into land and make such convenient purchase or purchases and settle the same on either of his sons as he shall judge the most deserving.'[130]

In 1748 Joseph Cranmer bought the great tithes of Newport, and thus he and his successors at Quendon Hall became lay rectors of the parish and responsible for the upkeep of the chancel of the church until Sir William Foot Mitchell surrendered his position in 1936.[131] In the following year Cranmer made another significant purchase, Pond Cross Farm (see fig. 28) with 340 a. of land, some of which was freehold and some copyhold of the manor of Newport Pond.[132] By the time of his death in 1763 he had acquired further small pieces of copyhold land including Wymarks Croft (8 a.) and 32 a. of customary land lying in the common fields in the manor, along with several freeholds.[133]

His son and heir Henry Cranmer continued to acquire property in Newport. In 1786 a map prepared for the owner of Shortgrove shows that Henry owned Pallett's Farm (184 a.) as well as the property he inherited from his father, including, on the High Street, Briscoe Cottage and the two cottages that later became The Paragon.[134] In June 1798 he

130 TNA, PROB 11/688.
131 Ibid., PROB 11/888; Newport PCC, Minute Book, 1936.
132 ERO, T/B 142/7.
133 Ibid.
134 Ibid., D/DU 205/19.

purchased for £850 the lands of John Sykes, a maltster and dealer who had been adjudged bankrupt. These lay mostly in Bury Field and Upper and Lower Standing, but also included 4 a. of pasture in Bulls Mead. In 1802 he was admitted as copyhold tenant to various lands formerly held by John Winter. Apart from 1 a. in Bulls Mead, the location of the lands was not specified.[135] At some point before 1813 the family added land and houses in the centre of the village including Belmont Farm and homestead cottages, which probably included the house now known as Belmont.[136]

At the beginning of the 19th century, Henry's mental faculties began to decline and he fell under the influence of a confidence trickster named James Winton, who insinuated himself into the household at Quendon by seducing the housekeeper's daughter, Margaret, who was married to James Greygoose (d. 1805), one of Henry's footmen. Margaret moved out to live with Winton, but when her husband died she returned to Quendon Hall to be with her mother, though she soon married Winton, and both then lived at the Hall. In May 1806 Winton persuaded Henry to grant him power of attorney to manage his affairs, so that he could receive income from the estate and begin the process of transferring some of the Cranmer property to himself and his wife.[137]

Henry's next of kin petitioned the Lord Chancellor for a commission of lunacy, which would investigate Henry's state of mind. The commission met at Stansted on 29 July 1806, and found that Henry had been of unsound mind since 13 May 1806, invalidating the power of attorney granted to James Winton. The receiver whom the inquiry now appointed to handle Henry's financial affairs was a solicitor from Cumberland named James Mounsey.[138]

Henry never recovered and died, childless and intestate, in 1810. Most of the estate passed to his cousin Martha Cranmer (d. 1813), also childless. Under the terms of her will most of the estate then passed to Anne Webb, a distant cousin. James Mounsey promptly married Anne Webb, and came to live at Quendon Hall.[139] Anne was the granddaughter of James Cranmer of Mitcham and thus a representative of the senior line of the family (and descended collaterally from the Archbishop), though through her mother rather than her father, William Webb. In 1813, the year she inherited Quendon Hall, she obtained a grant from the crown allowing her and her descendants to assume the name and arms of Cranmer.[140] In 1858 she held 158 a., and her relatives Mary and Henry Webb a further 317 a.[141]

Anne and her husband made some further small acquisitions of land in Newport, but the family's main contribution was in buying or building houses, including Pond Cross Farm House, built in 1852 for its tenant Thomas Shirley, and the cottages at the foot of Frambury Lane. The house in Newport High Street known The Georgians came into the ownership of the Quendon estate sometime between 1846 and 1864, and Anne Cranmer may have purchased this property too.[142]

135 Ibid., T/B 142/7.
136 NLHG Collections, transcripts of deeds of Belmont Farmhouse, in a private collection.
137 ERO, D/DYv 370.
138 Ibid., D/DYv 353–69, 371–3; TNA, C 211/5/C146.
139 TNA, PROB 11/1544.
140 Ibid., HO 38/15, 16.
141 Ibid., PROB 11/1544.
142 ERO, D/CT 252A, 398A; TNA, IR 29/12/243, IR 30/12/243.

Anne died childless in 1852 and most of her property, including the Newport lands, went to her niece Mary Anne, on condition that she and her family lived at Quendon Hall.[143] Mary Anne was married to Captain Henry Byng of the Royal Navy, a great-nephew of the Admiral Byng who was executed in 1757 for failing to engage the enemy during the Seven Years' War. Anne Cranmer required Mary Anne Byng to take the name of Cranmer, and her eldest son, Alfred Molyneux, was granted a royal licence to be known as Cranmer-Byng: his descendants still bear that name.[144] Mary Anne Byng did not long outlive Anne Cranmer, and thus in 1852 Alfred Molyneux Cranmer-Byng, who served as a colonel in the Grenadier Guards, inherited Quendon Hall and part of the estate, though some of it remained in the hands of his brother Henry Byng until he died in 1881.[145]

Dispersal of the Shortgrove and Quendon Estates

Quendon Hall Estate

The years either side of the First World War were marked by the dispersal of landed estates throughout England. Col. Cranmer-Byng at Quendon Hall seems to have got into severe financial difficulties in the late 19th century. Neither the Cranmers nor the Byngs had ever possessed great wealth: the Byng family had a long history of service in the Royal Navy, and in the 18th century the Cranmers had been lawyers and civil servants.[146] They were landowners on only a modest scale, and it may be that they were hard-hit by the agricultural depression of the late 19th century, which was particularly severe in Essex, where land values fell by 30 per cent between 1865 and 1895 and agricultural rents by 46.6 per cent between 1872 and 1911.[147] In a letter to the Local Government Board in 1899 Cranmer-Byng observed that his great tithes, 'commuted in 1836 at £280 per annum have now through rates and loss of tithe by the tithe act of 1891 dwindled down to less than £40 per annum.'[148]

In 1898 Col. Cranmer-Byng's son Lancelot, who was then living at Horham Hall near Thaxted, raised a mortgage of £12,000 secured on the Quendon Hall estate, and at the same time Col. Cranmer-Byng himself seems to have had difficulty paying some of his bills.[149] Eventually, by February 1906, he was unable to meet his obligations, and on 21 February he was declared bankrupt.[150] Shortly afterwards he became seriously ill and he died on 20 May 1906.[151] The Trustee in Bankruptcy put the contents of Quendon Hall up for sale in July 1906.[152] The sale marked the beginning of the end for the Cranmer-Byngs at Quendon and Newport. In the following year Lancelot Cranmer-Byng, who was no longer living at Quendon Hall, sold 14 lots of property in Newport, including

---

143 TNA, PROB 11/1392.
144 Ibid., HO 38/16.
145 *Return of Landowners*, 8.
146 *ODNB* 9, 309–18.
147 *The Agrarian History of England and Wales*, VII 1850–1914, ed. E.J.T. Collins (Cambridge, 2000), part I, 150–99, part II, 1939.
148 TNA, MH 12/3727.
149 ERO, D/F 35/12/25.
150 *The Times* 22 Feb., 7 Mar. 1906; *Saffron Walden Weekly News* 2 Mar., 16 Mar., 23 Mar., 27 Mar. 1906.
151 *Saffron Walden Weekly News*, 25 May 1906.
152 Sale catalogue kindly lent by Mr Bruce Munro; *Saffron Walden Weekly News*, 3 Aug. 1906.

Figure 29 *Sir William Foot Mitchell, 1859–1947. Owner of Quendon Hall estate 1908–47, MP for Saffron Walden 1922–29.*

The Georgians and The Paragon, and in 1908 he put the Hall itself and the rest of the estate on the market.[153] His own interests were intellectual and academic, and he made a distinguished contribution to western understanding of East Asian literature and culture.[154]

Quendon Hall and its remaining property, including its remaining lands and houses in Newport, were bought by Mr (later Sir) William Foot Mitchell. Like Sir Carl Meyer at Shortgrove, he represented the Edwardian plutocracy rather than the old landowning class. He was a businessman who had been a partner of Marcus Samuel, the founder of the Shell Oil Company. He spent many years in Japan developing his business contacts there and playing an important part in the integration of Japan into the world economy in the 1890s. Some years later he was a member of the group of financiers, including Carl Meyer of Shortgrove, who negotiated the sale of Japanese government bonds in London and New York during the Russo-Japanese war of 1904–5.[155] It may have been his connection with Carl Meyer which led him to buy Quendon Hall. Although he retained many business interests in England, he now lived at the Hall, where he described his recreations as riding and shooting.[156] Between 1922 and 1929 he served as MP for Saffron Walden (Newport's constituency), being succeeded by R.A. Butler.

The new owner was in a much stronger financial position than the Cranmer-Byngs, and he felt little need to continue the break-up of the estate. He sold Belmont (not Belmont Farm) in 1924, but otherwise he made no significant disposals of property in Newport. Indeed, ten years earlier, in 1914, he had financed the building of Hill View and Nolton Cottage, known as the Country Life cottages, at the foot of Church Street.[157]

Foot Mitchell died in 1947, and the Quendon estate passed to his son-in-law Sir Arthur Ellis, Regius Professor of Medicine at Oxford University. He gradually sold off more land and houses. He sold the pair of villas in Station Road called Buriton and Berwyn in 1951, the two parts of Headley House in 1953 and Hill View and Nolton Cottage in 1956. Even

153 ERO, D/DU 869.
154 L. Cranmer-Byng, *The Vision of Asia* (London, 2nd edn, 1930), ix.
155 R. Henriques, *Marcus Samuel: First Viscount Bearsted and founder of the Shell Transport and Trading Company 1853–1927* (London, 1960), 63–4; R. Smethurst, 'Takahashi Korekiyo, the Rothschilds and the Russo-Japanese War, 1904–1907' (http://www.rothschildarchive.org.lib.articles/AR2006Japan).
156 *Who's Who in Essex* (Worcester, 1935), 196.
157 *Country Life*, 1 Aug. 1914; J. Gordon, 'Newport's "Country Life" Cottages' *NN*, 31 (1989), 96–7; above, p. 34.

Figure 30 *Mrs Carl Meyer (1862/3–1930) and her children, by John Singer Sargent, 1896. Oil on canvas.*

after Sir Arthur sold Quendon Hall itself to Sir Robert Adeane in October 1956, he and his family retained substantial holdings in Newport. Belmont Farm was not sold until 1962 and between then and his death in 1966 he disposed of further small amounts of land. His executors sold Pallett's Farm and Pond Cross Farm in 1976. Sir Robert Adeane sold his estate to the earl of Inchcape in 1969. In turn, he disposed of much of the estate to Tower Investments in 1979–80, but the connection with Newport was not entirely severed. In 2006, for example, the Bowker Close houses were built on land which had belonged to the Inchcape Family Trust.[158]

158 NLHG Collections, copies of deeds and abstracts of title relating to transfer of the Quendon Estate to Sir Arthur Ellis from the executors of Sir William Foot Mitchell, 1947 (originals in private hands); Sale catalogue of Quendon Estate 1979 (copy kindly provided by Messrs Savills, Chelmsford).

Figure 31 *Pallett's Farm, High Street. An 18th-century former farm house.*

Shortgrove Estate

Houses in Newport which belonged to the Shortgrove estate came up for sale between the wars. In October 1920 J.C.T. Heriz-Smith auctioned most of the property in Newport which he had retained after selling Shortgrove Hall. The lots included Newport House, Monk's Barn, the house now called The Old Post Office, the Priory cottages, and the lordship of the manor. The sale realised over £5,200, but some properties which had failed to reach their reserve price were subsequently sold by private treaty.[159] Eighteen years later, after Thomas Place had sold Shortgrove Hall and adjacent parkland to C.H.A. Butler,[160] he put the rest of the estate up for sale in separate lots.[161] His agent wrote to all the tenants of these properties inviting them to buy their holdings by private treaty before any auction took place.[162] Some did so, though Place's Trust was still selling some freeholds in Newport in the 1940s.[163]

These disposals from both the Shortgrove and Quendon estates, particularly to sitting tenants as suggested by Place's 1938 letter, mark an important point in the transition from a village in which most property was owned by two substantial landowners to a community mainly of owner-occupiers, as it has remained since.

---

159 NLHG Collections, sale particulars 1920.
160 Above, p. 45.
161 NLHG Collections, Auction sale catalogue 1938. (The sale does not seem to have taken place.)
162 Ibid., letter from John D. Wood, Sept. 1938.
163 ERO, D/DU 775/23.

ECONOMIC HISTORY

THE ECONOMIC HISTORY OF NEWPORT, in recent centuries regarded as a village dominated by agriculture, is more complicated than it first appears. The earliest economic record, Domesday Book, suggests an agricultural community. A century or so later, however, Newport was clearly regarded as a small town with all the features that might be expected of a medieval urban community: markets, fairs, a hospital and a population engaged in trade. This community existed alongside the agricultural activity in the two manors of the parish, though Newport was still referred to as a town in the 16th century. Later, however, Newport assumed the character of a large agricultural village, though with the railway came 'urban' features such as a gas works and a maltings. It retained this character into the 20th century, though in the second half of that century and in the early years of the 21st century, it changed again and for most residents of Newport, where they live is not where they work.

Newport as a 'borough'

Domesday Book gives little indication of the nature of Newport as a settlement, and there is insufficient evidence to demonstrate any continuity between the Anglo-Saxon *burh* at Newport (if *burh* it was), and 12th-century Newport.[1] By then, however, it had acquired some urban characteristics. In 1164–65 it was described as a 'burgus', a borough;[2] in a number of records from the 13th and 14th centuries Newport is again described as a borough ('burgus'), and its urban status is suggested by the fact that the manor had a number of burgesses holding by burgage or rent-based rather than land-based tenure.[3]

The first Ordnance Survey 25" plan of the parish (1877) marks a 'castle' on the present (2014) site of the grammar school,[4] but no archaeological or documentary evidence has come to light which might confirm the Ordnance Survey's supposition. The 18th-century antiquary John Holman (perhaps mistakenly) suggested the existence of a castle.[5] In 1291 and again in 1321–5 there were 13 tenants who paid *wardpenny* annually.[6] Wardpenny was attached to certain tenures in the manor, and it may have related to guarding fortifications, perhaps one of the royal castles in Essex such as Colchester. It may, on the other hand, have related to the royal gaol at Newport, which is known to have existed from at least 1173.[7]

1   Above, pp. 8–9.
2   *Pipe R.*, 11 Henry II, 20.
3   TNA, JUST 1/229 m. 15d; C 132/42/1 m. 12; SC 6/1124/5; *Ministers' Accounts,* I, 48.
4   OS Map 1:2500 Essex sheet IX (16), 1877.
5   ERO, T/P 195/17/11, but *CRR* V, 8–10 John, do not support Holman's assertion.
6   ERO, T/B 3/1; TNA, SC6/1147/1.
7   *Pipe R.* 19 Henry II, 13.

In the second half of the 12th century, perhaps the most remarkable feature of Newport's urban status was briefly apparent. The Jews in medieval England were exclusively town dwellers, being unable to hold land, and under the protection of the king. Newport, as a royal manor, was clearly becoming an urban centre. Even so, it is surprising that a small Jewish community was established in the parish, engaged in money lending. Sometime between 1160 and 1163 Richard of Anstey, a Hertfordshire landowner, conducted a lawsuit against his cousin over the estate of her father William de Sackville.[8] He recovered the estate, but to cover his costs he had to borrow substantial amounts, mainly from Jews in eastern England. He borrowed a total of £11 10s. 0d. from 'Jacob the Jew of Newport', paying interest at a rate of 4d. in the £ per week on the first £6 10s. 0d. (87 per cent per annum) and 3d. in the £ per week on the rest. A little later he borrowed £4 10s. 0d. from 'Mirabella the Jewess' of Newport, who may have been Jacob's wife or daughter. Her rate of interest was 4d. in the £ per week, and Richard paid in interest to both of them a total of £10 17s. 4d. on money which he borrowed for terms varying from eight to thirteen months. These rates were not out of line with what other moneylenders charged to borrowers like Richard who had only a small amount of land as security, but Richard repaid his loans.[9] In 1173 Jacob was involved in an action for debt against William de Mountfichet,[10] but had died by 1183, for his son was in wardship that year.[11] It is possible that his family had connections with the Jewish community in Lincoln, rather than Cambridge, which was of course much closer to Newport. His son's guardian, Peitivin de Eye, accounted for the wardship at Lincoln from 1183 to 1185.[12] Another Jew, Mosse (Moses) was subject to the tallage of the Jews in 1192, but he evidently never paid. Perhaps he died, or possibly left the country.[13] With his death or departure the Newport Jewish community disappears from the records. The community was unlikely to have been large and was short-lived. It was not one of the 27 centres where an *archa* or registry for debts to the Jews was established, and the Jews of Newport did not contribute to the Northampton *donum* of 1194.[14]

The Jewish community was only one indicator of Newport's urban status in the Middle Ages. Tolls of the 'borough' (*burgus*) were worth £8 in 1272.[15] According to a survey of 1299 there were more than 20 places described as shops, though whether they were retail premises or workshops is not clear.[16] There were butcheries located in The Shambles, a bakehouse, four forges, and one inhabitant, Matthew Chapman, who was described as a merchant. There are several occupational surnames suggesting a variety of crafts, but even as early as 1300 a surname is not an accurate guide to occupation (though Chapman the merchant is suggestive). Flemings Lane, mentioned in 1299,

8   TNA, EXT 6/143 (formerly E 101/505/1); transcribed with an introduction by P. M. Barnes, 'The Anstey Case', in *A Medieval Miscellany for Doris Mary Stenton*, ed. P. M. Barnes and C.F. Slade, Pipe R., new series 36, 1960 (London, 1962), 1–24; *ODNB*, 'Richard of Anstey'.

9   H.G. Richardson, *The English Jewry under Angevin Kings* (London, 1960), 10, 67.

10   *Pipe R*, 21 (20 Henry II) 1173–4, 72.

11   Ibid., 32 (29 Henry II) 1182–3, 71.

12   Ibid., 34 (31 Henry II) 1184–5, 94.

13   Ibid., 40 (3 Richard I) 1191–2, 32, 173.

14   I. Abrahams, 'The Northampton "Donum" of 1194', *Jewish Historical Society of England*, Miscellanies Part I (1925), lix–lxxiv.

15   TNA, C 132/42/1 m.12.

16   ERO, T/B 3/1.

suggests that there may have been trade with or residents from Flanders. Sheep were important in the agriculture of the parish and Tilty Abbey, which owned property in the village, was heavily involved in the wool trade.[17]

In the early 14th century Newport was wealthier than most of its surrounding villages. In 1327 and again in 1334 the lay subsidy assesments show that Newport's wealth was comparable with that of Clavering, Takeley and Ashdon, and not much less than (Saffron) Walden itself. Its wealth probably derived from its varied commercial activities as well as agriculture, for it was not an important centre for the cloth or woollen industries.[18] By the end of the 16th century, however, leatherworking had become a significant industry, with some 20 per cent of the fathers of children baptised between 1591 and 1636 being engaged in the trade.[19]

Markets and Fairs

By the 12th century Newport had a successful market. When Geoffrey de Mandeville, earl of Essex, was granted the manor by the Empress Matilda in 1141, however, she gave him to right to remove the market from Newport to his town of Walden where he had a castle and which he hoped to develop as a commercial centre.[20] When King Stephen recovered power later that year he reissued Geoffrey's grant, but omitted the right to move the market from Newport. A market is recorded in 1254,[21] so it was presumably restored sometime before then, and market tolls appear in ministers' accounts in 1296–7.[22] By the 13th century, therefore, Newport had become a small commercial centre. In 1203 King John granted Girard de Furnival the right to hold a fair over the three days either side of the feast of Saints Peter and Paul (29 June).[23] Furnivall had custody of the manor at that time, but nothing is known of the fair thereafter.[24]

In 1227 Henry III granted St Leonard's Hospital the right to hold a fair on the feast day of St Leonard, 6 November.[25] The fair, known as Colt (or Cold) Fair was held in Hospital Field at the north end of the village, close to the boundary between the parishes of Newport and Wendens Ambo.[26] In the 14th century there is evidence for men from Clavering coming to Newport to sell livestock and buy commodities such as butter and tar, along with a jar to put the tar in.[27] In the 16th century, merchants from elsewhere in East Anglia traded saffron at the Colt Fair in the autumn, after the saffron harvest, and

---

17   Ibid.; above, p. 51.
18   Ward, *Lay Subsidy of 1327*, 46–56; R.E. Glasscock, ed.,*The Lay Subsidy of 1334* (London, 1975), 84–7.
19   B. Nurse, 'Occupations in Parish Registers: The Evidence from Newport, Essex', *Local Population Studies,* 52 (1994).
20   *Regesta Regum Anglo-Normannorum 1066–1154*, ed. H.A.Cronne and R.H.C. Davis, III (Oxford, 1969), no. 274.
21   J.H. Round, *Geoffrey de Mandeville* (London, 1892), 140–4; *Gazetteer of Markets and Fairs in England and Wales to 1516,* I (London, 2003), 134; R.H. Britnell, 'Essex Markets Before 1350', *EAH,* 13 (1981), 15–21.
22   *Ministers' Accounts*, 49.
23   *Rot. Chart*, 109.
24   *Cartae Antiquae* (Pipe R. new series 33, 1957), 60.
25   *Cal. Chart.* 1226–57, 62.
26   J. Chapman and P. André, *Map of Essex* (Colchester, 1777), plate I.
27   ERO, D/DP M1164. I owe this reference to the kindness of Mr Robert Wood.

there is evidence for this continuing into the 18th century.[28] The Colt Fair was important to the economic life of Saffron Walden as well as Newport.[29] William Harrison (Vicar of Radwinter, east of Saffron Walden), described it in 1587 as amongst 'the greatest marts in Europe'. Debts were settled there, and it was an important market for horses: Harrison commented on the sharp practices which the drovers engaged in before selling their horses.[30] The fair was abolished in July 1872, after it had acquired a reputation for drunken boisterousness.[31]

Agriculture, *c*.1086–*c*.1600

The Domesday survey of 1086 recorded two manors in the parish. Newport (often in subsequent centuries known as Newport Pond) had been held by King Harold before the Conquest and was held by King William in 1086. It was assessed at eight and a half hides with a *berewica* or outlier at Shelford (Cambs.).[32] This outlier, later the manor of Granhams,[33] was assessed at three hides and 46 a., and in 1086 was worth £25 16s. 0d. Newport would have been worth much more. The population of Newport had fallen immediately after the Conquest but had recovered and increased overall by 1086. Newport had 26 *villani* households (villeins, or customary tenants), having had 18 at the time of the Conquest and later, 15. In 1086 there were 13 households of bordars (eight in 1066, five later), and two households of slaves. This increase in population seems to have coincided with changes in the manorial economy. In 1066 the lord's demesne estate had arable land with two plough teams (*c*.200–*c*.240 a.) on his demesne, in 1086, just one. In 1066, the tenants had 8 plough teams, cultivating *c*.800–*c*.960 a., in 1086, 10, cultivating *c*.1000–*c*.1200 a. Arable cultivation was clearly only one part of the agricultural economy. The king's demesne had woodland with pannage sufficient for 100 pigs, 24 a. of meadow, ten cattle, one horse, 79 pigs and 102 sheep.

The second manor, Shortgrove, was in two parts. The part held by Robert Gernon had had six households of slaves in 1066 but only three in 1086. The manor had correspondingly declined. There were three plough teams working the lord's demesne at the Conquest and only two in 1086. The amount of arable land under cultivation had thus fallen from *c*.300–*c*.360 a. to *c*.200–*c*.220 a. though there remained 15 a. of meadow. The general decline was reflected in other demesne holdings. In 1066 there were three horses, three cows and 60 pigs: in 1086, none. The mill present in 1066 had gone but there remained 100 sheep and 11 of the 23 hives of bees present in 1066. The value of the manor had correspondingly fallen. It was worth £4 in 1066 and £3 in 1086.[34] The second part of the manor was held by Eustace, count of Boulogne. It seems that the count had doubled the area under cultivation from *c*.100–*c*.120 a. to *c*.200–*c*.240 a. and changed the

28   Ibid.
29   E. Allan, 'Chepyng Walden/Saffron Walden, 1438–90: A Small Town', (University of Leicester PhD thesis, 2010), 127, 131, 135. I am grateful to Dr Allan for permission to cite her thesis.
30   F.G. Emmison, *Essex Wills*, passim. W. Harrison, *The Description of England*, ed. G. Edelen (New York, 1994), 53, 308.
31   TNA, MH 12/3716.
32   DB, 973; above p. 9.
33   *VCH Cambs* VIII, 210.
34   DB, 1020; above, p. 37.

nature of tenure for his tenants. Where there had been one household each of villeins, bordars and slaves in 1066, in 1086 there were three households, all of bordars. As with the other holdings in the parish arable cultivation formed only part of the economy. There were 90 sheep in 1086, 11 pigs, three cattle, two horses and 9 a. of meadow. At the end of the 11th century, therefore, the agricultural economy of Newport was mixed, balancing livestock, mainly sheep and pigs, and an increasing amount of arable.

In the 13th century Newport was one of four royal demesne manors in Essex which the crown and its officials treated as a group for judicial and sometimes for administrative purposes.[35] The others were Hatfield Broad Oak, Havering and Writtle.[36] Newport manor was managed on the crown's behalf by the sheriff or by a royal keeper in return for the profits from managing the manorial resources. In April 1225, for example, the sheriff of Essex was ordered to purchase stock for the manors of Newport and Writtle,[37] and the timber resources of Hatfield Forest were used to repair the mills and other structures at Newport.[38] In 1222, Henry III ordered the Exchequer to recompense the keeper of the manor, Ralph de Tony, for sowing wheat and buying two oxen and two horses, presumably for ploughing.[39] Later in the same year, Henry ordered the sheriff to make a *bovarium* (byre) on the manor for housing plough oxen and horses, and to provide fodder for them.[40] In the following April the sheriff was ordered to sow 'our land of Newport' with oats and to repair the mills.[41]

In 1229 Henry III granted Newport to Walter de Kirkham for life.[42] Kirkham had been one of the accountants at the king's wardrobe,[43] but in 1229 he was appointed Dean of the College of St Martin le Grand, which no doubt explains his grant of the manor of Newport shortly afterwards, for the college already held Newport church. Kirkham's officials kept the manor in good repair, maintaining the mills and ensuring that the fishponds, an important asset, were well stocked with pike and bream.[44] Kirkham also had a new grange and a new mill built,[45] and the development of the manor in these years suggests that, in common with much of England at that time, the population of the manor was expanding and agricultural productivity increasing.

Kirkham was appointed dean of York in 1244 (and bishop of Durham in 1249),[46] but some time before then he must have given up his tenure of Newport, for in 1242 Henry III granted the manor to his brother Richard, created earl of Cornwall in 1227.[47] The grant of the earldom was to him and his heirs in perpetuity, thus creating a substantial

35   R.S. Hoyt, *The Royal Demesne in English Constitutional History 1066–1272* (Ithaca NY, 1950), 99–100.
36   Hatfield Broad Oak was known as Hatfield Regis from *c.*1190: P.H. Reaney, *The Place-Names of Essex* (Cambridge, 1935), 39.
37   *Rot. Litt. Claus.* I, 34.
38   *Close Rolls* Henry III 1229–30, pp. 307, 512–5; 1234–37, 249–50.
39   *Rot. Litt. Claus.* I, 505.
40   Ibid., 524.
41   Ibid., 542.
42   *Patent Rolls* Henry III 1225–32, p. 314.
43   *ODNB* 31, 798–9.
44   *Close Rolls* Henry III 1234–7, pp. 274, 388, 430.
45   Ibid., 70, 249.
46   *ODNB* 31, 798–9
47   *Close Rolls* Henry III 1237–42, p. 404; above, p. 49.

royal apanage. The manor was part of the ancient demesne of the crown, and Richard was authorised to levy tallage on the manor, as kings had done in the past.[48]

Under Earl Richard (d. 1272) and his son Earl Edmund (d. 1300), Newport was kept in hand as a demesne manor, and a more systematic analysis of the economy of the manor is possible for these years than for earlier or later periods. A detailed picture of the manor is given by several documents from the end of the 13th and early 14th centuries. An extent drawn up at Earl Richard's death recorded 229 a. of demesne land, 8 a. of hay meadow, and some pasture. There were two water mills and a windmill, together with a valuable fishpond. The labour services of the tenants were worth 66s. 7d. a year, though whether they were performed or commuted is not clear.[49] For the year 1296–7 a set of ministers' accounts survive.[50] They show that the demesne was almost exactly the same size (231 a. of arable); there were 20 a. of pasture, two watermills and one windmill, all of which were let at farm for a fixed return. A survey made for Earl Edmund in 1299 states that there were 221 a. of demesne land, of which 65 a. were in Kyngesdon Field, 76 a. in Kynerswel Field and North Madfield, and 80 a. in North Field and Grane Field.[51] There were 8a. of hay meadow and 10½ a. and half a rood of pasture, scattered amongst various fields in the manor. A valor of the manor, probably from Edward II's reign, records 231 a. of demesne arable, 9 a. of sheep pasture, 8 a. of meadow, and 10½ a. of pasture, with a grange, pasture and underwood at Birchanger.[52]

These accounts reveal that wheat and oats were by far the most important crops grown on the demesne lands. In 1296–7, 77 a. of wheat were sown, yielding 62½ quarters, and there were 72 a. of oats, producing 70 quarters and five bushels. A manorial account for some time in Edward I's reign provides another, very similar, picture of the yield of grain on the manor.[53] At that time 76 a. of wheat yielded 59 quarters and three bushels, amounting to 2½ bushels per acre. 66½ a. were sown with oats, yielding 63 quarters. Both accounts record small amounts of barley (perhaps for brewing) and dredge (a mixture of oats and barley). About half the wheat and oats were sold, and most of the rest retained for seed the following year; but some of the oats were used for animal fodder, and six bushels were used for *potagium* (probably porridge) for the *famuli* (paid workers).[54] A manorial account of 1323–4 shows a similar pattern to that of 1296–7, though with 3¾ bushels of peas.[55] By the 15th century, barley may have become a more important crop than it had been before the Black Death. In 1443 the Tilty Abbey Register records a malt mill,[56] and in 1488 a deed refers to a pond called a 'maltemylledame', presumably for the same mill.[57]

Newport's agriculture in the late 13th century was primarily arable. Demesne livestock in 1296 amounted only to six draught animals, three oxen, ten cows and a bull,

---

48   *Cal.Close,* 1264–68, p. 463.
49   TNA, C 132/42/1 m.12.
50   *Ministers' Accounts,* I, 48–54.
51   ERO, T/B 3/1.
52   TNA, SC 12/8/61.
53   TNA, SC 6/863/7.
54   *Ministers' Accounts,* I, 48–54.
55   TNA, SC 6/1147/1.
56   ERO, T/B 3/1.
57   Ibid., D/P 15/25/36.

four calves, 50 hens and three swans. It was profitable: the sale of grain, livestock and other produce (£19 9s. 3d.) together with the assize rents of the tenants (£11 12s. 10½d.), income from farming the mills (£8 for a half year), other dues, market tolls and profits of the court, and the sale of miscellaneous products such as cheese, brought in £53 8s. ½d. Money was spent on labourers' wages (some wage labour was required even where demesne labour services were performed), necessary repairs and maintenance, purchase of stock, and the lay subsidy of one twelfth levied in 1296.[58] However, all these costs amounted only to £6 15s. 2¼d., leaving a surplus of £46 12s. 10¼d., which was paid over to the receiver at Berkhamsted.[59]

There are no such detailed records for Shortgrove, but the Priory of St Bartholomew Smithfield compiled an extent of the manor in 1306.[60] This extent suggests that the agrarian economy of Shortgrove was very similar to that of Newport. In 1306 Shortgrove's demesne consisted of 240 a. of arable, 6 a. of meadow and 5 a. of pasture.[61] Wheat and oats were the main crops, with some barley, dredge, and peas and beans. There is no reference to livestock, apart from chickens, but two of the tenants had the occupational name *bercarius* (shepherd), suggesting that sheep rearing possibly played a more important part in the economy of the tenants than it did in Newport.

The extent allows comparisons between the way in which the two manors were managed. At the turn of the 13th century, both were dependent on the labour services of tenants. On Newport manor the tenant of each half virgate of land (probably about 15 a.) was required to cultivate 1½ a. of the demesne, ploughing in winter, sowing in spring with his own seed (and a further half a. with the lord's seed), and harrowing.[62] After the feast of St John the Baptist (24 June), each tenant was required to mow half an acre of meadow and carry the hay to the lord's grange. Lower down the social scale, the 15 cottagers on the manor were required to hoe 7½ a. of demesne land each, and they were required to reap and bind the corn. Then each virgater was required to take five cartloads of wheat and five cartloads of oats to the lord's grange in autumn. In addition to these services, each tenant was required to perform boon services for two days in each season. The work of harvesting the grain was largely the responsibility of the cottagers. They held less land than the virgaters, who had their own substantial holdings of land to harvest at the same time. The social stratification of the manor was thus, in theory at least, reflected in the different obligations of the tenants. However, the monetary value of each service was noted, and it is possible that a market existed in services, blurring the social distinctions between virgaters, cottagers, and men who may have been landless.

The extent of Shortgrove reveals an agricultural community of 62 adults, one third freeholders and two thirds villeins. The freeholders had holdings of at least 1 a., and some had much more: Goselinus the tanner, for example, held 6 a. and the Master of St Leonard's Hospital had 4 a. The size of the villein holdings was broadly similar. The labour dues were significantly heavier than on Newport manor. Villeins were obliged to perform services such as haymaking and, particularly, harvest work. The harvest obligations were substantial. Each villein was required to reap 2 a. of wheat and 2 a.

58   *Ministers' Accounts*, I, 49–53.
59   Ibid., I, 48–54.
60   E.A. Webb, *The Records of St Bartholomew's Priory Smithfield*, 2 vols (Oxford, 1921), 1, 431–6.
61   TNA, SC 12/8/61.
62   TNA, SC 12/8/61.

of oats, and to thresh 2½ bushels of wheat or peas or beans or barley or dredge, or 6 bushels of oats during the harvest season, and more during the autumn. Some tenants were required to work on the lord's demesne for one or two days each week, except at Christmas, Easter and Pentecost, and many were required to render chickens and eggs to the lord. The villeins could expect to receive cheese, bread and ale from the lord during harvest time, and were entitled to glean in the stubble after harvest. Each of the services had a monetary value, and the custom of the manor gave the lord the right to choose whether the tenant would perform his service in person or commute it for a cash payment.

Although records for Newport in the second half of the 14th century and the 15th century are scarce, a surviving account roll for 1355–6 provides some evidence for the impact of the Black Death of 1348–9.[63] The fishpond could not be let at farm because no one wanted it; the windmill was ruinous and no profit could be got from it (though the two water mills were still in use). A number of tofts and other places lay vacant and could not be rented; the farm of the toll bridge was reduced by about one third, presumably because there was less traffic over it, and the labour services of the villeins had been commuted for cash payments. In November 1379, Richard Neuman of Newport and others granted John Bole, his wife and two others two messuages, one mill, 153 a. of land, 4 a. of meadow, 4 a. of pasture, and 12s. 4½d. rent in Newport.[64] This may represent the transfer of the lease of the demesne from one group of Newport tenants to another. A reduction of rather more than one third in the acreage of the arable demesne (from c.220–230 a. to 153 a.) is comparable with other manors on good land in lowland England in the late 14th century, and so is the holding of the demesne by one or more tenants of the manor.[65] Newport's decline was not unusual.

The inflationary effect on wages of the decline in population was illustrated by a case from Newport in July 1378.[66] John Bole senior was accused of paying various men 6d. or 7d. per day and having made various payments in kind, including giving them free dinners. The Statute of Labourers mandated a rate of 4d. Bole was also accused of agreeing in advance to pay men 10d. a day in the autumn for harvesting and giving his ploughmen 20s. or 2 marks (26s. 8d.). The Bole family were wealthy: John was the son of Walter Bole, one of the two wealthiest inhabitants of Newport according to the taxation assessment of 1327.[67]

John Clobbe of Newport (who is not otherwise recorded) joined the Peasants' Revolt in 1381. He was among the Thaxted rebels who freed prisoners from the bishop of London's gaol in Bishop's Stortford and then moved on to Hertford, where they attacked the castle of John of Gaunt, duke of Lancaster. From Hertford they went to London, where Clobbe took part in the sack of Gaunt's Savoy Palace. Gaunt later took out a private prosecution against Clobbe and other rebels involved in the attacks on his

63   Ibid., SC 6/845/20.
64   TNA, E 210/4520.
65   *The Agrarian History of England and Wales*, III 1348–1500, ed. E. Miller (Cambridge, 1991), 13–15, 54–8.
66   *Essex Sessions of the Peace 1351, 1377–79*, ed. E.C. Furber, EAS Occasional Publications 3 (Colchester, 1953), 64.
67   *The Medieval Essex Community: The Lay Subsidy of 1327*, ed. J.C. Ward , ERO Publication 88 (Chelmsford, 1983), 51.

property.[68] Although the duchy of Lancaster had estates in north-west Essex,[69] there is no other evidence of participation in the revolt by men from Newport or its immediate neighbourhood.

The value of Newport continued to fall in the 15th century. A bailiff's account of 1450–1 recorded that the windmill was in a state of ruin and decay; the rent of the fishpond could not be collected because nobody held it; and the rent of a toft of the Master of St Leonard's Hospital was reduced from 2s. 3d. per annum to 9d. because it was in the lord's hands.[70] Under Edward IV and Henry VII the crown made some effort to manage the manor more efficiently. When Henry Bourchier was granted the manor for ten years in 1454–5 his farm was increased by 13s. 4d. from the previous sum of £23 6s. 8d., and it remained at this level for the rest of the century.[71] The demesne was now farmed by the royal grantee, and on several occasions provision was made for the repair of the windmill and the bridge in the manor.[72]

Newport and Shortgrove from the 17th Century to the Present Day

Manorial Customs and Tenant Landholding

A series of lawsuits around 1600 throws some light on the economy of the manor of Newport at that time. They all turned on the issue of inclosure, and suggest that by the late 16th century sheep farming played a larger part in the economy than it had done in the 13th and 14th centuries. In 1594 Geoffrey Nightingale accused two other farmers of enclosing a common pathway used for driving his sheep on to the common fields after harvest or when they lay fallow, and of trying to change the times when grazing had been allowed under the custom of the manor. Two years later Nightingale again complained, this time accusing the tenant of Hospital Farm of enclosing about 80 a. of common fields in Frambury Field and Bury Field, where he grazed his sheep and other tenants pastured their cattle after harvest.[73]

Even more contentious was the inclosure of Pond Cross Common by the then lord of the manor, the earl of Suffolk. He maintained that because the land included the now dried-up fish pond, which pertained to the lord, the Common was his property. This was contested by 37 tenants, who feared the loss of their right to pasture animals on the Common after the hay harvest had been taken. A compromise was reached in the Court of Chancery in July 1612, under which the Common would remain enclosed, but the tenants would retain their rights of pasture after harvest, and the lord would commute his right to the hay crop for a payment of £20 p.a. to the overseers of the poor of the parish.[74] The inclosure remained contentious, however, and there was another attempt to tear down the inclosure in 1643.[75] All three cases suggest a manorial community

---

68   H. Eiden, *"In der Knechtschaft werdet ihr verharren…": Ursachen und Verlauf des Englischen Bauernaufstandes von 1381* (Trier, 1995), 212–5; pers. comm. from Dr Eiden.

69   E.g. the manor of Quendon.

70   TNA, SC 6/845/21.

71   BL, Microfilm M2470, Roll 206.

72   Ibid., Rolls 211, 215.

73   TNA, C 3/246/22, 23.

74   Ibid., C 3/283/73; below, pp. 92–3.

75   *Journals of the House of Lords* VI, 21(28 April 1643).

determined to maintain its rights of common grazing and common pasture, and common access to the open fields. They also show the persistence of open field farming in which some fields lay fallow from time to time and all were used for animal grazing after harvest.

In 1652 the Shortgrove manorial court agreed to the production of a new rental for the manor.[76] The initiative seems to have come from the tenants, who shared the concern of the tenants on the manor of Newport Pond to maintain their customary rights and holdings. Their rents in 1652 amounted to £3 6s. 4d., and although Shortgrove was a much smaller manor than Newport Pond, the rental reveals the same pattern of customary tenants holding parcels of copyhold land, both arable and pasture, in open fields. There were, however, a number of closes of arable land, and some parcels which were laid out as hop gardens, for which there is no evidence in Newport.

The Newport manorial court was still being used in the late 18th century to settle property interests at the point when tenants died, as well as to resolve any disputes concerning the complex landholding in the common fields. After the death of John Wyatt in 1770, his heir, John Robbins of Little Hadham, surrendered the reversion of three acres of copyhold land in White Ditch Field with appurtenances to Stephen Haynes, whom Wyatt's widow had married. The court also recorded Haynes's tenure of a tenement on the High Street (he was described in the court record as a shopkeeper) and 4 a. in Hospital Field held as two separate plots. Haynes later surrendered his three acres in White Ditch Field to Thomas Mumford of Wimbish.[77] In 1788 the land passed again to Susanna Mumford, a spinster and perhaps Thomas Mumford's daughter.[78]

On the death of Giles Dent Knightley of Parsonage Farm in 1770 his widow, Sarah Knightley, took possession of a significant quantity of land spread across Newport, including plots of land in Bury Water Field, Bury Meadows, White Ditch Field, Bulls Mead and Bales Mead. Two years later, on 1 December 1772, Knightley surrendered 33 a. of her inheritance to George James Williams of St James's, trustee for the earl of Thomond, on condition that the surrender would become void on payment of £1,800 (with interest) by the following May.[79] The payment was made, and a few years later the lands were sold to Samuel Cole of Maldon, a maltster. Parsonage Farm itself was also put up for sale.[80]

Farming Practices

A map of 1727 shows that much of the land east of the river Cam and north of Bromley Lane, essentially most of the manor of Shortgrove, consisted of some open arable fields divided into strips, and some inclosures. The tenants enjoyed the right of sheepwalk over the land.[81] By the late 18th century, however, a substantial part of this land had been turned into parkland for Shortgrove Hall, entailing a substantial loss of arable land, with only the southernmost and northernmost part of the land shown on the 1727 map remaining in cultivation.[82]

76   ERO, D/DQ 14/135.
77   Ibid., T/B 142–7.
78   Ibid.
79   Ibid.
80   *VIT*, 81.
81   ERO, T/M 298/1.
82   Ibid., D/CT 252B; above, p. 39.

Newport experienced no such change, but in 1709 the tenants recorded the custom of their manor at a meeting of the manorial court. Rents were stated to be 6*d.* per annum for copyhold and 4*d.* per annum for freehold land, the right of the poor to glean the stubble before sheep were grazed was laid down, and it was forbidden to graze sheep or horses on the common, while each householder was to graze no more than two cows. Rights of way were to be protected, and Newport inhabitants were to be allowed to carry their goods over the toll bridge free of charge.[83] The customary rights of the tenants were upheld by a manorial court which still had some vitality.

A greater variety of crops was grown in the 17th and 18th centuries than in the medieval period. The 'fields looking merily with most lovely Saffron' that Camden recorded were still visible in and around Newport until at least the middle of the 18th century.[84] The 1727 map of Shortgrove showed one field devoted to cinquefoil (visible on map 4), and turnips were grown on the Audley End estate in 1697.[85] The sheepwalks, which were the subject of litigation *c.*1600, provided the raw material for woolcombing and yarn spinning for the worsted trade.[86]

Although Vancouver estimated that only a tenth of Essex parishes ever had any open fields, the majority of these were to be found in Uttlesford Hundred.[87] An irregular form of open-field agriculture persisted in Newport until 1861.[88] The larger farmers had substantial farmhouses in the centre of the village and held strips in the open fields beyond as well as enclosed plots. Wills and manorial records from the 18th century show that small farmers held parcels of land scattered across the open fields and in their own ownership. Philip Buck, a tanner, held 2¾ a. of land in Bury Field, ¾a. of arable in 'Whiteagefield', 1½ a. of copyhold land in hospital field, a pasture close of an acre, a messuage in Saffron Walden and various other small plots.[89] John Farnham's will in 1727 recorded that in addition to his messuage at Crown Inn, he held 2 a. of common land in Hospital Field and 1 a. of copyhold land all of which were in the occupation of William Cadmore.[90]

The open fields were made available for grazing after the harvest. Robert Milner passed 35 a. of land and also his right to pasture 150 sheep 'in commonable fields of Newport' to Joseph Cranmer of Quendon Hall in 1749.[91] Typically, some farmers held land in other parishes too, and the manorial court records frequently mention people outside of Newport who had interests in the village fields. William Clarke of Hatfield Broad Oak was admitted in 1771 to a mixture of freehold and copyhold land in Newport, Widdington and Sawbridgeworth following the death of his wife's uncle, Turner Poulter. This included an acre of Bury Water Field, a customary messuage or tenement with yards and appurtenances on Goosehill, a freehold messuage in Bellman Street (now Belmont

83   Ibid., D/DK M113.
84   Allan, 'Chepyng Walden'; *Ag. Hist. England*, V.I, 214.
85   *Ag. Hist. England*, V.I, 222.
86   G. Ball, *Land, Agriculture and Industry in North West Essex* (Saffron Walden, 2009), 33.
87   Vancouver, *General View of the Agriculture of the County of Essex* (London, 1795),185
88   John Hunter, *Field Systems in Essex* (Colchester, 2003), 11–13.
89   ERO, D/ABR 11/215.
90   Ibid., D/ABR 19/302.
91   Ibid., T/B 142–7.

Figure 32 *Harvesting at White Ditch Farm, 1910.*

Hill) and other freehold land.[92] The court for 1793 confirmed the right of Thomas Havers of the Bulse Farm in Wenden to graze up to 120 sheep and three rams on the common field.

No entry was recorded for Newport in the 1801 crop returns, but in neighbouring parishes, wheat and barley predominated, alongside oats, peas, beans and other crops.[93] Vancouver observed that in north-west Essex parishes there tended to be a single crop, with little meadow or pasture but instead 'good crops of wheat, oats, peas, and beans' on the frequent fallows, 'besides a very considerable quantity of excellent barley, malted upon the spot for the London market, where it is said to be in high esteem'.[94] This was true in Newport, where a maltings was built in the mid 19th century.[95] At the time of tithe commutation in 1839, Newport parish was recorded as having 1,199 a. 2 r. 5 p. in arable, 425 a. 3 r. 12 p. in grass, and 43 a. of woodlands.[96] Wheat (303 a.), barley (196 a.), oats (106 a.), and turnips (90 a.) predominated amongst the arable crops.[97]

Farm buildings were located in the middle of the village, from where labourers would venture out to work individual intermingled strips. The manorial court resolved issues such as rights of way across the common fields. In 1747 it was recorded that manorial tenants were entitled to 'a cartway for carrying out dung and fetching corn home from further end of Bury Lane along Ten Acres Hedge to White Ditch Field and also to another

92   Ibid.
93   Ward, 'Essex Farming', 185–201.
94   Vancouver, *General View*, 12.
95   Ball, *Land, Agriculture and Industry*, 33; below, p. 76.
96   ERO, D/CT 252A.
97   TNA, IR 18/2444.

cartway from further end of Bury Lane the side next the [Town] of [Rusplat] Hedge to another part of White Ditch Field.'[98]

In 1839, Newport had four main open fields (Bury Field, Hospital Field, White Ditch Field and Whole Furrow Field) and various other areas of common such as Bulse Common and Ley Common, both at the time laid to arable. Conversely on occasion portions of the open fields may have been left to grass, as suggested by the description of the one and a half acres of meadow in Bury Field owned by Giles Dent Knightley in 1768, the point at which he mortgaged his landholdings.[99] The largest of the open fields were owned in severalty, and mostly farmed by tenants or under-tenants. Bury Field in 1839 was 208 a. 1 r. 18 p. in extent, of which William Charles Smith of Shortgrove, Lord of the Manor, owned by far the largest proportion (113 a. 0 r. 17 p.). The tithe apportionment lists seven separate owners of land in Bury Field, and 12 individual occupiers. The next biggest open field was Whole Furrow Field at 122 a. 0 r. 23 p. of which Smith owned 90 a. 1 r. 16 p.

Arable land formed 1,158 a. out of 1,665 a. cultivated. There were 592 separate plots identified on the Tithe Award map, most of which were tenanted by farmers. The largest landholdings were held by William Charles Smith (951a. 1r. 15p.), Anne Cranmer (157a. 3r. 27p.) and Stephen Robinson (126a. 2r. 33p.). Smith was recorded as having 231 a. in hand, most of which was the plantations and pasture of Shortgrove, while Anne Cranmer farmed 48 a. for herself. Most of the land in Newport, therefore, was farmed by tenants. There were five tenants with holdings of more than 100 a. in 1839: Joseph Livings (297 a.), Dudley Gayford at Hospital Farm (276 a.), David Skipper (158 a.), John Hayden (143 a.) and Charles Belsham (103 a.).

The inclosure award of 1861 dealt with 824 a. 3r. 18p. of land, suggesting that roughly a half of Newport's total area was still being farmed in common by the middle of the 19th century.[100] The unusually late date of the inclosure is indicative of the irregular nature of the open field system practised in Newport. In 1861, individual owners were given allocations of landholdings to compensate for the loss of plots of arable land in the large open fields, and for common grazing rights that they had hitherto enjoyed over the commonable meadows and on the stubbles after harvest. William Smith remained the largest landowner, claiming more than half of the land that was apportioned through the inclosure award (439 a. 0r. 28p.). Common rights that were compensated for typically included the right to graze cattle on Newport common and rights of sheepwalk over the open fields. Institutional owners as well as individual landlords were recognised in this way. The trustees of the Congregational church, for example, were awarded 101 a. in the inclosure award while the Gace's Charity trustees were awarded 17 a. 3 r. 2 p.

The pattern of arable farming changed little until the early 20th century. Wheat was generally the predominant crop, though barley and, to a lesser extent, oats were also important, with turnips and beans. Sheep rearing remained important until the early 20th century, with a herd of over 800 in 1866 and more than 1,000 in 1900. Cattle and pigs were also important, along with poultry.[101] Although inclosure did not greatly change the types of crop grown, it probably hastened the consolidation of landholdings

98   ERO, T/B 142–7.
99   Ibid.
100 Ibid., Q/RDc/53.
101 TNA, MAF 68/23, 696, 1266, 1836, 2121, 2406.

into fewer hands. The number of people listed as 'farmers' in local trade directories fell from nine in 1855 to five in 1894.[102]

More rapid change took place in the 20th century, especially after 1950. Sheep rearing had almost entirely disappeared between 1900 and 1910; there were no sheep at all in 1950, and the numbers of cattle and pigs also fell sharply. Wheat (311 a. in 1988) and barley (197 a.) remained important crops, but oats and turnips were no longer grown by 1980. On the other hand, sugar beet was grown from the 1930s, and oil seed rape from 1980, albeit on a small scale (15 a. in 1988).[103]

The process of consolidation of holdings continued into the 20th century. By 1941, three quarters of Newport's agriculture was in the hands of three principal farmers. The largest of these operations belonged to J.G. Turner, who farmed on behalf of Sir William Foot Mitchell of Quendon Hall. Along with 115 a. of wheat and 110 a. of barley, Turner grew a diversity of crops including oats (38 a.), sugar beet (30 a.), potatoes (28 a.), rye (20 a.), clover (20 a.), beans (12 a.), turnips and swedes (10 a.), kale (10 a.), peas (5 a.), mangolds (5 a.), mustard (5 a.) and flax (5 a.). He also held 42 a. of grass and 10 a. fallow. C.B. Hill at Pond Cross Farm was also a tenant of William Foot Mitchell and had 69 a. of barley and 43 a. in wheat along with quantities of oats, potatoes, sugarbeet, mustard and grass. More than half of Newport's land was farmed by these two farmers, while Barnard Brothers at Parsonage Farm also recorded substantial quantities of wheat (61 a.), barley (47 a.), peas (19½ a.), clover (17½ a.) and sugar beet (9½ a.).[104]

Employment

Most, but not all, of Newport's working population in the 18th and early 19th centuries were employed directly or indirectly in agriculture. The 1830 survey recorded 195 families living in 176 houses, of whom two fifths (81 families) remained chiefly employed in agriculture. Of the others, 65 families were occupied in trade, manufacture, and handicrafts, and 11 were categorised as 'wholesale merchants, capitalists, bankers, professional persons and other educated men'.[105] A high level of exemption from the hearth tax in the later 17th century may have been indicative of this mixed economy, with poorer artisan labourers living and working alongside farm workers.[106]

By the latter part of the 19th century Newport had a small elite of farmers who had extensive acreages and provided substantial employment. G.H. Barnard of Parsonage Farm had 1,332 a. and employed 46 men, 13 boys, one engine man (for the threshing machine), one wheelwright, one blacksmith and one clerk. Thomas Shirley farmed 529 a., employing 25 men and six boys, John Edwick had 366 a. and employed 13 men and six boys, while Dudley Gayford farmed 290 a. employing 12 men and three boys. Shirley was also a builder and property developer, and played a prominent part in the life of the village.[107]

---

102 Comparison of *Post Office Dir. Essex* (1855) with *Kelly's Dir. Essex* (1894).

103 TNA, MAF 68/2406, 2970, 3510, 3940, 4311, 4680, 5171, 5697, 6106.

104 TNA, MAF 32/849/352.

105 Monk, *Inhabitants*.

106 French, *Hearth Tax*, 41.

107 Census Returns, 1861–1901; above, p. 10.

Figure 33 *Rickyard of Barnard's Farm, photograph taken c.1904.*

Sheep husbandry played an important role well into the 19th century. Between 1698 and 1715, 8 per cent of Newport workers were woolcombers.[108] Cloth was fulled in the water near the ford in Bury Water Lane and stretched on frames in the Tenterfield.[109] Woolcombing was in decline by the first half of the 18th century.[110] The last procession to commemorate St Blaize's day on 3 February was said to have taken place in 1778, and involved a route from Saffron Walden to Newport and Littlebury.[111] The last woolcomber (Robert Brooks) was recorded in the 1841 census.

As might be expected of a village of Newport's size and prominence, a number of trades were practised. Henry Crane of Newport was described as a 'victualler' when his land was reapportioned after his death in 1748.[112] In 1839, Newport boasted bakers, blacksmiths, boot and shoemakers, bricklayers, butchers, carpenters, coopers, corn dealers, gardener, grocers and drapers, hairdresser, maltsters and corn merchant, painter, saddler, wheelwright, nurseryman and vet. Three straw hat makers were named (Sarah Johns, Elizabeth Norman and Mary Osborne) and six inns listed (the Coach and Horses, Hercules, Rose and Crown, Star, Three Colts, and Three Tuns).[113] Diverse professions continued to appear regularly in directories that were published in the second half of the 19th century. There was a marked decline in the number of shoemakers listed, from seven in 1855 to three in 1894. Other professions listed include an architect (Edward Barr, recorded as living in the village in 1882), a landscape painter (Edgar Longstaffe, also living in Newport in 1882), a higgler (William Willett, recorded in 1874), and a lime

---

108   *VIT*, 52.
109   Ibid.
110   Ball, *Land, Agriculture and Industry*, 66.
111   J. Player, *Sketches of Saffron Walden and its Vicinity* (Saffron Walden, 1845).
112   ERO, T/B 142/7.
113   *Pigot's Dir. Essex* (1839).

burner (William Fennell, recorded in 1855 and 1874 but not thereafter). By 1882 there was enough work for Joseph Searle to earn his keep as a chimney sweep.[114]

For women, the main form of employment throughout the 19th century was domestic service. In 1861 over half the 96 women whose employment is given in the census were in service, and although by 1901 the number was slightly less than half, service and ancillary occupations such as laundress, ladies' help, and ladies' companion still accounted for most of the employed women. A few were employed in the retail and liquor trades (an assistant publican at the Star and a victualler at the Three Tuns, for instance), and the Primary School employed female teachers, while a number of women (14 in 1901) worked, mainly from home, as dressmakers. But there was no fundamental change in the pattern of female employment over the second half of the 19th century.[115]

Although Newport retained its agricultural aspect into the 20th century, employment in agriculture diminished sharply, especially after 1945. In 1940 32 people worked in agriculture, but there were only nine employees by 1970 and three by 1988. Otherwise the farms were worked by farmers themselves, their partners and wives: a consequence of mechanisation.[116] In 2001 only 28 people were employed in any way in agriculture.[117]

19th and 20th Century Industries

Gas

In rural parishes such as Newport the establishment of a gas works depended not just on a ready supply of coal, after the railway came in 1845, but also on changes in company law in the mid 19th century which made possible the establishment of limited liability companies having as few as seven directors.[118] Previously such companies had been regarded as partnerships, in which the partners had unlimited personal liability.[119] A small company such as the Newport Gas Company thus became a less risky proposition.

In January 1867, therefore, the Newport Gas Company was incorporated under the provisions of the 1862 Companies Act.[120] The Company had seven directors: Thomas Shirley, John Edwick and David Skipper, all described as farmers; Thomas Crane, builder, George Robinson, surgeon, George Barnard, coal merchant, and John Chapman, the vicar of Newport. The object of the company was to build a gas works and provide a gas supply to Newport and its neighbourhood. The initial capital was £2,000, consisting of 400 shares at £5 each.[121]

Within a year all the shares had been taken up. Thomas Shirley was a director and initially the largest shareholder, with 66 shares. The other directors had 113 shares between them, of which the Vicar had 12. The remaining shares were bought by a further 31 people, from a variety of occupations and social backgrounds. W.C. Smith of

114 *Post Office Dir. Essex* (1855); *Kelly's Dir. Essex* (1874, 1882, 1894).
115 Census returns, 1861–1901.
116 TNA, MAF 68/3940, 4310, 4680, 5171, 5697, 6106.
117 http://www.neighbourhood.statistics.gov.uk (Newport).
118 T.I. Williams, *A History of the British Gas Industry* (Oxford, 1981), 8–10; Joint Stock Companies Act 1856 (19 & 20 Vict. c.47); Companies Act 1862 (25 & 26 Vict. c.89).
119 Williams, *Gas Industry*, 8.
120 TNA, BT 31/1322/3435.
121 Ibid.

Figure 34 *Aerial view of the railway, with goods siding, the gas works, and (at extreme right) the Maltings. Photograph probably c.1920.*

Shortgrove bought 20 shares; C.K. Probert, solicitor, six; Samuel Peacock, master at the Grammar School, five; and Sydney Perry, the Congregational minister, also five. Other shareholders, however, included a bricklayer, a publican and a retired publican, a butcher, a blacksmith, and James Drage the stationmaster. All but six of the initial shareholders were Newport residents.[122]

The gas works was completed by the beginning of September 1867, with a gas holder which had a capacity of 7,500 cubic feet.[123] The works were sited close to the railway on the east side of Newport station, and a siding was constructed to serve it.[124] At a vestry meeting in June 1867 Thomas Shirley, who was a churchwarden as well as one of the directors of the gas company, successfully proposed that the Vestry should levy a rate under the terms of the Lighting Act 1833 to pay for street lighting. A lighting rate was approved annually by the vestry and then (from 1894) by the parish council to pay for 26 street lamps.[125] Some private householders had gas lighting installed in their houses as soon as the supply was available. C.K. Probert, one of the shareholders, had 16 lights in Newport House, and Thomas Shirley lit every room in his Pond Cross Farm house, with

122 Ibid.
123 *Chelmsford Chronicle*, 27 Sept. 1867, p. 6.
124 OS 1:25 000 Map, Essex IX (13) (1st edn, 1877).
125 ERO, D/P 15/8/2, 3; NPC, Minute Books *passim*.

another light in the farmyard. A gas main was also laid to Quendon Hall, which was lit up for the first time on 22 September 1867, 'the first day of shooting.'[126]

By 1872 the number of shareholders had been reduced from 43 at the end of 1867 to 27, with Thomas Shirley now holding 102 shares. By 1877 he had 122, and after the issue in 1884 of a further 400 shares at £1 each he had 244 shares, rising to 264 in 1893. David Gayler's holding increased from 15 in 1867 to 51 in 1872 and 122 in 1888. By 1898 the stationmaster, James Drage, who had bought five shares in 1867, held 97 £5 shares and 147 £1 shares. He now described himself in the company register as a 'gentleman.' In place of popular capitalism a small group of dominant shareholders, able to control the company, had emerged by the end of the century.[127]

The only company accounts to survive are for 1908. By far the greater part of the company's income – £454 11s. 4d. – came from gas sold to private customers. The adoption of the incandescent mantle, invented in 1885, had made domestic gas lighting safer and more popular. The income from gas sold for street lighting, however, amounted to just £55. Expenditure, mainly on coal and wages, was only £257 9s. 4d., and thus the accounts showed a healthy surplus.[128]

In 1909 the directors and shareholders agreed to sell the company to the Bishop's Stortford District Gas Company, and to put the Newport company into voluntary liquidation.[129] By an Act of Parliament in 1910,[130] several small rural companies, including the Newport company, were merged in the Bishop's Stortford undertaking, and, significantly, the newly enlarged company was empowered to supply electricity. The gas works seems not to have been a large employer; there was a manager and a resident foreman, but the census returns provide no further information.

The merger did not lead either to the immediate closure of the Newport works or to the provision of a public electricity supply. In June 1931 the North Metropolitan Electric Power Supply Company acquired a controlling interest in the Bishop's Stortford Company, and in November of that year it decided to close the Newport works, along with other small gas works which had belonged to the Bishop's Stortford company. Gas was henceforth provided for the village by a pipeline from Stansted and Bishop's Stortford, and the gas mains were renewed at the same time.[131] Two small gasometers remained on the site for some years, along with a cottage and a maintenance depot. Upon nationalisation of the industry in 1948 the Bishop's Stortford Company became part of the Eastern Gas Board. The site of the Newport works was cleared and sold in 1968. Only the former manager's house now remains.

The closure of the Newport works and the laying of a pipeline from Bishop's Stortford may have enabled Newport to retain its gas supply when other rural communities that were not linked to a major source of supply lost theirs. Villages which had never had a gas supply were unable to persuade regional gas boards to lay new mains over long distances. When the manufacture of coal gas ended in the late 1960s and natural gas took

126 *Chelmsford Chronicle*, 27 Sept. 1867, p. 6.
127 TNA, BT 31/1322/3435.
128 Ibid.
129 Ibid.
130 10 Edw. 7 & 1 Geo. V c.17; *London Gazette*, 26 Nov. 1909, 29 July 1910.
131 *Centenary of the Bishop's Stortford, Epping and District Gas Company 1835–1935* (1935), 5–6.

Figure 35 *Newport Maltings, Station Road. Opened by G.H. Barnard in 1855. Date of photograph unknown.*

its place in the early 1970s, Newport had the infrastructure in place to enable the parish to be converted to natural gas.

In the summer of 1990 British Gas laid a high-pressure mains pipeline from its terminal in Norfolk to east London. The pipeline passed under the M11, London Road (B1383), and the railway line at the southern end of the parish, just north of the road from London Road to Widdington.[132]

Other Industries and Businesses

The railway provided direct employment: in 1861 there was a station master and seven other employees, rising to 12 by 1891; but it also proved a catalyst for other developments (see fig. 2). In 1855, ten years after the arrival of the railway, G.H. Barnard opened a maltings in Station Road, next to the station. It remained in use until 1982, and over the following seven years it was converted into a number of small industrial and business units. Some of these were in their turn converted into residential accommodation in 2012.[133]

132 NLHG Collections, letter from the Librarian of the Eastern Gas Central Library, n.d., *c.*1990.
133 Census returns, 1861–1901; pers. obs. by author.

Barnard, however, was much more than a maltster. He was described in 1874 as a 'coal merchant and farmer.'[134] His family owned Parsonage Farm until 1909, and had a coal yard at the station. In the 1881 census he described himself as a coal merchant employing ten men and a bricklayer with one man and a boy, as well as being a farmer.[135] In the 19th as in the 14th century, Newport acted as a centre for supplying the surrounding villages with commodities needed in agriculture.

In the first half of the 20th century Ginger's timber yard occupied a large area on the west side of the High Street (now Bullfields and part of Cherry Garden Lane). In the 1930s it was the largest employer in the village, but it was closed in the 1960s.[136] After the Second World War the principal industrial development was the chalk quarry near to the railway line on the southern side of the village. Some extraction took place before the war, but planning permission was granted in 1949 and by 2012 22,000 tonnes was produced during the six months of each year (April to September) when it operated. The chalk is used mainly for agricultural purposes.[137] Adèle Meyer established the Carnation Nurseries in the early 20th century, and used the profits from them to fund her work with mothers and babies in the village.[138] Until the early 21st century there was a small horticultural industry, with two nurseries producing tomatoes, cucumbers and peppers under glass. Towards the end of the 20th century, some of the land on which the nurseries stood was used for small business units, and later there was some housing development there.[139] Of the 82 businesses examined in a survey of 1986, the majority were in retail, marketing or other services.[140] Taking into account both the teaching and the ancillary staff, the schools were probably the largest employers in the village in the late 20th and 21st centuries. Most of the teaching staff and most of the secondary pupils, however, live outside the village, so it is not clear how large a contribution education makes to the village economy.

134 *Kelly's Dir. Essex* (1874).

135 Census return, 1881.

136 C. Gordon and J. Bines, 'Ginger's Timber Yard', *NN*, 50 (1998), 38–40; below, pp. 157–8.

137 http://www.needhamchalks.co.uk/locations;newport.

138 'Carnation Growing: A Visit to Lady Meyer's Nurseries' (*Garden Life* 8 Feb. 1913), 297; below, pp. 84–7.

139 Above, p. 76.

140 C. Murphy, 'Newport in 1986: The Living Village', *NN*, 26 (1986), 4–7.

SOCIAL HISTORY

SOCIAL STRUCTURE TO C.1600

ON MANORS SUCH AS NEWPORT, which formed part of the ancient demesne of the crown (as the concept emerged in the late 12th century), the obligations of the villein tenants were generally lighter than was usual on seigneurial manors. This may have arisen partly because the demesne tended to be smaller on royal manors (this seems to have been true of Newport), but also because their rights were more firmly entrenched in law than they were on other manors.[1] In 1086 the tenants on the manor of Newport had ten ploughs to the lord's one, suggesting that most of the land was held by the tenants for their own benefit.[2] Despite the place-name, Newport, being suggestive of an urban foundation, Domesday Book gives the impression that it was an agricultural community.

By 1299 Newport had some of the characteristics of a town, and there was substantial social stratification on the manor.[3] There were 84 burgage tenements, of which 26 were in the hands of only three men, who no doubt sub-let most of them. The survey lists eleven *terrarii* or freeholders, who held between them 22½ virgates (675 a., assuming a virgate was *c.* 30 a.). There were substantial inequalities amongst them: three held about 400 a. between them, but six no more than 30–40 a. each. There were also great variations in the burgage holdings of the *terrarii* or freeholders: John Revel, for instance, one of the *terrarii*, held 15 burgages; the heirs of Stephen Clerk held eight and a half, and John Overbridge held three. Stephen Rokesle, another freeholder, had a burgage and three shops, and was wealthy enough to contribute to the 1313 and 1327 lay subsidies.[4] The freeholders were not necessarily the wealthiest group, however: of the 15 listed in 1299, only four of them (or their descendants) paid tax in 1327, and some of the virgaters may have been able to accumulate enough personal wealth to pay tax. There was no direct correlation between tenurial status and wealth. The surveys and valuations present a snapshot of manorial society, and manorial court rolls do not survive, so it is possible that a land market existed whereby some freeholders acquired virgates to hold by what later became known as copyhold tenure, and the same may have been true of some cottagers or their families.

The same survey records a group of five tenants who held by serjeanty. This was a free tenure, which carried the obligation to perform certain services which were not specified in the survey. Free tenants on ancient demesne of the crown were, however, liable to tallage, even if the manor was let at farm, and from time to time payments (usually

1   Hoyt, *Royal Demesne,* 192–207.
2   DB, 973.
3   ERO, T/B 3/1.
4   ERO, T/B 3/1.

about £7) were made by the men of Newport.[5] By the end of the 13th century tallage was gradually replaced by a system of parliamentary taxation, but the manors on the ancient royal demesne paid parliamentary taxes – the lay subsidy – at a higher rate than other rural communities.[6]

In the early 16th century there was a group of ten to fifteen men, holding both freehold and copyhold land, who were significantly wealthier than the rest of the inhabitants of Newport. In 1524, for example, nine men and one woman (a widow) had land and goods worth £10 or more a year, while at the other end of the social scale just under half the inhabitants were wage earners who earned at least £1 a year and were thus liable for tax in that year; with, no doubt, many others who earned too little or had too few possessions to be taxable.[7] Social differentiation, however, was gradual: there was no clear distinction between the wealthy elite and those below them. The social scale tapered gradually downwards, and degrees of wealth varied substantially; the poorest, though, were the most numerous.

Some of the wealthier families had extensive material possessions and derived their wealth from a variety of sources. The Stanes family are a particularly good example: Alice Stanes, a widow who died in 1535, left her husband's smithy and its equipment along with land, cattle and sheep, to her son Richard, who was amongst the wealthy tax-paying elite at the end of Henry VIII's reign.[8] His son, also Richard, who died in 1602, amassed substantial holdings of property. He had over 50 a. of land in Newport and Widdington and six messuages, along with a great variety of household goods, implying considerable wealth and a high standard of living. He depended mainly on land for his income, though he was also a landlord and produced malt, probably from his own barley.[9] Stephen Nightingale (d. 1565) derived his living from his trade as a glover as well as his possession of 25 a. of land.[10] Some village officers were chosen from this elite: in 1524, for example, the two constables, John Howland senior and George Adam, had lands and goods worth £10 and £6 13s. 4d. a year respectively.[11]

SOCIAL STRUCTURE FROM C.1600

The 16th-century evidence does not bear out the description of Newport in Joyce Frankland's will as a 'great and poor town'.[12] If it was poor, it may have been a temporary phenomenon, a consequence of the economic difficulties of the latter part of Elizabeth I's reign. Evidence from the Hearth Tax in the second half of the 17th and early 18th centuries suggests that perhaps 10–20 per cent of the inhabitants were secure in their wealth, and regularly paid rates as well as the Hearth Tax; some were assessed for as

5   *Pipe R, passim.*
6   R.E. Glasscock, *The Lay Subsidy of 1334* (London, for the British Academy, 1975), xiv, 87; *Lay Subsidy of 1327*, 51.
7   TNA, E 179/108/155, 171.
8   WAM, Wyks p. 288; TNA, E 179/109/281.
9   *Essex Wills*, Commissary Court 1596–1603, no. 942.
10 Ibid., 1558–66, no. 126; TNA, E 179/109/281; E 179/110/348.
11 Ibid., E 179/108/155.
12 Below, p. 103.

many as 10 hearths. These men were churchwardens, overseers of the poor, village constable, and trustees of Gace's charity. Below them, however, was a much larger group subject to fluctuating economic circumstances, perhaps because they were wage labourers in agriculture or crafts such as leatherworking. Newport remained, as in the 14th century, somewhat wealthier than many surrounding villages. In the 17th century, for example, Giles Dent father and son had sufficient wealth generated from London trade to purchase the Shortgrove estate and build the Hall.[13]

In the 19th century, too, the village had an elite of prosperous entrepreneurs such as Thomas Shirley and G.H. Barnard who took advantage of the opportunities offered by the coming of the railway to establish businesses and engage in property development.

Figure 36 *Charles Kentish Probert (1820–88), solicitor, antiquary, and holder of several offices in the village. He lived at Newport House in the High Street (see fig. 37).*

---

13   French, 'Hearth Tax', 54–64 and 410–11; ERO, D/P 15/25/55–7; for Dent, see above, p. 38.

Figure 37 *Newport House, High Street. A substantial Georgian house, residence of C.K. Probert until his death in 1888.*

These men, like their 17th-century counterparts, tended to monopolise the various local offices, and as new bodies, such as the School Board, were set up in response to government legislation, they were represented on these as well.[14] There was also an emerging middle class, such as the solicitor C.K. Probert (d. 1888), who lived at Newport House and was involved in a wide range of activities, holding numerous positions of importance in the village (see fig. 36).

A significant difference, however, between Newport after *c.*1750 and the village in earlier centuries was the presence of important resident landholding families, the Cranmers (later Cranmer-Byngs) at Quendon Hall and the Smiths and their successors at Shortgrove. These families played the part expected of them in the life of the community, for example as trustees (later governors) of the Grammar School, as patrons of the church (the owner of Quendon Hall was the lay rector), and as leading figures in social life. Of particular significance for Newport, however, were the philanthropic activities of the earl of Thomond and his agent in the late 18th century, the Smiths in the early 19th century, and Adèle Meyer in the early 20th century.

14   Below, p. 96, 99.

PUBLIC HEALTH

In the 1770s, possibly on the initiative of his steward William Smith, the earl of Thomond, owner of Shortgrove, supported making Newport an early centre for the practice of inoculation against smallpox. Inoculation had been practised in England from the early 18th century, and in Newport two old ladies began inoculating some of the labouring poor of the parish in 1772. Their initiative aroused the concern of some of the leading people in the village, however, including William Smith. Smith raised his concern in a letter to Lord Thomond on 1 March 1772 in which he said that several of those who had already been inoculated were in favour of inoculating all the poor. Others, however, argued that the two old ladies had set an 'imprudent example' by inoculating parishioners in private houses rather than in places specifically set aside for inoculations.[15] Nonetheless, a survey showed that about 130 had already been inoculated, and there were about 140 more who were willing to be done. That left only four families who, Smith said, 'were not willing to be innoculated (*sic*) so they must take their chance.'[16]

Smith observed that the husband of one of the ladies 'has been a pretender to surgery but is superanuated' (*sic*), and on the strength of this she charged 2*s.* 6*d.* for each inoculation. Her colleague had been a smallpox nurse, and she charged only 1*s.* for each inoculation. Smith went on to say that the parish's reputation might suffer if the ladies were allowed to continue and 'any accident' happened. He therefore commissioned Mr Welch of Stansted Mountfichet, a doctor, to carry out the rest of the inoculations for a fee of 20 guineas. Instead of requiring each family to pay for their inoculations, he expected the trustees of Gace's charity and the parish vestry to meet the cost, 'with anything that your lordship (Thomond) pleases to contribute.' We do not know, however, how much Lord Thomond contributed.[17] The inoculations took place between 8 and 14 March 1772, and were remarkably successful: on 29 March Smith reported to Lord Thomond that only one death had occurred, 'a sucking child belonging to your Lordship's shepherd.'[18] Newport was not the only rural community to practise mass inoculation in the last three decades of the 18th century,[19] but it was unusual in that there was apparently no local epidemic which prompted the initiative.

By the beginning of the 19th century, when vaccination for smallpox began to replace inoculation (outlawed in 1840) the death rate declined significantly, but epidemics still occurred from time to time. One method of dealing with the disease was to establish 'pest houses', buildings in which sufferers could be nursed and, more importantly, isolated from the rest of the community. In June 1810 the vestry bought a copyhold cottage on the north side of Bury Water Lane to use as a pest house. There is no evidence about how often it was occupied by victims of smallpox, but it was sold in 1850 and was later pulled down; the land was used as a county council depot for many years, and

---

15   PHA, K5/7. Extracts from these letters are quoted by kind permission of Lord Egremont. See also J.R. Smith, *The Speckled Monster* (Chelmsford, 1987), 50, 65.

16   PHA, K5/7.

17   Ibid.

18   Ibid.

19   P. Razzell, *The Conquest of Smallpox* (Firle, Sussex, 1977), 113–39.

developed for housing in 2012.[20] The sale of the pest house perhaps suggests that the incidence of smallpox was declining, mainly no doubt because of vaccination, which became compulsory in 1853.[21] Although outbreaks of smallpox still occurred from time to time in the later 19th century and beyond, no cases are known in Newport.

Information about epidemic disease is sporadic before the Public Health Acts of the early 1870s. Occasional outbreaks of diseases such as typhoid, probably caused by poor sanitation, led the vestry in 1850 to authorise a rate of 3*d.* in the £ to allow the surveyor of highways to build sewers, which emptied into the river.[22] The 1872 Public Health Act, however, created rural sanitary authorities, with a medical officer of health (MOH) appointed for each authority by the Boards of Guardians. In 1874 the Medical Officer for the Saffron Walden Rural Sanitary Authority expressed concern about the drainage system in Newport. Five cases of typhoid had been reported that summer, all men who worked at Shortgrove and shared the same privy, thought to be the source of the outbreak.[23] Sewage still discharged into the river, and the MOH recommended that Mr Smith at Shortgrove should be required to lower his dam on the river so that 'filth is allowed to flow away' and not stagnate.[24] A more far-reaching drainage scheme was proposed but came to nothing, and discharge into the river remained a problem, particularly during the dry summer months when there was sometimes insufficient flow on the river to flush the sewage away.[25]

In 1898 Saffron Walden Rural District Council prepared a comprehensive plan to improve both the sewage system and the public water supply, so that it was sufficient to flush the sewage system,[26] but it was successfully opposed by Col. Cranmer-Byng, on whose land the pumping station for a proposed reservoir would have been erected. He said that the proposed scheme was too expensive, and that a sewage system with a flushing water supply was totally unnecessary. He even went so far as to call for the removal of the MOH to another locality 'where he may find scope for his costly and uncalled-for sanitary improvements.'[27] The rural district council felt unable to go ahead: the Local Government Board commented that the council lacked the courage to carry out the scheme in the face of such opposition.[28] The board consoled itself with the argument that the problem with the water supply in Newport was not so great as to make the project urgent, though some experts disagreed. During the period 1892–9 no deaths from enteric fever had been recorded, and only one case of the disease had occurred.[29] In 1891 and 1892, however, there were outbreaks of diphtheria, and in the 1892 epidemic three children died.[30] A public water supply was finally installed in 1932.

20 ERO, D/P 15/8/4; TNA, MH 12/3707, 3708.
21 3 & 4 Vict. c. 29; 16 & 17 Vict. c. 100.
22 ERO, D/P 15/8/2.
23 TNA, MH 12/3717.
24 Ibid, MH 12/3727.
25 Ibid.
26 Ibid.
27 Ibid.
28 Ibid.
29 Ibid.
30 Ibid., MH 12/3723.

In 1925 the MOH reported that Newport urgently needed a drainage system and an improved water supply. The parish council agreed to support such a scheme provided it did not entail more than 6*d.* in the £ on the rates, and in the following year the village approved the proposal at a parish meeting, provided sufficient funds became available.[31] Not until 1932, however, were there sufficient funds for the installation of a mains water supply and the construction of a sewage works, on Water Lane.[32]

The annual reports of the MOH regularly recorded cases of the usual infections of childhood, such as measles, scarlet fever and whooping cough. Deaths from these diseases were rare, though in 1892 the young daughter of Luther Mitchell, head teacher of the Council School, died of scarlet fever.[33] Amongst the adult, and especially the elderly, population respiratory and cardiac diseases were the most frequent causes of death, along with occasional accidents inseparable from the work of a largely agricultural community.[34]

Despite the prevalence of childhood infectious diseases, infant mortality in Newport in the latter part of the 19th century was low by national standards. In 1888 the infant mortality rate was 6.6 per cent of all live births, less than half the national average, as the MOH reported.[35] In the following year, at 6.3 per cent, it was lower than at any time over the previous 16 years, and apart from an occasional, and unexplained, increase (for example in 1898), it remained at roughly this level until the First World War.[36] In other respects, however, child health remained a problem, and poor nutrition, poor dental care, and the lack of helpful advice to pregnant women and nursing mothers attracted increasing attention in the early years of the 20th century.[37]

SOCIAL WELFARE

Both public and private initiatives played their part in improving child health. The 1906 Education Act allowed local education authorities to provide school dinners for pupils, and in the following year local authorities were required to appoint school medical officers with powers to examine children.[38] In the early 20th century, however, the most important contribution was made by Adèle Meyer. Born into a wealthy Jewish family in London in 1862 or 1863, she was the wife of Carl Meyer, who had bought the Shortgrove estate in 1903 (see fig. 30). By the beginning of the 20th century she had become involved in various campaigns to improve the position of women. She sympathised with the suffragettes, but her main interest was the betterment of the working conditions of many women, especially those in the garment trades. In 1909 she published a book jointly with Clementina Black which was the outcome of a year's investigation into the work of

31   NPC, Minute Book 1915–61, 81–2, 91; Parish Assembly Minute Book, 171–2.
32   NPC, Minute Book 1915–61, 127–8.
33   NCPS, Log Book 2 (1882–1914).
34   TNA, MH 12/3715-3727; ERO, D/B 2/OFF2/65.
35   TNA, MH 12/3723.
36   Ibid., MH 12/3723-3727; ERO, D/B 2/OFF2/65.
37   See, for example, G.R. Searle, *The Quest for National Efficiency: a Study in British Politics and Political Thought, 1899–1914* (Oxford, Blackwell, 1971).
38   6 Edw. VII c.57.

women in these trades. At the same time she became involved with the St Pancras School for Mothers in London.[39] The School provided advice on infant care and nutrition for pregnant women and nursing mothers, and its teachers went into the homes of young women to teach them domestic subjects, particularly cookery. In November 1910, when she was Chairman of the St Pancras School, she established a health centre along similar lines at Martin's Farm (now Tudor House), Newport.[40] She rented the house (which had belonged to the Shortgrove Estate until 1907), and financed the centre throughout its existence from the proceeds of her carnation nurseries. She brought from London one of the teachers from the St Pancras School, Florence Petty, known as the 'Pudding Lady', and appointed her as Health Visitor in Newport (see figs 38 and 39).[41]

She first of all set up a Girls' Club, where girls were encouraged to take part in music, drama, sewing, dancing and cookery lessons.[42] Perhaps inspired by the example of Conrad Noel, the socialist vicar of Thaxted, she introduced Morris Dancing in 1911, and this attracted boy scouts as well, 'with entirely decorous and successful results.'[43] She also initiated the provision of dinners for the school children. The children were given meal tickets at school, and came down to Martin's Farm for their dinners. The cost, borne by Lady Meyer, was estimated to be 1*d*. for each pupil's food and for the gas used in cooking.[44]

She also founded a 'Welcome Club', as a similar club at St Pancras had been named. This was a mother and baby clinic, where mothers brought their babies to be weighed, and receive advice about nutrition. Each mother paid 1*d*. per month, and Florence Petty encouraged them to talk not just about their infants but also about their school-age children, so that any problems could be picked up. They also discussed problems reported to the Centre by the School Medical Officer.[45]

In July 1911 Lady Meyer added a dental clinic to the facilities of the Centre.[46] The introduction of medical inspection of school children revealed the poor dental health of many of them; both Lady Meyer and Florence Petty believed that poor dental health led to many other illnesses, so the dental clinic's work was therefore educational and preventative, as well as clinical. The service was not free: the dentist, who visited the Centre from Saffron Walden, charged 12*s*. 6*d*. per hour, and anaesthetics were administered by the village doctor, Arthur Browne, for a fee of 5*s*. per case. In the six months from July to December 1911 the dentist treated 134 patients, of whom 51 were school children; 44 extractions were performed with anaesthetic and 37 without! The

39   *British Medical Journal,* 13 June 1908, 1462; Mrs Carl Meyer and Clementina Black, *Makers of Our Clothes* (London 1909).

40   Essex Education Committee, Report of School Medical Officer 1911, ERO C/DO 10/3; *Rearing an Imperial Race*, ed. C.E. Hecht (London, for the National Food Reform Association, 1913), 121–4, 273–4, 403–9.

41   *Imperial Race*, 405–6; Miss Bibby, Miss Colles, Miss Petty and Dr Sykes, *The Pudding Lady: A New Departure in Social Work* (London, for the St Pancras School for Mothers, n.d. [*c*.1911]), 100–3.

42   *Imperial Race*, 406.

43   Ibid.

44   Ibid., 406–7.

45   Ibid., 407–8.

46   Ibid., 408–9.

Figure 38 *Lady Meyer's Health Centre for mothers and infants at Martin's Farm (now Tudor House), Bridge End. Photograph taken c.1910–14.*

Figure 39 *Penny dinner children at Lady Meyer's Health Centre, Martin's Farm (now Tudor House), c.1912.*

County Medical Officer said in his report for 1911 that the clinic 'is much appreciated by the village.'[47]

The climax of Lady Meyer's work came in 1912, when she instituted a 'National Health Week', which was to begin with special church services in all the participating communities. The services were to be followed by sessions devoted to the discussion of topics such as general hygiene, mothercraft, cooking, and the relationship between temperance, sanitation and health.[48]

Although the Health Centre was a private venture, Lady Meyer and Florence Petty worked in close co-operation not only with the village doctor, but also with the local Nursing Association, which provided a nursing service for Newport and the neighbouring villages. The Association was founded in 1906, and by 1911 Lady Meyer was President of this too. The service was free for those on parish relief; others paid a subscription which varied from 2s. to 10s. a year, depending on income. The Nurse's hours and duties were laid down in some detail, and she was provided with accommodation and a bicycle.[49]

Much of the provision for health care in the village seems to have revolved around Lady Meyer's dynamic personality in the years before the First World War. The Nursing Association, which was separate from Lady Meyer's Health Centre, continued until it was subsumed in the National Health Service in 1948.[50] It is not clear, however, what happened to the Health Centre itself during and after the First World War. The Meyers incurred some hostility during the war because of Sir Carl's German origins, and the Centre may therefore have closed. Sir Carl died in 1922, and two years later his widow sold the estate and moved away from the village.[51] Dr Browne, who practised from his home, Belmont House, remained the village doctor until 1939. His successors practised from home until the 1970s, when the Newport practice acquired 55 Wicken Road for use as a surgery. In 1982 a new, purpose-built surgery was opened in Frambury Lane. It was designed by the architects Fitzroy Robinson of Cambridge, and in 1995 it was extended to accommodate the many ancillary services that the practice now provided.[52]

POOR RELIEF

The Old Poor Law

Under the Poor Law legislation of 1601, Overseers of the Poor were elected annually by the parish meeting in open vestry, and operated under the supervision of the Justices of the Peace. They were responsible for the setting and raising of a parish poor rate and the distribution of relief both in cash and in kind. This was recorded in the Parish Books along with the distribution of money under the several parish charities and the placing

47   Ibid., 409; ERO, C/DO 10/3. Adèle Meyer became Lady Meyer in 1910.
48   ERO, C/DO 10/3.
49   'A Local Nursing Association', NN, 3 (1975), 6–7.
50   C. Gordon, 'Nurse Dutton', ibid., 15 (1981), 25–31.
51   Above, p. 44.
52   J.R. Glennie, 'The New Surgery', NN, 17 (1982), 55–7; idem, 'Newport Surgery is 30 Years Old', ibid., 77 (2012), 22–3.

of apprentices and bastardy cases. Saffron Walden borough records include orders for the removal of paupers from Newport to Saffron Walden and *vice versa*.[53] There was also a parish almshouse adjacent to the first workhouse. A death there was recorded in 1632 and five further deaths and two births between 1700 and 1749.[54]

This workhouse was established by the parishioners meeting in Vestry in 1709. It may have been in the house purchased that year from William Burling for £8 by the vestry for town use.[55] Its precise location is not known, but the messuage 'late in the occupation of Elizabeth Pigg spinster and now of the town and called or known by the name of the workhouse' was situated between the tenement of the Wyatt family to the north and Belmont Street to the east.[56] Its purpose was reformatory: the removal of 'Idleness and Debauchery of a stupid Ignorance and Neglect of both human and divine duties' by housing and putting to work persons over 14 years old who were not yearly hired as servants and those claiming alms. It may therefore have been linked to the long-standing Puritan presence in the village.[57]

Reformatory workhouses are often associated with the work of the late 17th and early 18th century Societies for the Reformation of Manners. The Newport workhouse is therefore relatively early. The house had rooms above for beds and below for work, which was to be primarily the spinning and preparation of wool. It was anticipated that the poor would already have their own spinning wheels and reels. Those unsuited to this work would make tilepins, shoemakers' pegs, butchers' skewers and thatchers' spindles. Inmates who abused the work requirement were to be sent to the House of Correction, and swearing, lying, stealing, obscenity and the neglect of the Sabbath were to be severely punished. The house was funded through a rate of 1s. 6d. in the £ and the earnings from the sale of the spun wool and other work. The first master was Edward Turner, webster. By 1735 the master was a Mr Steward. In 1737 there were ten residents: five women, two men and three children. In 1738 there were 11 residents: six women and five men, of whom seven had been resident the previous year.[58]

Nevertheless, the annual cost of poor relief rose from £54 19s. 10d. in 1707 to over £200 towards the end of the century.[59] Dissatisfaction was expressed in 1754 about rising poor rates when 'the Majority of such Inhabitants in Vestry assembled as are taxed to the Maintenance of the Poor' objected to William Clarke's raising of a 1s. 5d. in the £ rate against an allowed rate of 1s. 4d. and his 'unequal assessment'. In 1755 their case was heard at the county Quarter Sessions, though the outcome is unknown.[60]

Towards the end of the 18th century the workhouse had become unsatisfactory, and the almshouses in Bury Water Lane were 'ruinous, confined and unwholesome.' In August 1793, the earl of Thomond at Shortgrove offered to remove and rebuild them.[61] A vestry unanimously accepted the proposal for a new room 40ft by 18ft on land given

53   ERO, D/B 2PAR5 series.
54   Ibid., D/P 15/8/1.
55   Ibid., D/P 15/8/4.
56   Ibid., D/DYv 60.
57   ERO, D/P 15/8/4; below, pp. 134–5.
58   ERO, D/P 15/8/4, D/DYv 43.
59   ERO, D/P 15/8/1.
60   ERO, D/P 15/8/4.
61   ERO, D/P 15/8/4.

at Bull's Hole in what is now Bury Water Lane.[62] Five years later, in 1798 Thomond built
a new workhouse 60ft by 16ft 'as a common working room for the poor inhabitants'
adjacent to the new almshouses (see fig. 40). Thomond funded the planting of elm
trees to provide fuel, and herbs, potatoes and cabbages were grown in the workhouse
garden.[63] The old poorhouse and almshouses were pulled down. A further cottage near
the toll bridge, apparently used as a poorhouse, was also to be demolished. The deed for
the new workhouse was signed by Thomond, the churchwardens and overseers, and 19
other parishioners. These included such leading figures as the magistrate George Pochin,
and the vicar, Revd Bell, together with the Independent minister Revd Bryant and one
woman, Sarah Knightley.[64]

However, the cost of the Poor Rate continued to climb, as it did generally during
the economically depressed years of the Napoleonic Wars. A return to a Parliamentary
commission gives the cost to the parish under several headings. The net cost of poor
relief was £482 5s. 9¼d. in 1801 and £606 10s. 8½d. in 1817, rising to £729 16s. in 1823
and falling to £587 5s. in the following year. In the early 1830s it rose again, to an average
of £827 between 1830 and 1834.[65]

The New Poor Law

Under the 1834 Poor Law Amendment Act, responsibility for the relief of the poor
passed to the new Poor Law Union of Saffron Walden, paid for by parish poor rates
passed to the Union. The Union was administered by a Board of Guardians and a new
Union workhouse was built at Radwinter Road, Saffron Walden.[66] A Newport Overseers'
Account Book for 1837–48 records Poor Rate receipts and payments in outline only. The
largest payment was to the Board of Guardians, at typically between £100 and £130 per
quarter, offering little saving over the Old Poor Law. There were also small payments
for the maintenance of a parish building (thatching and bricklaying) and in respect of
occasional removal, vagrancy and bastardy cases. In 1846 money was also set aside to
assist pauper emigration which had been discussed at the Vestry in January and February
of the same year.[67] From 1840 deaths in the Union Workhouse are fairly regularly
recorded in the Newport burials register and the 1881 census recorded six Newport
inmates: three older men (John Beckwith, blacksmith, 67, William Buck, agricultural
labourer, 62, and George Wright, agricultural labourer, 77) and three children (Walter,
William and James Luckings aged one, five and seven). According to oral testimony,
the Bury Water Lane accommodation was described as still being in the early years of
the 20th century 'a type of workhouse…They were single rooms to let at six shillings a
week'.[68] The old parish workhouse building is now privately owned cottages (nos 1 and 2

62   Ibid.
63   Ibid.
64   Ibid., D/Q 14/147.
65   Ibid., Q/CR 1/9/25; House of Commons Parliamentary Papers, Select Committee on Poor Rate Returns,
     1825 and 1830–4.
66   4 & 5 Will. IV c.76.
67   J. Cooper, *The Well-Ordered Town. A Story of Saffron Walden, Essex 1792–1862* (Clavering, 2000), 82–3;
     E. Sanders and G. Williamson, *Littlebury: a Parish History* (Parish of Littlebury Millennium Society,
     2005), 182–3; *VIT*, 121.
68   ERO, D/P 15/8/2; Newport Parish Registers.

Figure 40 *View of rear of Bury Water Cottages, Bury Water Lane, where the parish workhouse was situated from 1798 until its closure following the Poor Law Amendment Act, 1834. All the cottages are now private residences.*

Bury Water Lane). It still is marked by the 1798 plaque on the south wall recording the Wyndham donation (see fig. 40).

The workhouse system was abolished by the Local Government Act 1929.[69] Saffron Walden Union workhouse became a Public Assistance Institute under the control of Essex County Council. In 1932 Newport Parish Council campaigned vigorously against the rural district council's plan to move this facility to Takeley, on the southern boundary of the district, and the Isolation Hospital from Saffron Walden to Braintree some 25 miles away, on the grounds that the increased travel distances would cause serious hardship to the families of Newport inmates.[70] After the Second World War the Saffron Walden Public Assistance Institute closed and became St James' Hospital. It was converted to residential accommodation in the early 21st century.

CHARITIES

Gace's Charity

On 23 November 1520 John Covill and Agnes his wife conveyed his farmhouse and lands in Newport, called 'The Gaces' after a previous landholder, to trustees.[71] The rents and profits were to be used to assist those inhabitants of the village who had suffered misfortune. The farmhouse, demolished in 1880, was situated on the higher ground

69   19 & 20 Geo. V c.17.
70   NPC, Minute Book, 129–31.
71   *Report of the Commission Concerning Charities*, 32, pt 1, 1837, 801–3; below, p. 133.

above Belmont Hill on the site of the present Gace's Acre.[72] The land attached, which provided most of the income, has varied from about 41 a. in the early 18th century to 40 a. in 1871 and 35 a., mostly in White Ditch Field, in recent years. A small proportion of its income now comes from investments in government stock.[73]

In 1718–24 the churchwardens and others claimed in Chancery that the Trustees were favouring their friends and awarding grants to those who did not need them. Although the vestry had no say in the administration of the charity, new trustees were ordered to be appointed and funds, assessed by the court at £48 5s. 3d., had to be handed over. The legal costs, reduced to £225 19s. 5d., but still far greater than the income of the charity, were required to be paid by the defendants.[74] Following the action in 1726, the terms for awarding grants were clarified. The Trustees resolved that income should only be distributed to persons 'such as by loss of cattle, goods or chattels, or through sickness, fire, wind or any such misfortune shall be reduced to poverty or want'.[75]

In the 19th century the charity came under the supervision of the Charity Commissioners, who approved a scheme of 12 June 1877 which confirmed that the charity was designed for exceptional cases of distress and sickness. After the reform of local government in 1894, and in face of opposition from the trustees, a new scheme was adopted on 30 May 1917 which placed the charity under the control of the parish council to the extent that a majority of the trustees (five out of nine) had to be appointed by the council.[76]

In the 18th century the income available for distribution was less than £20 a year, and by the middle of the 19th century it was still less than £50 per annum, though it increased gradually in the course of the 20th century.[77] Many individuals who suffered illness or losses especially of livestock and trade were helped with small amounts, varying from 3s. to £5 from the 17th to the 19th centuries. Recipients increased from about 20 in the early 18th century to a peak of 82 in 1832, including a few 'decayed tradesmen' who were assisted over several years. The trustees responded to the potato famine in 1847 with a special grant of £5 to the local subscription fund to relieve the hardship suffered by many families in the parish.[78]

For most of the 20th century grants were given under the 1917 scheme which did not permit regular payments. It supported medical care, providing nurses and midwives, and making donations to institutions such as dispensaries so that local people could benefit from their services. Aid in kind such as fuel, clothes and food could be supplied and local Provident clubs established for the same purpose could be supported. Temporary relief in money might be given as a loan.[79] In 1919, the practice of making public annual

72   ERO, D/P 15/25/30, 15/25/80.
73   Ibid., D/P 15/25/1, A12122 Box 1; *Return of Owners of Land, 1871*, Essex, 10.
74   ERO, D/P 15/25/53.
75   Ibid., A12122.
76   Scott Sanderson, 'Gace's Charity', *NN*, 38 (1992), 42; ERO, A12122.
77   ERO D/P 15/25/1-2; http://www.charity-commission.gov.uk. Financial information is © Crown copyright.
78   ERO, D/P 15/25/2.
79   Sanderson, 'Gace's Charity'.

payments on Hock Monday (the second Monday after Easter) was discontinued in favour of payments on application throughout the year.[80]

In 2014 the charity was governed by a scheme approved by the Charity Commissioners in November 1975, and amended in March 1999. Its objectives remain the relief of poverty in the village of Newport by making grants to needy individuals, who may apply at any time during the year. Between 2008 and 2012 its yearly average income was £2,896, and its average expenditure £2,824 per annum. In addition to its investment income it received some small grants from other sources, such as Uttlesford District Council's New Homes Bonus scheme. [81]

Lettice Martin's Charity

In 1562 Lettice Martin, a widow from Chrishall, established a trust, and at her death about 1575 she left an estate of around 78 a. for the benefit of the poor of Chrishall and 32 other parishes in Essex including Newport. Newport's share of the income was 13s. 4d., and Lettice Martin's intention was that every poor householder in the village should receive 1s. each year.[82] The churchwardens in Newport, who were given the responsibility for distributing the funds, preferred to give smaller amounts to more people. In 1664, two years' income was brought from Chrishall to Newport and 71 people were given 4d. and six people 6d. each. By the 19th century, the practice was to limit the recipients to widows and widowers, and between 26 and 60 persons received between 1s. and 2s. each.[83]

In 1901, the estate was sold by order of the Charity Commissioners, and Newport's share of the proceeds, £105 15s. 1d., was reinvested. By 1992 the value of the fund was £6,281, and £10 each was paid to 29 widows and widowers. With such small funds at their disposal, most of the other parishes who benefited from Lettice Martin's gift have amalgamated the charity with other parochial charities, but in Newport it has maintained a separate existence, perpetuating the donor's name.

Between 2007 and 2011 its income was £306, and expenditure £271.[84] At the end of 2011 the fund amounted to £6,489. Although there is no scheme governing the charity, grants are still paid to widows and widowers, with the distribution taking place in the parish church each May: 29 widows and widowers benefited in 2011, though the number fluctuates from year to year. The charity has also received grants from the Newport Business Association and Uttlesford District Council's New Homes Bonus scheme.[85]

Pond Common Trust

The Pond Common Trust has its origins in the outcome of a Chancery lawsuit in 1612 between the earl of Suffolk, lord of the manor of Newport Pond, and 36 tenants of the manor, led by Matthew Stanes.[86] As part of the settlement of the suit, the earl agreed to

80   VIT, 136.
81   http://www.charity-commission.gov.uk. Financial information is © Crown copyright.
82   Jane Cox, 'The Lettice Martin Charity', NN, 48 (1997), 165–9.
83   ERO, D/P 15/8/4.
84   http://www.charity-commission.gov.uk. Financial information is © Crown copyright.
85   Information from the charity's correspondent in Newport. The New Homes Bonus Scheme is a central government grant administered by UDC.
86   TNA, C 3/283/73; above, p. 66.

pay £20 a year to the overseers of the poor, for distribution amongst the tenants. Six of the 'most substantial men of the town of Newport' were to advise on the distribution.

Until 1860 the money was distributed amongst those having common rights.[87] In that year, however, the churchwardens took counsel's advice about the propriety of distributing the money in this way. He advised them that they should no longer do so, but should hold the money in trust for the benefit of all the inhabitants of the parish.[88] In 1873 the Commissioners drew up a scheme for the Trust under which its income was to be applied to the maintenance of the church clock and also to the erection and maintenance of public pumps or drinking fountains, for the benefit of all the inhabitants of the parish.[89]

The need to maintain the parish pumps ceased with the coming of a mains water supply in 1932,[90] but the Trust's income continued to be applied to the maintenance of the clock and the payment of an honorarium (not always claimed) to the clock winder.[91] Between 2007 and 2011 the income of the Trust amounted to £3,412, and expenditure to £2,628. It would, however, be insufficient if major expenditure on the clock were needed.[92]

LEISURE AND RECREATION

Following inclosure in 1861, a 4a. field on the Common was allocated to the Churchwardens and Overseers 'as a place for exercise and recreation for the inhabitants of the said parish'. This was initially the responsibility of the Surveyors of Highways. Rents from the ground were applied to the highway rates until the Commons Act of 1876, after which they were used to improve recreation grounds or for the purchase or rent of additional recreational space. The field was depastured by sheep for an annual rent of £4 to £5 and occasionally mown for hay in the summer.[93] From 1865 the ground was managed by a committee.

The marshy ground by the river Cam was subject to flooding in the winter and rush growth in the summer. In 1877 the committee replied to the Inclosure Commissioners that it was 'occasionally used for cricket by the village lads and boys and would be more used if more conveniently situated'. Their reply originally included a suggestion that there was a more centrally-located field owned by the Shortgrove estate but that it was not known whether the owner was willing to effect an exchange. This answer was deleted from the final version.[94] In 1878 a shed was erected for the cricketers and in 1883 the ground was improved by the removal of a dam and scouring to prevent flood damage. Road scrapings were also spread and lime trees planted on the boundary.[95]

---

87   ERO, D/P 15/8/1,4.

88   NPC, *Newport Pond Common Charity*, typescript with no author or date, probably *c.*1950–60.

89   TNA, CHAR 6/2/3.

90   Above, p. 83.

91   R. Holmes, 'The Pond Common and Lettice Martin Charities', *NN*, 25 (1986), 71.

92   http://www.charity-commission.gov.uk. Financial information is © Crown copyright.

93   ERO, D/P 15/8/2, 15/8/3, D/Q 25/27; Q/RDc 53A; 39 & 40 Vict. c.56.

94   ERO, D/Q 25/27 items 2, 10.

95   Ibid., D/P 15/8/3.

Figure 41 *First football match at the recreation ground, Aug. 1984 (White Horse v. S.V. Cranheim of Tübigen, Germany).*

Figure 42 *Newport Cricket Team. Winners of John Davidson Trophy, Sep. 2012.*

In 1894 the parish council acquired responsibility from the vestry for the recreation ground where, in addition to sports, celebrations and other events (such as circuses) were held. Flooding from the river remained a perennial problem and the minutes record the regular need to keep the surrounding ditches and river course free of blockages. Neighbouring tenants also had to be reminded to keep their boundary fencing in repair to prevent invasions by hens.

At this time the ground seems to have been used primarily by the cricket club which now had a pavilion there, although by 1928 this was ruinous and was demolished. The football club, on the other hand, had to request permission to use it each season, perhaps a reflection of the different social make-up of each team. Children's play equipment was erected there in 1919.[96] In 1963 the parish council raised with the rural district council the need for an additional recreation ground to meet the needs of the growing population. An affordable site at Frambury Lane was eventually found in 1972 and planning permission gained in 1973.[97] The purchase price was met by a £10,000 loan from the Public Works Loan Board. The new cricket and football pitches were available for use in 1985 and 1986 and a Club House opened in 1992 (see figs 41 and 42). A Croquet Club was founded in 1984, and in 2014 it had three lawns and a Club House.[98]

In the late 19th and early 20th century many non-sporting organisations were established in the village. Some were branches of nationwide movements, such as the Band of Hope, which flourished from the 1880s onwards despite (or perhaps because of) the nine pubs in the village c.1900.[99] The Newport Working Men's Club was founded in 1917 as a club for returning servicemen. Now known as The Newport Club, it has remained on its original site in the centre of the village, and from 1996 women could become members in their own right.[100]

A branch of the Women's Institute was inaugurated in 1918, with an initial membership of 70. It remained active and important, especially during the Second World War, until social changes in the late 20th century led to declining membership, and it was wound up in 2004.[101] It had a drama group, which co-existed with the Newport Amateur Dramatic Society, founded in 1921, and the Newport Amateur Theatrical Society has continued to mount productions into the 21st century. The Mothers' Union met weekly from the beginning of the 20th century, but here too social changes had their impact, and in the late 1950s the Ladies' Fellowship (later the Ladies' Social Club) was started for young mothers who did not wish to join the Mothers' Union.[102] A significant feature of the social and cultural life of the village from c.1950 has been the diminishing role of the church.

For young people, a drum and fife band was formed in 1883, which played at Shortgrove and Quendon as well as in the village, and a Boys' Club was opened in 1889 with a Girls' Friendly Society somewhat later, both of which were affiliated to the parish

96   NPC, Minute Books and Assembly Minute book, *passim.*

97   ERO, D/J 52/2/2.

98   *VIT,* 174–5.

99   Newport Parish Magazine, *passim.*

100 J. Murphy, 'The Newport Club', *NN,* 56 (2001), 82–4.

101 A. Moule, 'A Brief Record of Newport Women's Institute', ibid., 4 (1975), 37–8; V. Bright and E. House, 'Newport Women's Institute 1918–2004', ibid., 67 (2007), 102–3.

102 J. Brace and J. Peters, 'The Ladies Social Club: How it Began', ibid., 29 (1988), 113.

church.[103] After the establishment of a Newport boy scout troop, associated with Baden-Powell's nation-wide movement from 1911,[104] the Boys' Club seems to have been less important. A girl guide troop was not, however, formed until 1930.[105] A scout hut, Jikes Hall, was built on the recreation ground in 1985.

For those with more academic interests, the Duodecimo Society, founded in 1891, provided an opportunity for a group of 12 like-minded men (women were not admitted until the 1990s) to meet regularly and discuss topics of the day. Its members reflected the increasing presence of middle-class professionals in the village during the 20th century, though some were not residents of Newport. As with the Women's Institute, however, social changes at the end of the 20th century led to a declining membership and it was wound up in 2005.[106] The Newport Art Group was established in 1981 and holds annual exhibitions, while the Local History Group, founded in 1977, has carried out extensive research into the history of the village, and since 2004 has organised an annual programme of talks on local history.[107]

For all these activities, the provision of suitable premises was essential, and even more protracted than the creation of a second recreation ground was the search for a village hall. In the 1880s C.K. Probert was one of a group of prominent people in Newport who sought to establish a trust with funds to finance the building of a parish hall and reading room. James Bailey of Shortgrove, amongst others, made a financial contribution; the Barnard family gave the trust the proceeds from the sale of a piece of their land, and eventually the proceeds financed the purchase from J.C.T. Heriz-Smith of a plot on the east side of the High Street for a building which opened in 1898. The trust's funds were insufficient, however, to cover the running costs of the hall, and Percy Bailey, James's heir, soon bought the building. In 1912 he sold it to Sir Carl Meyer for £200.[108] Sir Carl hoped that the parish council would then buy it, but they did not have sufficient funds to do so.[109] The matter was raised again in 1919 and in June 1930 when a resolution was made to proceed with negotiations and fundraising and a sub-committee was set up for the purpose, but the asking price (£750) was prohibitively high and the project collapsed once more. In the meantime the Congregational Church hall was used for public meetings and social events.[110] In 1940 the subject was again on the agenda as the parish hall was understood to be on the market. Again, available funds (£120 to £130) were thought to be inadequate and in wartime it was unlikely that more could be raised.[111] In 1940 the parish hall was acquired by Essex County Council and used as a school canteen during the war, and a youth club.[112]

103 Newport Parish Magazine, *passim*.
104 Ibid., May 1911.
105 *VIT*, 151.
106 G. Elcoat, 'The Duodecimo Society, 1891–1991', *NN*, 35 (1991), 78–9; R. Helmore, 'The Duodecimo Society 1891–2005', ibid., 69 (2008), 10–11.
107 *NN*, passim: reports from 1981 onwards.
108 NLHG, Village Hall Deeds..
109 NPC, Parish Assembly Minute Book, 97–9, 105–7.
110 Ibid., Minute Books, *passim*.
111 Ibid., Minute Book, 116; Parish Assembly Minute Book, 194–6, 241.
112 *VIT*, 147.

From 1950 fundraising began in earnest to build a hall on a site on Station Road donated by Benskins Brewery. The new hall, substantially built by volunteer labour, was completed in summer 1960. In 1978, trusteeship of the hall was transferred to the parish council.[113]

EDUCATION

Education Before 1839

There is sporadic evidence for elementary education in Newport before the development in the 1830s of a system of public finance for schools in England and Wales. In 1676 Samuel Pack of Newport, described as a 'gentleman', was indicted for teaching boys and girls in a house in the parish before he had obtained a licence to teach. This may have been a dissenting academy, but it does not appear on the database of these academies.[114] In the 18th century, the parish registers record the occupation of three men as 'schoolmaster': Thomas Clerk (1706), Thomas Wallace (1780), and Benjamin Digby (1730) who was described as 'a petty schoolmaster'. William Hollingsworth (1735) was described as 'Master of the Writing School'. Although there is no evidence that these men actually taught in Newport, some form of elementary school probably existed there because candidates for entry to Newport Free Grammar School had to be able to read and write.[115]

In the replies to the bishop of London's visitation articles in 1778, it was stated that 'we have some schools for teaching little children'. In 1810 the vicar stated that in addition to the Grammar School there were two day schools with 35–40 pupils each, but the dissenters had no school apart from a recently-established Sunday school.[116] There were still two day schools in 1818, one of which had 36 girls supported by Margaret, wife of Joseph Smith of Shortgrove, along with 24 others whose parents paid for them. The other school had 22 girls and four boys supported by Mrs Smith and ten supported by their parents.[117]

In 1830 the vicar of Newport, Edward Gould Monk, compiled a census of the parish. He recorded everyone's name, occupation, age, whether they attended church, and whether each person 'reads, writes, or goes to school'.[118] It is not clear what 'goes to school' signified: it may mean no more than that they attended Sunday school, but it must have included pupils at the Grammar School. Nonetheless, the census shows that just over half the 244 children between the ages of four and 14, 124 (61 boys and 63 girls) experienced some form of education. In some families all or most children between four and 14 had some education, while in others none did. This may reflect the different inclinations of families, but also the ability to pay whatever fees were required.

---

113 NPC, Minute Book, 219, 333; ERO, D/J 52/1/1, 208.

114 TNA, ASSI 35/11/72; http://www.english.qml.ac.uk/drwilliams.

115 Newport Parish Registers, baptisms 1706, 1735; burials 1730, 1780; W.T. Phillips, 'The History of Newport (Essex) Grammar School', Durham M.Ed. thesis (1968), 121–2.

116 LPL, Fulham Papers, Lowth 5 ff. 434–7; Randolph 11/48.

117 *VIT*, 94.

118 Monk, *Inhabitants*.

By 1833 there were seven schools in the parish. One was Newport Free Grammar School; two were Sunday schools; and the remaining four had 80 pupils between them, of whom 29 were boys and 51 girls. Children were educated largely at the expense of their parents, though a few private individuals continued to provide some financial support.[119]

The County Primary School and its Predecessors

In 1838 Revd Monk proposed to establish an Anglican Sunday school, but the National Society for promoting the Education of the Poor in the Principles of the Church of England refused to make a grant merely for a Sunday school.[120] In the following year, however, strongly urged by the Society, Monk submitted a proposal for a daily and Sunday school with 86 pupils, 43 boys and 43 girls, with a fee of 1*d.* per week for each child.[121] This time he was successful; the National Society agreed to guarantee £25 of the total cost, and W.C. Smith of Shortgrove offered land for the building. Monk had considered applying for a grant from the Privy Council Committee on Education, but he was not prepared to accept the Council's inspectors, who might not be adherents of the Church of England.[122] Nonetheless, the school was opened in January 1840. It was funded by subscriptions and by payments from the children's parents.[123] The school was

Figure 43 *Plaque originally on the front of the old primary school at the corner of School Lane and Wicken Road. Now displayed outside the present school building on Frambury Lane.*

119 *Abstract of Answers and Returns Relative to the State of Education in England and Wales,* I (HC 62, 1835), 284.
120 LPL, National Society Records, Newport File NS/7/1/909, pieces 1–4.
121 Ibid., NS/2/2/1/1/4, piece 6, p. 29.
122 Ibid., pieces 7–12, pp. 137–8.
123 Ibid., piece 13; LPL, *Returns to the General Inquiry made by the National Society into the State and Progress of Schools for the Education of the Poor in the Principles of the Established Church* (1849), 14–15; *White's Dir. Essex* (1848), 620.

built on a cramped and inconvenient site and was bounded on two sides by a wide road (Wicken Road), with a pond just beyond a small garden at the rear of the building.[124] There was no room for a playground, let alone a teacher's house, and by 1848 Monk and his fellow-trustees planned a more substantial schoolroom on a more spacious site with accommodation for 45 boys, 45 girls, and 15 infants, with an adjacent house for the mistress. The estimated cost was £708 2s.[125] William Smith once again donated the site, on the corner of Wicken Road and School Lane. Over £500 was raised by local subscription, much of it from Elizabeth Glyn, William Smith's sister and widow of the vicar of Henham.[126] The vestry agreed to donate materials from the Cage, the village lock-up, which they intended to demolish.[127] Monk now agreed to accept the Council's inspection regime, and the Council accordingly made a grant of £100.

The new school opened in autumn 1849 and remained affiliated to the National Society until 1874, when a meeting of the ratepayers agreed to set up a school board for Newport under the 1870 Education Act. The Board was constituted on 14 April 1874,[128] and the managers and trustees of the National School subsequently agreed to transfer the school and its buildings to the Board, on condition that the schoolroom could be used on Sundays for a Sunday school.

In 1870 average annual attendance was 45; by 1876 it had risen to 68, and in 1881 it was 93.[129] In 1882 inspectors reported that numbers had 'increased satisfactorily', and recommended that the infants should now be taught in a separate department.[130] However, attendance declined in the autumn of 1884 when several families left the village 'as there has been a reduction in the number of employees on the Shortgrove estate since the decease of W.C. Smith Esq.'[131] It may have been partly for this reason that the School Board attempted to secure the closure of the one remaining dame school in the village. Following the 'voluntary' closure of the dame school five pupils were admitted in December 1884, and another four in January 1885, but the Head Teacher (Luther Mitchell) commented that 'there are a few more who ought to come.'[132] By the following year average attendance had risen to 131.[133]

Payment of fees remained a problem for some families. In April 1891, for example, Gace's charity paid the fees of three children who had not attended because their parents were unable to pay, though, in general, chronic non-attendance was rare. The 1891 Education Act allowed parents to insist on free education, but the virtual abolition of fees did not produce a sudden increase in attendance. In 1891 attendance was 146, but in 1895 it was 133, though in 1899 it had recovered to 154.[134] In March 1897 the School

124 TNA, C 54/12308, mm. 24–5.
125 Ibid., ED 103/13/64, pp. 943ff.
126 Ibid., p. 953, and inscription on commemorative plaque: fig. 43, p. 98.
127 ERO, D/P 15/8/2.
128 ERO, D/P 15/8/2; *London Gazette*, 17 Apr. 1874, 2146.
129 TNA, ED 2/170; *Reports of the Committee of Council on Education* (1870–1), 456; (1875–6), 533; (1880–1), 578.
130 NCPS, Log Book 2 (1882–1914), 6 Nov. 1882.
131 Ibid., 26 Sep. 1884.
132 Ibid., 1 Dec. 1884, 4 Jan. 1885.
133 *Report of the Committee of Council on Education* (1885–6), 514.
134 Ibid. (1890–1), 590; Board of Education, *Schools in Receipt of Parliamentary Grants 1899–1900* (1900), 73, 526–7.

Figure 44 *Children and Staff of the Council School, with Luther Mitchell, Head Teacher, 1915.*

Board drew up plans for the further enlargement of the school, and a new room, to accommodate 60 infants, was duly opened on 28 February 1898.[135]

Essex County Council, as the Local Education Authority (LEA), assumed responsibility for the school in 1902.[136] Day-to-day matters were now under the control of school managers rather than a school board, but at Newport much the same people continued in office. The vicar, Revd George Tamplin, who had been chairman of the school board, became the first chairman of the school managers.[137]

Attendance remained a problem at the beginning and end of the harvest each year, and the school had to arrange its summer holiday around the harvest season, which varied from year to year.[138] Between 1908 and 1914 Adèle Meyer of Shortgrove arranged 'vacation schools' during the summer holidays. They lasted for three weeks, and were very successful. In 1910, for example, over 80 children out of 148 on the school roll took part, and in 1914 some 69 children participated. It was valuable for parents who would be heavily involved with the harvest, but there is no record of what the children were taught, nor whether any payment was required. The scheme ceased after the outbreak of war in 1914.[139]

135 NCPS, Log Book 2, 12 March 1897.
136 2 Edw. VII, c.42
137 NCPS, Log Book 2, 23 Dec. 1903.
138 ERO, E/MM/353/1, pp. 69–70.
139 NCPS, Log Book 2, 1908–14, *passim*.

Shortly before the outbreak of the Second World War, the school was designated as a centre for the reception of evacuees who were to be billeted in the village, and on 3 September 1939 a group of mothers and young children arrived from Woodford. The Managers noted on 4 October that there were 29 evacuees on the roll, along with 101 local children.[140] The number of local children had been reduced, however, by the withdrawal of 16 children who lived in Wicken Bonhunt. A temporary school was established for them there during the blitz, but it closed in autumn 1942, when air raids had become much less frequent.[141]

There were 14 evacuees at the school in January 1940 and only nine in April; but once the blitz started the number increased substantially. There were at least 50 on the roll between October 1940 and October 1941, and they were described in the Managers' minutes as 'government and private evacuees': many, no doubt, fugitives from the bombing in London.[142] There is no evidence that the school suffered any bomb damage, but air raid warnings were frequent from late August 1940 until mid June 1941, and a shelter was dug in the boys' playground.[143] By the autumn of 1942, however, the situation had eased considerably. The number of evacuees was now only in the 20s, the Wicken children had returned, and the number on the roll reached 136 by July 1943.[144] When the Managers met for the first time after the end of the war in Europe, on 19 July 1945, they recorded that there were 125 children on the roll, including ten evacuees, whose parents had evidently decided to remain in Newport.[145]

Under the terms of the 1944 Education Act,[146] the LEA envisaged that the school should be a Junior School providing primary education for 100 children of five to 11 years of age. In order to bring the accommodation up to the required standard, a hall would have to be provided at a cost of £50 for the site and £7,000 for the building, though this would not be done until 1951 at the earliest.[147] The school retained some of the characteristics of an elementary school until 1950. Even though the leaving age was raised to 15 in 1947, children still left at age 14 until 1950.

The number of children admitted each year between 1945 and 1960 fluctuated between 19 and 34, but in the 1960s and 1970s, as the population of the village doubled, admissions increased. They reached 39 in 1970–1, 40 in 1971–2, 31 in 1972–3, and 40 again in 1973–4. There had been substantial housing development in Cherry Garden Lane and adjacent roads in these years, and these addresses started to appear in the school admissions register as new families moved into the village.[148]

By the early 1970s the school building had become too small. In 1961 the Managers had proposed erecting an entirely new building, but it was repeatedly delayed, and in the late 1960s the large building on the east side of the High Street, formerly the Parish Hall, then the Youth Centre and now a private house, was taken into use again as a dining hall

---

140 ERO, E/MM/353/1, p. 22.
141 NCPS, Log Book 4 (1936–65), 13 Sept. 1939, 19 Oct. 1942.
142 Ibid.; ERO, E/MM 353/1, pp. 81–95.
143 NCPS, Log Book 4, *passim*; ERO, C/W 1/2/61, 62.
144 ERO, E/MM 353/1, p. 105.
145 Ibid., p. 113.
146 7 & 8 Geo. VI c.31, section 35.
147 ERO, E/MM 353/1, p. 128.
148 NCPS, Admissions Register, 1946–86.

and also as a classroom. Parents, however, objected because of the danger to children in crossing a busy main road (at that time the A11 London–Norwich trunk road) to get there from the school, so a temporary classroom was erected on part of the Head Teacher's garden. (He was compensated with part of the adjacent field, leased from G. Barnard.) The lower junior class was now transferred back to the school, and meals were again served in the school building itself.[149]

In 1971 plans for a new building were revived, and a new school was built on a new site on Frambury Lane about half a mile from the existing building. On 14 January 1974, the Head Teacher, W.H. Ingham, wrote in the Log Book that 'we opened in the new school in Frambury Lane this morning.'[150]

Newport Free Grammar School

There is no conclusive evidence for the existence of a school in Newport before the foundation of Newport Free Grammar School in 1588. Although there was a guild of Corpus Christi at Newport nothing is known about it before the lay subsidy returns of 1524[151], and there is no record of it keeping a school as it did elsewhere in Essex.[152] On the other hand, on 20 August 1581 Nicholas Harvey, schoolmaster, witnessed a grant of land in Newport; but it does not follow that he taught at an otherwise unrecorded school in the village.[153]

The foundation document of the Grammar School is the will of Joyce Frankland,[154] dated 20 February 1587, the year of her death. She was a wealthy but childless widow,

Figure 45 *Newport Free Grammar School, as it was in 1907.*

149 Ibid., Log Book 5 (1965–83), 3 Nov. 1967 to 10 Feb. 1968.
150 Ibid., 14 Jan. 1974.
151 G. Martin, 'Medieval Essex Gilds', in *Essex Heritage*, K. Neale, ed. (Oxford, Leopard's Head Press, 1992), 41.
152 TNA, E 179/108/171.
153 ERO, D/P 15/25/39; Newport Parish Registers, Burials, 1594.
154 TNA, PROB 11/70.

who made bequests to several institutions, including Brasenose College Oxford and two colleges at Cambridge, Emmanuel and Gonville and Caius. Her Newport bequest arose from a suggestion by Geoffrey Nightingale, tenant of Pond Cross Farm in Newport. He was educated at Christ's College Cambridge, and at Gray's Inn, where he may have encountered Joyce Frankland's son, who entered the Inn in 1576 but died in 1581.[155]

Geoffrey Nightingale was a neighbour of Thomas Sutton, who in 1611 founded Charterhouse School. In 1569 Sutton had acquired the lease of the manor of Littlebury, and he nominated Nightingale as one of the founding governors of Charterhouse. The first Master, appointed in 1613, was John Hutton MA, vicar of Littlebury, and another governor, appointed in the following year, was William Byrd DCL, who also had connections with Littlebury.[156] There was, perhaps, a group of clergy and educated gentry in north-west Essex who shared an interest in the establishment of new schools.

According to Joyce Frankland's will, Nightingale had told her that Newport was 'a greate and poore towne', and that the inhabitants had a Town House (the former Corpus Christi Guild Hall) which they wanted to use as a school house, but lacked the ability (i.e. means) to do so.[157] Mrs Frankland accordingly left to Nightingale and four other inhabitants of Newport an endowment to £23 10s. a year, which was to be held in trust for the 'erection, maintenance and fynding of a free grammer schoole within the saide towne of Newporte.'[158]

The Newport Trustees, with Dr Legge, Master of Gonville and Caius College Cambridge, drew up the statutes which formed the basis for the government and conduct of the school until the promulgation in 1874 of a new Scheme under the Endowed Schools Act of 1869.[159] Dr Legge not only prescribed the curriculum and day-to-day routine of the school, but he also laid down certain general principles for the admission and education of pupils. In particular, he required the Master to teach rich and poor equally, and that the children of paupers should be given priority in admission, provided they were capable of being taught and were already able to read and write. The Master of Caius was required to consent to the appointment of the Master, and to conduct an annual visitation of the school.

The management of the endowment in the 17th and 18th centuries, which included property in Distaff Lane, near St Paul's in London, gave rise to some difficulties which led to litigation in Chancery and a commission of inquiry under the earl of Suffolk in 1662. The Commission recommended that the existing Trustees should be replaced by a newly-constituted body consisting of two of the three surviving Trustees and eight others, 'honest and substantial' inhabitants or landowners and proprietors in Newport.[160] Endowment income was henceforward to be received by the Trustees, who would pay the Master, the Usher, and the Visitor; no property was to be leased for more than 21 years, and the Trustees and the Visitor were to follow the admissions policy set out in Joyce Frankland's will and the original statutes.

---

155 J. Foster (ed.), *The Register of Admissions to Gray's Inn, 1521–1889* (London, 1889), 38, 50.
156 G.S. Davies, *Charterhouse in London* (London, 1921), Appendix D, 352.
157 TNA, PROB 11/70, f. 7.
158 Ibid., ff. 7–8.
159 Gonville and Caius College Cambridge Library, Ms. 714A/570A, ff. 1–8.
160 TNA, C 10/64/5, no. 5; ERO, D/Q 25/47.

Towards the end of 18th century, however, the conduct of the school itself gave rise to some concern, particularly on the issue of whether the curriculum should be exclusively Classical. In 1793 the Trustees took advantage of the resignation of the Master, James Buck, to review the syllabus and the arrangements for the admission of pupils.[161] They interpreted Joyce Frankland's will as above all providing education for the children of the poor of Newport, even if few of them could benefit from an education solely in Latin and Greek. The reforms they implemented were intended to ensure that this principle was upheld, even if it meant conceding that the school might acquire some of the characteristics of an elementary school, with children being taught English, writing and arithmetic.[162]

The new Master, Revd Thomas Bell, had to agree to teach those boys who were sent by the Trustees not only Latin and Greek (if required), but also 'reading English grammatically', writing, arithmetic, merchants' accounts (bookkeeping), geography and 'other branches of English literature'.[163] These boys, who would number up to 50, were to receive a 'modern' education, with Classics playing only an optional part. He also had to agree to give his whole time to educating these boys, and at no time take any other scholars, or any boarders.

Bell remained until his death in 1828, and the Trustees then appointed Revd Edward Gould Monk as his successor. Monk's family was North American. Like his father, he had been born in Nova Scotia, though his mother came from a family long-established in Boston which had moved to Nova Scotia after the end of the Seven Years' War. Monk was appointed Headmaster on 1 April 1828, more than three months before his appointment as vicar of Newport.[164]

Monk asked the Trustees to remove the restriction on the number of paying scholars in the school, arguing that the free scholars would benefit 'both in their education and manners by being united in the school with boys of a superior rank', and that he would be better able to teach Latin and Greek if he could admit more such pupils, some of whom would be boarders. The Trustees agreed, on the understanding that the boarders were not to form a separate, and perhaps academically superior, group.[165]

The account books show that the Trustees were careful and meticulous in their duties, and their scrupulous management ensured the School's survival. This was publicly recognised in 1836 when the Charity Commission investigated the endowment, and 'spoke favourably of the general management of the Trustees.'[166]

A Royal Commission on charities was established in 1819, and in May 1836 it began to consider the Newport Free Grammar School Trust. After a thorough investigation into the management of the endowment the Commissioners were satisfied, but they suggested a number of changes in the way in which the income, estimated at about £220 a year, should be allocated. They proposed that the number of free scholars, which had remained notionally at 50 for many years, should be increased to 60. They accepted the

161   Ibid., D/Q 25/41.
162   Ibid.
163   Ibid.
164   CCED, 'Edward Gould Monk'; below, p. 139.
165   ERO, D/Q 25/42.
166   ERO, D/Q 25/42.

Figure 46 *Newport Free Grammar School, c.1900.*

case for taking boarders, in the belief that they would 'tend to raise the character of the school and the endowment.'[167]

The Commissioners' most important recommendation was that the existing school house should be demolished and a new one erected on the same site, to be paid for from the capital in the repair fund, which stood at £673 5*s*. 5*d*. The new building would have a schoolroom capable of accommodating 80 pupils, and would provide room for boarders, who were still to be taught in the same room as the free scholars.[168] All these recommendations were approved by the Trustees, and a draft scheme was approved by Chancery later in the year.[169]

Plans for the new building were drawn up by William Ward of Saffron Walden in 1836, and it was erected in 1838–9. Ward practised as an architect, surveyor, and builder. He had carried out repairs to the church in 1834, and is known to have worked on a

167 Ibid., D/Q 25/69; *Report of the Commissioners for Inquiring Concerning Charities* xxxii I (1837), 798–802.
168 *Report Concerning Charities*, 801.
169 Ibid., 801–2; ERO, D/Q 25/42.

Figure 47 *Church House, Church Street, previously Newport Free Grammar School.*

number of other churches in the area, including Chrishall and Stansted Mountfitchet.[170]
The new building, of red brick, cost £488 3s. 0d., and the builder was Joseph Wedd.[171]
It was originally L-plan, and the range along the churchyard consisted of a cloister on
the ground floor with schoolroom above. The style was a simplified Tudor-Gothic, with
arched heads to the openings on the ground floor and hoodmoulds over the windows.
On the first floor there are two east-facing canted oriel windows. The gables had
decorative bargeboards and originally carried little pinnacles.[172] The building was sold in
1878–9, following the opening of the new buildings by W.E. Nesfield, and after passing
through a number of hands was purchased by the vicar for the use of the parish church
in 1910. It was renovated in 1990–1 and in 2014 was known as Church House.[173]

The new building was ready for occupation in October 1839, with 43 boys on the
register, 23 of whom came from Newport.[174] Monk does not seem to have tried to achieve
the full complement of 80 envisaged under the 1836 scheme: with only one assistant such
numbers might have been an impossible burden. The periodic visitations by the Master
of Caius suggest that the school in the new building was well conducted,[175] and for the

170 Pigot & Co., *Royal National and Commercial Directory and Topography of the Counties of Essex Herts
      Middlesex* (1839), pp. 68–9; LPL, Incorporated Church Building Society files 1049, 1488, 1696.
171 *VIT*, 95.
172 ERO, D/Q 25/11.
173 Ibid., D/Q 25/29, T/B 301; *NN*, 35 (1991), 113; *VIT*, 117.
174 ERO, D/Q 25/42.
175 Ibid., D/Q 25/42, 25/2.

time being the related questions of the number of boarders and the subjects to be taught in the school seem to have been settled.

The changes in the character and curriculum of the school under James Buck, Thomas Bell and Edward Gould Monk had been accommodated within the framework of Dr Legge's statutes. In 1851, however, under Monk's successor as Headmaster, Revd John Wisken, the Master of Caius as Visitor to the school promulgated a series of amendments to the statutes, which he called 'Rules for Government of the School.' Preference was still to be given to boys from Newport, but the age of entry was raised from seven to eight. After some consideration the Trustees decided not to introduce fees at this stage but they agreed on changes to the curriculum. The boys were to be taught 'Writing, Reading, Arithmetic, together with Elementary Mathematics, good manners, and all other instruction and learning fit to be taught in a Grammar School.' The provision of elementary education was formally recognised, but there was no explicit requirement in the Rules to teach Latin or Greek.

These issues were, however, overtaken by events. The Schools Inquiry Commission (generally known as the Taunton Commission), set up in 1864, reported on Newport Free Grammar School in 1867.[176] They classified it, according to the numbers who stayed on over the age of 14, as a second grade school, with at least 10 per cent of its pupils over that age. They also classified it according to the social composition of its pupils as B and C, which meant that it drew its pupils from the 'middle and lower classes of society.'

They proposed that the school should charge a fee of 6*d.* per week per pupil, but poorer pupils should be granted scholarships paid for out the endowment, and thus the Founder's intention would, at least to some extent, be maintained. They noted that the Headmaster was allowed to take up to ten boarders, but recommended that 'in such a poor town as Newport' this number should not be increased, and it would be better if the rule allowing boarders were to be abolished. The Commissioners' recommendations were embodied in a new scheme for the school, approved in 1874.[177] Tuition fees of between £3 and £6 a year could be charged, and boarders were to be admitted. A minimum of £60 a year from the endowment was to be used to provide exhibitions for pupils, preference being given to boys who had attended public elementary schools. The curriculum was to cover a range of modern subjects, with Latin only as an option. Apart from free education for some poor scholars from Newport, little remained of Joyce Frankland's original intentions.

In other respects the scheme embodied some of the more general policies of the Commission.[178] The Trustees were to be replaced by a Governing Body of 11 people. The Master of Caius and two governors appointed by the magistrates of Essex were to hold office *ex officio*. Four representative governors were to be elected by the Vestry of Newport (introducing the principle of election to the governing body), and five co-opted governors were to be appointed by the surviving Trustees. The scheme also stated that women could be governors, and article 39 permitted the Governors, if and when the Trust's funds were sufficient, to provide buildings for a girls' school, though this never happened.

---

176 *Report of the Schools Enquiry Commission 1867–8*, xiii.
177 *Charity Commission Accounts and Papers* 17 (1874), 361–70.
178 *Schools Enquiry Commission* 1, chapter vi.

The scheme authorised the Governors to spend up to £1,500 on enlarging and improving the school buildings and erecting a residence for the Headmaster with accommodation for about 20 boarders. Although the existing school premises had been in use for only 35 years, the Governors nonetheless decided to build an entirely new school, on a new site, financed by the sale of the Distaff Lane properties in London.[179]

The architect for the new school was William Eden Nesfield. Nesfield is best known for his domestic work; indeed he was one of the leading architects of the so-called Domestic Revival or 'Queen Anne' movement of the 1870s. Most of his non-domestic work is to be found in north-west Essex: the restoration of Radwinter church, 1867–70, and in Saffron Walden Market Place the restoration of the Rose and Crown, 1872–4, and the building of Gibson's Bank (now Barclays), 1873–5.[180] Nesfield's design was stylistically different from many of the grammar schools being rebuilt at this time, which tended to look to the date of their original foundation, the 16th century, for inspiration. As a result Nesfield's school is more advanced than, for example, Edward Burgess's new building for Saffron Walden Grammar School (now Dame Johane Bradbury's School) of 1881, and more akin to the London Board Schools of the 1870s and Basil Champneys' Newnham College Cambridge of 1874–5.[181]

Nesfield's building was loosely in the style of the 17th century, combining aspects of a collegiate building with those of a manor house. It was built mainly of red brick, round a courtyard with a covered inner walkway like a cloister. The entrance to the courtyard was on the east side, in the middle of what was originally a screen wall. Opposite the entrance was the dining hall (a classroom in 2014), with dormitories above lit by two large dormers with shaped gables. There was modest decoration in the form of brick aprons below the dormers and coved eaves between them. In the middle of the wall was a pedimented niche. On the north side was the original schoolroom (a library in 2014), with small classroom beyond. This range originally terminated in a half-hipped roof, with the little octagonal, domed bell-turret at the east end of the ridge. On the south side was the headmaster's house, noticeably more domestic in character and making reference to the local Essex vernacular tradition. The first floor is jettied and has panel pargetting instead of brick. On the south side is a three-storey porch, originally the garden entrance, of which the top storey is also jettied and pargetted (see figs. 45 and 46).[182]

The contract drawings were signed in 1876, the contractors being George and Frederick James Whiffin of Saffron Walden, with whom Nesfield had previously worked.[183] The grounds were laid out by William Chater, nurseryman of Saffron Walden, whose other works included the formal gardens at Shortgrove Hall. The buildings were completed in 1878. The original character of Nesfield's building has been compromised by subsequent additions, although those of the first half of the 20th century were more or less in keeping in terms of style and materials. Particularly damaging to Nesfield's design

179 ERO, D/Q 25/44, 83.
180 A. Saint, *Richard Norman Shaw* (London, 2010), 166; J. Bettley and N. Pevsner, *Essex* (New Haven & London, 2007), 632, 665–6.
181 M. Girouard, *Sweetness and Light: the 'Queen Anne' Movement 1860–1900* (London, 1977), 64–76; Bettley & Pevsner, *Essex*, 660.
182 *Essex Review*, 15 (1906), 73–82.
183 ERO, D/Q 25/75, 96, 97; J. Physick and M. Darby, *Marble Halls: Drawings and Models for Victorian Secular Buildings* (London, 1973), p. 185 (contract drawings for the Rose and Crown, Saffron Walden).

was the replacement of the screen wall across the east side of the courtyard by the single-storey block of 1926–7, designed by the County Architect's Department.[184] By this time the classroom on the north side of the courtyard had been extended to the east to form a First World War Memorial Hall, part of a more ambitious scheme prepared, but not fully executed, by W.J. Kieffer, 1919–21. The east end of the Memorial Hall is distinguished by its pedimented centre and tall round-arched window.[185] On the north side of the schoolroom, a single-storey laboratory was added in 1895–6 to designs by G.E. Pritchett of Bishop's Stortford, and in 1913 a classroom beyond by H.H. Dunn of Cambridge. These were raised to two storeys in 1936 and 1920 respectively, rather overpowering Nesfield's buildings.[186] Dunn also designed, in 1913, a masters' sitting room at the south-west corner of the dining hall, with bedrooms on the first floor.[187] In 1911–12 a London architect, James S. Cooper, designed another laboratory on the west side of the west range, as well as a 'manual training room' or woodwork shed; it replaced a stable. The laboratory was still standing in 2012.[188]

The scheme of 1874 brought about a decisive break in the continuity of the school's history. The connection with Caius College was all but severed: the Charity Commissioners exercised the powers that had been the Master of Caius', though he remained an *ex officio* governor, and the endowment was vested in the Official Trustees of Charitable Lands. Over the next 50 years the School became increasingly dependent for funding on the Board of Education and Essex County Council, and with funding came a gradual extension of external influence and control, particularly from the Local Education Authority for Essex, established under the 1902 Education Act.[189] The Board's inspectors questioned the school's efficiency and the need for the Saffron Walden area to have two 'second grade' schools. The LEA had doubts about the school's future, thinking that when the present Headmaster retired the school 'would probably cease to exist.'[190] In 1905, therefore, they turned down a request from the school for a grant, and proposed that Newport and Saffron Walden Grammar Schools should be amalgamated as one foundation, with boys in Newport and girls in Saffron Walden.[191] This proposal was successfully resisted and in 1909 the Board of Education accepted the school's application for recognition as a secondary day school and placed it on their grant list. From 1910 until the Board ceased its direct grant in 1928 the school received just over £13,000.[192]

In 1913 the Board of Education advised the school to apply once again for grant aid from the LEA, on the ground that it had greatly improved.[193] The school was successful, though it received just £100 a year from 1915 to 1920. However, in 1922 the school was classed as a 'Deficiency Grant School', and LEA funding sharply increased, replacing the

184 ERO, D/Q 25/75.
185 Ibid.; *Builder* 122 (1922), 868.
186 ERO, D/Q 25/75, 99, 102; F. Thompson, *Newport Grammar School Essex* (Newport, Essex, 2nd edn 1987), 88; rainwater head with W.J. Kieffer's initials dated 1920.
187 ERO, D/Q 25/75, D/Q 25/102.
188 Ibid., D/Q 75/25, D/Q 25/100.
189 2 Edw. VII c.42.
190 ERO, D/Q 25/46, p. 88; TNA, ED 35/795.
191 ERO, D/Q 25/46, pp. 150–1; TNA, ED 35/795.
192 TNA, ED 35/795; ERO, D/Q 46, p. 170, D/Q 25/77, pp. 8, 13.
193 Ibid., ED 35/795; ERO, D/Q 25/77, pp. 109–10.

Board's grant after 1928. In 1933 the school received £2,734 from Essex, and between 1915 and 1934 the county granted the school over £17,000 in total, together with some small grants for specific purposes.[194]

The Inspectors reported in 1930 that the school 'displays a vigorous intellectual life which is often found very hard to bring into being in schools similarly circumstanced', but the Governors were becoming uncomfortable with the degree of external control that LEA funding entailed. In particular, they wanted to maintain their own admission examination,[195] but the LEA threatened to withhold grant from 1 April 1934 if the Governors did not agree to admit pupils on the basis of the County's examination. Faced with a deficit of over £3,000 for the year 1932–3 they had little choice but to comply. They reached a compromise agreement with the LEA, under which they retained limited control over admissions, but they had to agree to close the boarding house (The Links), which by then had only 12 pupils.[196]

The Governors regarded this as a capitulation, and sought to return to being a direct grant school. They enlisted the help of the MP for Saffron Walden, R.A. Butler, a school governor, but while publicly supportive he was sceptical in private about the Governors' intentions. The Board turned down their request to rejoin the direct grant list on the ground that it would entail extra expenditure,[197] noting privately that 'there is clearly still an extraordinary atmosphere of hostility on the part of the Governors to the LEA and this seems to be warmly reciprocated.'[198] Thereafter the LEA was the school's main source of funding, and the school accepted the degree of control which funding entailed.

The school remained open throughout the Second World War, maintaining a roll of about 220. In 1940 the Headmaster managed to prevent the premises from being requisitioned by the Air Ministry, though the Ministry did take over the premises of Saffron Walden Grammar School, which did not reopen as a grammar school after the war.[199]

The 1944 Education Act renewed the question of the school's status and its relationship with the LEA.[200] Theoretically the school could have chosen to become independent or seek readmission to the direct grant list, but in September 1946 the Governors applied for recognition by Essex LEA as a voluntary controlled school for 210 boys aged 11 to 18. The articles of government laid down that the LEA had the power to determine admissions; the LEA was obliged to take account of the views of the Headmaster, but retained ultimate control.[201]

In the late 1950s and early 1960s the growth of the population of north-west Essex and the national trend towards more pupils staying on into the sixth form led to

---

194 ERO, D/Q 25/77, pp. 129–30, D/Q 25/116.
195 Ibid., D/Q 25/79, pp. 163–5.
196 Ibid., A9193, Box 1; TNA, ED 35/4197.
197 ERO, D/Q 25/116, A9193 Box 1. Butler told the Board of Education that he was helping to raise funds 'at the request of the Governors', and was 'subordinating (his) own instinct that it may be necessary for (the school) to enter the county scheme.' (Note of meeting 30 Apr. 1935).
198 TNA, ED 35/4197.
199 ERO, A9193 Box 1. A detailed account of this episode, written from first-hand knowledge, is by Thompson, *Newport Grammar School* (2nd ed.), 100–1.
200 7 & 8 Geo. VI c.31, sections 9, 12.
201 ERO, A9193 Box 1.

proposals for the enlargement and reorganisation of the school. Although the Governors continued to oppose the admission of girls, expansion of the school went ahead and in 1967 it was enlarged to a three-form entry with 414 boys on the roll.[202] In 1965, however, government required LEAs to prepare plans for reorganising secondary education along comprehensive lines.[203] The Governors did not resist reorganisation in principle, but said that they would prefer the school to be a full 11–18 age range comprehensive school.[204]

The main concern of the Governors and Headmaster was to ensure that reorganisation maintained academic standards, and, in particular, a viable sixth form. Like the Governors of many other grammar schools they debated how many entry forms were necessary to produce a viable sixth form, but in the event they accepted that from September 1976 the school would become a four-form entry mixed-ability boys school.[205] The Headmaster won a victory over the name of the school: in March 1976 he drew attention to the provisions of Joyce Frankland's will, and the LEA agreed that the school should be known as Newport Free Grammar School.[206] In 2014, however, the School's name was changed to The Joyce Frankland Academy, Newport.

As the school grew in size in the second half of the 20th century, many new buildings were erected. The first of any significance was the Assembly Hall of 1957–8, a flat-roofed building of unrelieved austerity designed by Clifford E. Culpin. It was free-standing, and positioned to the north-east of Nesfield's block, but so close to it that it obscured the view of the older buildings from the road.[207] Later extensions, which form the Performing Arts Block (a music suite to the south and a drama studio to the east), have further reduced the view of the pre-war buildings, though their pitched roofs have somewhat softened the Hall's outline.[208]

Culpin also designed C Block, a two-storey classroom block along Bury Water Lane to the east of the main school buildings, 1957–9.[209] The Science and Technology Centre, designed by Lyster, Grillet and Harding, replaced a number of existing buildings and opened in 1997.[210] Other buildings by the same practice include the Sixth Form Centre (1998), and the Sports Hall (2002, extended in 2009) on the north side of Bury Water Lane.[211] A single-storey extension was made to the east end of the original headmaster's house in 2006–7 to provide a new entrance and reception area.[212]

North of Bury Water Lane a classroom block and gymnasium opened in 1968, and in 1977 another block, designed by the County Architect's Department, was added. The single-storey building is a good example of the construction system, known as MCB, which was then the standard for Essex schools. The rough finish of the external

202 ERO, E/MM 355, pp. 36, 54.
203 Department of Education and Science, *The Organisation of Secondary Education* (1965).
204 ERO, E/MM 355, p. 101.
205 ERO, E/MM 914/1, pp. 151–5.
206 Ibid., pp. 159–60, 175.
207 Ibid., D/Q 25/104.
208 *NN*, 25 (1986), 35; 29 (1988), 65; 31 (1989) 54; 33 (1990), 121; plaques on buildings.
209 ERO, D/Q 25/104.
210 Plaque on building.
211 Plaque on buildings; http://www.lgharchitects.co.uk (accessed 31 Jan. 2012).
212 Uttlesford District Council, planning application UTT/1394/06/LB, approved 9 Oct. 2006.

panels was intended as a concession to the local tradition of pargetting, seen on the headmaster's house as well as older buildings in Newport.[213]

By 1982 the number of pupils had risen to 768,[214] but under the 1976 reorganisation the school remained single-sex. Before reorganisation, Newport girls who passed the 11+ exam went to the Herts and Essex High School in Bishop's Stortford, and after reorganisation to the increasingly successful Saffron Walden County High School. In April 1991 however the LEA and Governors agreed that Newport should become a coeducational school. In September the first 57 girls were admitted to year 7 (the first year), together with 68 boys. After 405 years the daughters of Joyce Frankland took their place in her school alongside her sons.[215]

213 *Architect* 123 (1977), 20–1.
214 Thompson, *Newport Grammar School* (2nd edn), 117.
215 Rosemary Hughes, 'Newport Welcomes Girls', *NN*, 40 (1993), 32–3.

LOCAL GOVERNMENT

MANORIAL ADMINISTRATION

IN THE 12TH CENTURY, and probably for as long as Newport remained a royal demesne manor, it was grouped with three other demesne manors in Essex (Hatfield Regis, Havering and Writtle) for judicial purposes. Although Newport had its own hallmote, the hallmotes of the four manors sometimes held joint meetings before the sheriff to deal with matters which he placed before them.[1] Even when the keeping of the demesne was taken out of the hands of the sheriff and given to a *custos dominicorum* in 1236 the four Essex manors were still treated as a unit for some judicial purposes.[2] When Henry III granted the manor of Newport to his brother Richard earl of Cornwall in 1242 it became part of the earl's bailiwick of Berkhamsted, where the manorial officials accounted and where the earl's exchequer was located.[3] Administering the manor was a source of profit for its lord: the income from the view of frankpledge in 1296–7 was 8s. and the total profits of the court amounted to £4 14s.[4]

The court rolls for Newport Pond show that view of frankpledge continued to be held at the meetings of the manorial court during the 17th, 18th and 19th centuries, though the rolls give no details. It is not clear whether the men of Newport formed one single tithing for the whole of the manor, as happened on other Essex manors. The court continued to exercise jurisdiction over minor misdemeanours, and the custom of the manor was occasionally recorded in the rolls, most notably in 1709 when the level of entry fines and relief was recorded, along with the penalties for breaches of the bye-laws about grazing livestock on the open fields after harvest and on the common. A little earlier the vicar, Edmund Tatham, had codified and commuted some of the tithes.[5] This may be no more than coincidence, but it may reflect a wish for a greater definition of rights on the part of both the lay lord of the manor and the church.

There is no evidence for the election of the constable by the Newport manorial court until the 17th century. By then, the constable was regularly chosen and sworn by the court, along with the pinder and the aletasters and breadweighers. Even though they were elected and sworn at the manorial court, they presented their accounts to the parish vestry. Their detailed accounts do not survive, and they were recorded only in

1   *CRR*, I (Richard I–John), 77.
2   TNA, E 371/7 m.5, cited in Hoyt, *Royal Demesne*, 160–1.
3   *Ministers' Accounts* I, xix.
4   Ibid., 49.
5   ERO, D/DK M113.

abbreviated form in the vestry book.[6] They were usually chosen from amongst the better-off tenants and freeholders in the village: in 1524 the two constables, John Howland and George Adam, were amongst the wealthiest in terms of taxable goods, and in the 17th and 18th centuries the office generally rotated amongst a small group of men.[7]

VESTRY GOVERNMENT

Prior to 1659 there is only scattered evidence of the way in which the parish was administered. For example, Essex Quarter Sessions records provide early examples of the work of the Surveyors of Highways (an office created by the Highways Act 1555) and Overseers of the Poor, but evidence for parish government by the parishioners meeting in vestry only begins with a Parish Book started in 1659.[8]

Newport was an open rather than select vestry, but the Parish Books do not indicate whether attendance was restricted to those who paid rates or whether women were excluded. In 1688 there were 25 names (some of them subsequently deleted) to a resolution to hold monthly meetings. In 1703, some 17 inhabitants meeting in vestry, including the vicar, Edmund Tatham, made a similar agreement, the overseers being authorized to spend 2s. on each meeting.[9] By the 1730s minutes were typically signed off with around 10 names. There was sometimes a vote on an issue: for example, an agreement in October 1730 to support the bastard child of Francis Gigney was passed 'nemo contridaconte' (*sic*).[10]

The vestry was responsible for the selection of parish officers (two Churchwardens, two Overseers of the Poor, rising to four by the late 18th century, Surveyors of the Highways and Constables); the raising of the various local (Poor and Church) and county rates and the national Land and Window Taxes; the collection and distribution of charity monies; the local administration of the Poor Laws; and the repair and maintenance of the highways. There are also occasional references to the militia and, in 1810, during the Napoleonic Wars, to the 'procuring a man for the Army'. From 1874 the vestry both elected four governors to the Grammar School and set up a School Board which took over the management of the National School.

Although there are no details of the process of officer selection, a list of inhabitants 'capable of bearing office' over a rotating six-year period was made in 1689.[11] Vestry members were generally drawn from wealthier residents or those who had lived in the parish for some years.[12] Among those who served the various offices several times in Newport was the largest ratepayer at the time, Giles Dent, whose name always headed lists of signatures.

6   Joan Kent, 'The English Village Constable, 1580–1642: The Nature and Dilemmas of the Office', *Journal of British Studies*, XX (1980–1), 30–3; ERO, D/P 15/8/1.
7   TNA, E 179/108/155.
8   ERO, D/P 15/8/1.
9   Ibid.
10   Ibid.
11   Ibid., D/P 15/8/1.
12   H. French, *The Middle Sort of People in Provincial England 1600–1750* (Oxford, 2007), 113–6, 133–6.

Office-holding and participation were not restricted to men or to members of the established church. Overseers of the Poor included the Quaker Matthew Day (1682, 1689 and 1696) and, in the first half of the 18th century, three women: Day's widow Rebecca, widow Jane Whipham and Rebecca Wyatt, the Days' daughter. Ann McKeeg was among the parishioners who signed off the accounts of the Surveyors of Highways in December 1727 and Sarah Knightley served as Overseer in 1795. In 1800 Revd Bryant, the Congregational minister, served as Surveyor of the Highways. In 1794 the minutes recorded conflict over the election of the churchwardens. The disputatious vicar, Revd Bell, proposed John Capp. This was put to a vote and the old churchwardens were re-elected, Bell's being the only vote cast for Capp. Bell unsuccessfully sought redress at the Bishop's visitation, but did persuade the Archdeacon, Revd William Gretton, vicar of neighbouring Littlebury, to put Capp's name in the presentment. The Newport vestry agreed not to pass Capp's accounts.[13]

During the 19th century the parishioners in vestry were typically described as 'ratepayers' rather than, as previously, 'inhabitants'. This may reflect a drift towards an oligarchy of the better-off residents and a perception of the rising burden of both rates and duties on the vestry. The minutes in this period mainly consist of records of rates raised and the church restoration project of the 1850s. They do, however, suggest a number of ways in which the parish and its institutions and appearance were changing. In 1847–8 a dispute arose with the Eastern Counties Railway over the rating of the railway and station, goods shed and cottage. In 1857 an agreement was reached with the company on sharing the costs of construction of a new bridge. In 1879 the railway was again the subject of a dispute, this time over the company's proposal to alter the roads at the crossing for the delivery of goods, and in 1867 the Lighting Act of 1833 was adopted on a vote of 25:4 with one abstention. A sum of £65 was agreed as the annual sum to be raised by the Inspectors to light the parish.

THE PARISH COUNCIL

The Local Government Act 1894 abolished vestry government, replacing it in parishes with a population of over 300 by annually elected parish councils.[14] The first parish meeting was held on 4 December 1894. It was described in the parish magazine for January 1895 as 'very largely attended. But the proceedings were conducted in a most quiet and orderly manner.' James Bailey, the new owner of Shortgrove, was voted Chairman and six further councillors were elected by a show of hands, 'no poll being demanded', from a field of 17 candidates.[15] The first meeting of the new council was held on 20 December 1894.

Under the 1894 Act, women had the right to attend meetings, elect and stand for election. In December 1912 four women were among the 42 who attended a meeting which rejected a scheme to purchase the parish hall from Sir Carl Meyer. In March 1919 Miss Emma Perry was the first woman to be elected to the council. There were 19

13   ERO, D/P 15/8/4.
14   56 & 57 Vict. c. 73.
15   The list of candidates, proposers and seconders, and numbers of votes cast, is given in NPC, Parish Meeting Minute Book, 1894–1944.

women among the 65 electors present at the meeting.[16] Expansion of the council was first raised in 1949 and in 1958 the parish council made a request to Essex County Council that the number of councillors should be increased from seven to nine. This was agreed, and nine were duly elected in May 1958. In 1974 the number of councillors was again increased to 11.[17]

The business of Newport Parish Council initially continued much as under the old vestry system. However, the process of centralising the administration of local services under elected County Councils (created in 1888), Rural and Urban District Councils (also created under the 1894 Act) and other statutory bodies continued. The Local Government Act 1972 rationalized the three levels of local government. Parish Councils retained minor taxing and spending powers, their role being primarily that of assessing local opinion and conveying it to the Counties and Districts.

The 20th-century minutes of the parish council and Annual Meeting reveal local anxiety over some of the impacts of modernisation, especially the growth of motor traffic, with numerous incidents of vehicles causing damage to lamp posts and walls. Speeding though the village was first raised as an issue in 1924 when a speed limit of 10mph was suggested. There were also calls for extra signage, white lines, road widening and a bypass. By 1950 parked cars had become a problem, especially on Elephant Green, and in the 1960s some parishioners began to campaign for a pedestrian crossing on the High Street, which was eventually installed in 2009.[18]

Rapid development in the village and wider local area was causing concern by the second half of the 20th century,[19] and was accompanied by a growing interest in the conservation of the village's historic environment. In 1961 a *News of the World* advertising hoarding by the railway line was a cause of complaint. In 1968 Elephant Green was successfully registered as common land (and the parish council registered as owners in 1974) and there was a prompt response to the adoption of a Conservation Area.[20]

The parish council was also involved in other community activities. Allotments had existed in the parish since at least 1858 when they are shown on the inclosure Award map, and during the First World War the council established new allotments in Frambury Lane (but received only a poor level of subscription to War Savings Certificates compared to other parishes).[21] Between the wars it played a large part in the creation of the Newport Fire Brigade, and during the Second World War it was the focus for the war effort, organising measures against air-raids and invasion, 'communal feeding' and a Food Control Emergency Plan.[22]

---

16   Ibid., Minute Book, 212; Parish Meeting Minute Book, 107, 132.
17   Ibid., Minute Book (unpaginated); ERO, D/J 52/2/1.
18   NPC, Minute Book, 75, 99, 105, 114; ERO, D/J 52/2/1.
19   Below, p. 158–9.
20   NPC, Minute Book (unpaginated).
21   ERO, Q/RDc/53A.
22   NPC, Parish Meeting Minute Book 1894–1944, 248; NPC, Minute Book 1915–61, 175.

ADMINISTRATION OF JUSTICE FROM C.1600

Quarter Sessions and Assizes were held at the county town of Chelmsford, but some petty sessions before the Justices of the Peace (JPs) were held in Newport (among other Uttlesford parishes) from at least the 16th century.[23] In 1670 the sessions were held at the Bull Inn and in 1708 at the Red Bull.[24] The Justices in petty sessions supervised the work of Overseers and Surveyors of Highways of the hundred and heard presentments from the Constables of Newport and other parishes on matters such as breach of the Sabbath, failure to attend divine service, bastardy, vagrancy, and the regulation of alehouses. They also heard minor criminal cases (often in their own home and on the sworn evidence of lesser property owners or the constables) and had the power to commit cases to the Quarter Sessions. Geoffrey Nightingale and Giles Dent both served as Justices during the 17th century.[25] At the local level the justice system therefore played an important part in the social control of the lower classes by the local elite and middling sort, alongside such institutions as the 17th-century church courts and the 18th-century workhouse. The petty sessions were consolidated in the Saffron Walden Division under the Petty Sessions Act 1828.[26] They still met at Newport police station in the mid 19th century.[27]

From at least the 17th century Newport had a parish 'cage' for the detention of minor offenders. It stood in Church Street, on the site of Grigman's, the messuage John Lythall, the vicar, had left to the poor of Newport and other parishes in 1587.[28] There was also a pillory, which in 2014 is displayed in Saffron Walden Museum. The county House of Correction (occasionally referred to as the 'bridewell') in Newport is known to have existed in 1692, and in 1697 the keeper presented a petition to the Easter Quarter Sessions for an increase in salary from £10 a year which 'did not afford him a competent subsistence, nor a sufficient stock to manage the same'. Its prime purpose was to confine and 'correct' by setting to work those who were idle, disorderly, vagrants, or had committed minor offences. This House of Correction was leased to rather than owned by the county, but in 1749 the county purchased the freehold.[29]

The Quarter Sessions records indicate the sort of men and women who were sent to the House.[30] In Michaelmas 1763, for example, a whole calendar of prisoners detained since midsummer listed seven persons: five men and two women. They were relatively local apart from two from the Brentwood area. Four of the men were labourers and one a cordwainer. They had been committed for short terms (up to one month) for a range of minor offences: deserting their families leaving them chargeable to the parish, begetting a chargeable illegitimate child without indemnifying the mother's parish, unspecified misdemeanors, 'rude and disorderly' behaviour and assaulting the constable in Thaxted. Female inmates were often imprisoned for thefts of basic items that seem to

---

23   The earliest recorded was Sept. 1574: ERO/Q/SR 51/88, 89.
24   Ibid., Q/SR 423/37, 534/41. The two inns were separate buildings.
25   Ibid., Q/SR 211/99, 401/57.
26   7 Geo. IV c.43.
27   *White's Dir. Essex* (1863), 702.
28   ERO, D/P 15/8/2; LMA, DL/C 358 f. 382r.
29   Ibid., Q/SBb 183/9, 185/8.
30   Ibid., Q/SBb 232/9.

have been born of extreme need. Between Michaelmas and Christmas of the same year, for example, Elizabeth Brookes of Newport, widow, was in the House, sentenced to three months' hard labour for the theft of wood from Charles Phillips, farmer of Newport. She may have been recently widowed (Richard Brooks, labourer, was buried in February 1763) and was described as a pauper in her own burial entry.[31]

A 1774 report to the Quarter Sessions indicates that by this date the House had fallen into disrepair. It now had a purpose beyond the original aims of these institutions. It was 'much more used than formerly' and had 'become of great utility to the county and objects both of punishment and confinement are frequently sent thither from very remote and distant parts of the county'. As there was the opportunity to purchase the adjacent house and yard for £63, rebuilding on a larger plan with a proper house and offices for the keeper, working room and yard was recommended as the best option.[32]

A plan for a new building was drawn up in the following year, at an estimated cost of £647 3s. 5d. It is not known who was responsible for the design, which was examined and approved by the county surveyor, William Hillyer. The scheme was approved in April 1775, by which time the estimate had risen to £887, plus the £63 for the purchase of the site from Philip Martin and his wife. Payment of the balance due to the workmen was authorised in October 1775. Further work was ordered at the same time: to build a wall separating the women's section from the men's, and to sink a well with a pump, in accordance with an estimate prepared by Hillyer.[33]

The building survives, and in 2014 is named The Links. It is constructed mainly of red brick, but has a front of white brick with rusticated quoins. It has a three-bay centre with a pediment, with a further bay set slightly back to each side. The windows have semicircular heads, as does the doorway, which has a rusticated surround. In the tympanum of the pediment is a stone panel carved with leg-irons and chains to denote the building's purpose. The plan is a half-H, with two wings parallel to the road joined by a range on the north side. The front range contained the keeper's apartment and a room for the justices, with lodgings and workrooms on the other two sides of the courtyard. The windows were unglazed, but had shutters.

By the date of the rebuilding there was growing national concern at the conditions in which prisoners were held, and the prison reform movement of the late 18th century led to some improvement in the conditions under which inmates were held in the Newport House. The prison reformer John Howard visited the House in 1776, and wrote a moderately favourable report on conditions there.[34]

Howard's campaigns led to a closer involvement of the local elite in the running of prisons and regular reporting to the county, though in Newport the visiting justices were often in conflict with the county over the use to which the House was put and the sort of prisoners housed there. From 1790 a surgeon attended the prisoners regularly, reporting to the Quarter Sessions.[35] The prime concern was the presence (or, more typically, absence) of infectious fevers, but he also addressed such matters as the general

31 Ibid., Q/SBb 237/6; Newport Parish Burial Register.
32 ERO, Q/SBb 277/9, 17.
33 Ibid., Q/SO 12, 286, 309, 374–5, 397, 414.
34 John Howard, *The State of Prisons in England and Wales* (Warrington, 1777), 220–1, and idem., 1812 edn., 430–1.
35 ERO, Q/SBb 340/77.

health of the prisoners (often weak), and their nutrition. The spiritual and moral needs of prisoners were met by the appointment in 1805 of Revd Bell of Newport as Chaplain to the House: his duties included the provision of prayers and a sermon on Sundays and giving spiritual advice to the prisoners. Concern for welfare and decency also led to the provision of basic clothing for convicted prisoners.

In 1830 the Quarter Sessions proposed to 'discontinue' the Newport House, which had again fallen into disrepair and was housing some 'hardened and dangerous convicts' considered likely to influence the minor offenders traditionally sent there.[36] The proposal was vigorously opposed by the local justices. Lord Braybrooke drew attention to the changed local conditions, observing that there had been an increase in population in the district, there were 'evils inseparable from agricultural distress leading to occasional disturbances', and a rise in petty theft. In early December 1830 there was a series of rural riots in villages close to Newport: Wenden Lofts, Arkesden, Clavering and Henham. A total of 26 men involved were held in the Newport House of Correction where Braybrooke had attended 'to dispose of the rebels committed yesterday'. Unsurprisingly, the court decided against closure, even before the December riots.[37]

The Newport House was nonetheless too small to meet the standards of separation, work and discipline expected of modern gaols that were, it was hoped, to be 'schools of industry and virtue, instead of the very nurseries of crime'.[38] The Inspectors' report for 1838 conceded that the local crime rate had reduced but maintained that the House was a vital means of suppressing 'tumult', citing its use during the 1830 agricultural riots. However, it was generally 'very defective' and, moreover, appeared inefficient. The Inspectors suggested that since a new gaol was planned for Saffron Walden, the Newport House should be closed and a district prison created in its place.[39]

Although no district gaol was built in Saffron Walden, a large new county prison had opened at Springfield, Chelmsford in 1830, and the County Police Act, 1839, gave JPs the power to establish police forces in their counties.[40] Essex appointed its first chief constable in 1840,[41] and the Newport House of Correction was closed in 1841. The closure order stated that the opening of a gaol at Springfield had made the Newport House of Correction redundant, and at its closure it had only five prisoners, one of whom had absconded.[42] The prisoners were transferred to Chelmsford, and in August 1841 the building reopened as Newport police station.[43]

The building remained in use as a police station until June 1886, when it was sold to the Grammar School for £440. The school used it for a variety of purposes, including a boarding house, before conversion to flats in 1953.[44]

---

36   Ibid., Q/SBb 501/7.
37   Ibid., Q/SBb 502/45; Cooper, *The Well-Ordered Town*, 125, 128–36.
38   J.J. Gurney, *Notes on a visit made to some…prisons with Elizabeth Fry* (London, 1810, reprinted London 2000), 3, p.v.
39   *Third Report of the Inspectors appointed to visit the different prisons of Great Britain* (London, 1838), 224–36; *Fourth Report* (London, 1839), 147–52.
40   2 & 3 Vict. c.93.
41   M. Scollan, 'The Making of a Chief Constable', *History Notebook* 12 (Essex Police Museum, n.d.).
42   ERO, Q/SBb 544/22, 544/61/1.
43   Ibid., Q/SBb 544/61/1.
44   Sale catalogue in archives of Messrs Cheffins.

HIGHWAYS

Under Tudor legislation, responsibility for highways maintenance was placed on individual parishes using four days of compulsory direct labour by householders, supervised by the Justices.[45] In 1654 the inhabitants of Newport were presented for a list of failures to keep some highways in repair, such as the Bury Water Bridge, Bonhunt Lane, a common roadway from Newport to London and Bonhunt Bridge, a footbridge from Newport to Clavering. In 1662 a list of non-performers was again presented at the Quarter Sessions.[46]

Highways rates were usually amalgamated within the accounts of the constables in the Parish Books. More costly highways repairs were however sometimes noted there, for example Giles Dent's disbursements as surveyor in 1684 and 1685 (payments totalling £6 11s. 8d. for labour and mending of Wenden Bridge, and Wants Bridge on the road to Widdington) and a large bill of £36 13s. 10½d. in 1799 for gravel, stone picking, carting, blacksmithing, labour and bricks (from Quendon), again largely for Wants Bridge.[47] The 1817 parliamentary return lists the annual sums raised in 1801 to 1817. Over this period they rose from £45 2s. 0d. to £60 0s. 6¼d.[48]

In 1857 the vestry agreed with the Eastern Counties Railway to pay half the cost of building a new brick bridge to replace the wooden one over the river Cam on Debden Road, and a road from the turnpike to the station, provided this did not exceed £100. The railway company was to own and maintain the bridge, and the parish the road. Thomas Shirley of Newport was contracted to build the bridge and to undertake any repairs for 25 years for £200. In 1858 the railway company was released from its maintenance obligation on the grounds of the public benefit to the parish of the bridge.[49] The Vestry noted that the dissolution of the Turnpike Trust in 1870 created additional work for the Newport surveyors, and in 1876 it employed a man full-time on highways work, including the widening of the bridge by the Hercules public house to 20 ft, the cost again borne 50:50 by the parish and the railway company.[50] In 1880 a collector of the Highways Rate was appointed at a salary of £17 a year.

The Local Government Act of 1894 passed responsibility for highways from the parishes to the newly-created elected rural district councils and the Local Government Act 1929 passed it to county councils. Newport Parish Council then became a conduit for the passing of information on the need for repairs and of requests for highways alterations to Essex County Council, although it retained responsibility for some of the footpaths in the parish.

45 2 & 3 Ph. & Mary c.8.
46 ERO, Q/SR 362/33, 394/14.
47 Ibid., D/P 15/8/1, 15/8/4.
48 Ibid., Q/CR 1/9/25.
49 Ibid., D/P 15/8/2.
50 Ibid., D/P 15/8/2, 3.

FIRE SERVICE

Shortly before the outbreak of the First World War the parish council discussed the possibility of forming a fire brigade.[51] Nothing was done until in 1932 the provision of a mains water supply to the village made the establishment of a fire brigade more feasible, and in that year a parish meeting agreed to establish and manage a fire brigade for the village.[52] It was to be financed partly by subscriptions from residents, and partly by a grant of £100 from the Pond Common Trust.[53] The men were all volunteers, and 14 offered their services initially.[54] In 1933 a committee was appointed to manage the brigade. This committee was independent of the parish council, and had the power to levy charges on all who needed the services of the brigade.[55]

This arrangement lasted for five years, but in 1938 the Fire Brigades Act placed all brigades under local authority control, and required that their services should be provided free of charge.[56] Saffron Walden Rural District Council thus assumed responsibility for the Newport brigade, but in 1941 under the Fire Services (Emergency Provisions) Act all brigades came under the control of central government, and were assisted by the Auxiliary Fire Service. In 1947 the Fire Services Act transferred responsibility to county and county borough councils, and since then, Newport brigade has formed part of the county fire and rescue service, staffed by retained men.[57] From its foundation the brigade has been based at the fire station on the north side of Debden Road, west of the bridge over the railway. Since the opening of the M11 its importance has increased because access via the emergency interchange west of the village allows the brigade to respond quickly to accidents on the motorway.[58]

PARLIAMENTARY ELECTIONS

From 1406 adult (over 21) male holders of freehold property in Newport worth at least 40s. a year were entitled to two votes each for two county members of Parliament in parliamentary elections.[59] Until 1832 polling took place in the county town of Chelmsford, some 30 miles from Newport. The earliest poll book recording voting in Essex is for the general election of August 1679, when all six Newport voters polled for Sir Eliab Harvey and Sir Thomas Middleton, the defeated Court candidates. The number

---

51 NPC, Fire Brigade File, citing NPC Minutes; the Minute Book for this period is missing.
52 E.J. Ellis, 'Newport Fire Brigade 1932–1960', *NN*, 14 (1980), 47–67; the author was one of the original volunteers.
53 Ibid.
54 NPC, Fire Brigade File.
55 Ellis, 'Fire Brigade', 47.
56 NPC, Fire Brigade File.
57 1 & 2 Geo. VI c.72; 4 & 5 Geo. VI c.22; 10 & 11 Geo. VI c.41; *Introduction to the Essex Fire Service* (ERO, C/DB 3/4, n.d.).
58 Above, p. 18.
59 8 Hen. VI c. 7.

of Newport voters increased gradually: 30 in the 1694 by-election, 45 in the 1710 general election, and 30 in the 1763 by-election for example.[60]

The property qualification meant that most voters were drawn from the ranks of the better-off artisans and tradesmen, and were likely to have served in at least one of the parish offices. A few held freeholds in the parish but were not resident there or even in the county. Equally, some Newport residents voted by reason of a freehold in another Essex parish. Both the Anglican and Independent ministers sometimes polled (for example Edmund Tatham in 1715 and 1722, John Rix in 1774, Edward Gould Monk and James Hopkins in 1830).

The 18th-century poll books provide some evidence that polling of Newport freeholders was organised locally by 'party'. In the only election with a 'full' field of four candidates (1768) all 14 Newport voters voted for 'party' slates. In elections where there were three candidates for the two seats (1722, 1734, 1774) the Newport voters were either 'plumpers' (i.e. they exercised only one of their two votes, wasting the other) or 'straights' (voting for two candidates in alliance). It is often suggested that local landowners influenced voting significantly in pre-reform elections. In the 1763 by-election contest between John Luther and John Conyers, the first county election since 1734, a correspondent of John Strutt, a key supporter of Conyers, reported that Lord Thomond of Shortgrove Hall was being leaned on to back Conyers by his relative Lady Egremont.[61] A total of 24 of the 30 Newport voters did indeed vote for Conyers compared to only seven for Luther. Henry Cranmer at Quendon Hall also voted for Conyers in 1763, though Sir John Griffin Griffin at Audley End supported Luther.

This pattern had apparently broken down somewhat by 1830, the eve of reform, when 20 Newport freeholders polled in a three-cornered general election contest. A total of 16 plumped for Charles Western of Kelvedon (a reformist Whig who supported the abolition of slavery); one each plumped for 'True Blue' Tory John Tyssen Tyrrell and William Pole Wellelsey (standing as an independent with the aim of splitting the long-standing Whig/Tory compromise by which each party took one of the two county seats); one voted Western/Wellesley and one Western/ Tyrrell.

The 1832 Reform Act introduced registers of those qualified to vote on the enlarged franchise. The Act also divided Essex into two seats, the Northern and Southern Divisions, Newport falling into the former.[62] The Northern Division register for 1832 was published together with the votes cast in the general election of December 1832.[63] There were 34 Newport men registered, of whom 33 voted, a total lower after reform than in some 18th-century elections. Just over a half of these (17) had voted in the unreformed election of August 1830.[64] Of the new voters, eight were tenants: a shoemaker, baker, carrier, butcher and four farmers.[65] Apart, perhaps, from the inclusion of William

60   ERO, D/DKw 04; LIB/POL 1/1, 1/2, 1/6; http://www.historyofparliamentonline.org.
61   ERO, T/B 251/2/1: microflims of political correspondence of John Strutt and Col. J.H. Strutt, 1750–63. (Cited by kind permission of Lord Rayleigh.)
62   2 & 3 Will. IV c.45.
63   ERO, LIB/POL 1/16/1.
64   *The poll for two knights of the shire* (Chelmsford, 1830).
65   Sir John St Aubyn (whose illegitimate son had eloped with the wife of one of the candidates, Tyrell, in 1827 and had been cited in the ensuing criminal conversation and divorce proceedings) has been excluded from this number.

Patman, a labourer and freeholder, reform had made little impact on Newport's electoral demographics. Most of the votes cast, including those of Sir John St Aubyn and the five known dissenters, were for Western and Thomas Brand (24 and 22 respectively), who stood in the 'old Whig' interest, and had supported the 1832 Act and reform more generally. They were, however, defeated by the Tory protectionist alliance of Tyrell and Alexander Baring, for whom seven men voted as 'straights' including William Smith of Shortgrove.

The 1867 Reform Act made little difference to the rural franchise, but the county of Essex was further divided into three divisions, West, East and South. Newport was in the West Division.[66] The 1884 Redistribution of Seats Act created a parliamentary borough of Saffron Walden, which included Newport within its boundaries, returning a single MP.[67] Newport remains (2014) in the Saffron Walden parliamentary constituency.

66 30 & 31 Vict. c. 102.
67 48 & 49 Vict. c. 23.

RELIGIOUS HISTORY

PAROCHIAL ORGANISATION

FROM THE 7TH CENTURY until 1845, Newport formed part of the diocese of London.[1] In 1845, along with the other Essex parishes of the London diocese, it was transferred to the diocese of Rochester, and in 1877 to the diocese of St Albans, which was formed from part of the enlarged diocese of Rochester. In 1914 all the Essex parishes of the St Albans diocese became the newly-created diocese of Chelmsford. Newport remains (2014) part of that diocese.[2] In 1882 the suffragan see of Colchester was revived, and in 2014 Newport fell within the Colchester Episcopal Area.[3]

Probably from the 12th century onwards, diocesan bishops delegated some of their authority to archdeacons, and Newport fell within the archdeaconry of Colchester. The archdeaconry was divided into a number of deaneries, of which Newport was one, despite its church being exempt from episcopal visitation until 1550.[4] The *Taxation of Pope Nicholas* (1291) lists 13 churches under the deanery of Newport,[5] and the *Valor Ecclesiasticus* (1535) lists 19 rectories and vicarages, together with the priory of Bearden and the Hospital of St Leonard in Newport.[6] Newport has remained part of the archdeaconry of Colchester, but in 1907, while within the diocese of St Albans, the deanery was reorganised as the deanery of Newport and Stansted. It is now part of the deanery of Saffron Walden.[7]

THE PARISH CHURCH OF ST MARY

St Mary's Church dates from the first half of the 13th century. Its importance is indicated by the fact that it is cruciform, with transepts, and by its large size. (see figs. 48, 50 and 51). The windows of the north aisle, although restored or renewed, indicate

1   Pamela Taylor, 'Foundation and Endowment: St Paul's and the English Kingdoms, 604–1087', in *St Paul's: The Cathedral Church of London 604–2004*, ed. D. Keene, A. Burns and A. Saint (New Haven and London, 2004), 5–16 and map at p. 6; Below, p. 130.

2   F. A.Youngs Jr., *Guide to the Local Administrative Units of England* 1 (Southern England) (London, 1979), 146, 776, 780–1, 783–4; *VCH Essex* I, 81–3.

3   G. Hewitt, *A History of the Diocese of Chelmsford* (Chelmsford, 1984), 156–7.

4   *Cal. Pat.* 1549–51, 171–2; R. Newcourt, *Repertorium or an Ecclesiastical Parochial History of the Diocese of London*, II (London, 1710), 426–7; *Taxatio Ecclesiastica* (London, Record Commission, 1810), 8–29.

5   *Tax. Eccl.*, 23, 28.

6   *Valor Ecclesiasticus,* I (London, Record Commission, 1810), 440 and map of Newport deanery at end of vol. I.

7   Youngs, *Guide*, 776, 784.

Figure 48 *St Mary's Church, Newport, from the south.*

a date of *c.*1390. They may, however, represent alterations to a 13th-century structure. The external fabric includes a putlog hole that is partly lined with a fragment of what appears to have been the stone shaft of a Saxon churchyard cross. It is carved with a simple interlace pattern of two threads and has a roll-moulding along one side.[8] Like most churches in the area St Mary's is built of flint and pebble rubble with some stone; the dressings are of limestone and clunch. The south aisle was built (or rebuilt) in the early 14th century, and the north aisle in about 1390. A west tower was added in the middle of the 14th century. At about the same time the upper part of the chancel walls was rebuilt. A vestry was added in the 14th century on the north side of the chancel, and the two-storey south porch. The porch has a large window on the south front lighting the upper room, flanked by niches, and angle buttresses that rise to crocketed pinnacles. Late in the 15th or early in the 16th century the clerestory was added to the nave, and in the 16th century a clerestory of red brick windows was added to the chancel (see fig. 48).[9]

A number of furnishings have survived from the pre-Reformation church, the most important of which is the portable altar chest (see fig. 49). It dates from the latter part of the 13th century. The lid of the chest, when raised, forms the reredos, with paintings of the Crucifixion, the Virgin, St John, St Peter, and St Paul, each within a cusped arch. It is a very early example of oil painting on wood. The front has three friezes of ornament, circles, shields, and lozenges, the latter filled with 19th-century copies of ornament cast

8   Secker, 'A re-used Anglo-Saxon cross shaft fragment', 222–3.
9   RCHM(E) *Essex* I (1916), 198.

Figure 49 *Portable altar chest in St Mary's Church, latter part of the 13th century. The lid of the chest, when raised, forms the reredos, with paintings of the Crucifixion, the Virgin, St John, St Peter, and St Paul, each within a cusped arch. A very early example of oil painting on wood.*

in pewter.[10] The octagonal bowl of the font is probably 13th century, and its oak cover is 15th century. Also of the 15th century is the lectern, another rare survival. It has an octagonal base and stem, tracery panels, and tracery in the triangle between the top book-rests. The book-rests themselves appear to have been replaced in 1837. The chancel screen is 15th century, but it and the font were restored in 1858–60.

The church building was somewhat neglected after the Reformation, but not unusually so. Archdeacons' visitations in 1633 and 1686 noted a number of defects to the fabric. Some time in the 17th century a singing gallery was erected at the west end of the nave.[11] Benjamin Hughes, vicar 1780–96, disfigured the angels that supported the nave roof by cutting off their heads.[12] The process of repair began in 1826, when £190 was spent, but the building was still considered 'partially dilapidated' and further improvements were carried out in 1834–6 by the architect William Ward of Saffron Walden. As well as general repairs and repaving, this included providing new seating,

10 J. Alexander and P. Binski (eds), *Age of Chivalry: Art in Plantagenet England, 1200–1400* (London, 1987), 347.
11 ERO, D/P 15/8/1; TNA, PROB 11/888.
12 H.T. and T.S. Norris, 'Newport Angels', *NN*, 78 (2012), 30–1; *VIT*, 72; Hughes's responsibility is not established beyond doubt.

Figure 50 *Engraving of St Mary's Church Newport, from T.K. Cromwell,* Excursions in the County of Essex, *London, 1818.*

increasing the number of sittings from 273 to 499. The estimated cost of the work was £275, towards which the Incorporated Church Building Society provided a grant of £150.[13]

The major restoration, however, took place during the incumbency of Revd John Chapman, 1850–76. By 1850 the church was said to be in a very poor state; the tower had been struck by lightning in the 18th century, the stonework generally was crumbling, and many of the windows were broken or bricked up.[14] Work began in 1856 and was completed in 1860. In 1856–8 the tower was rebuilt by W. Brown of Kings Lynn under the direction of the architect G.E. Pritchett of Bishop's Stortford. It was ostensibly a faithful copy of the old one, although a keen local critic, Revd J.H. Sperling, thought that the walls had been unnecessarily thickened and the proportions spoilt.[15] Then the nave clerestory was rebuilt under the direction of the clerk of works, Mr Whitehead, with eight new three-light windows; in the process a Doom painting over the chancel arch was discovered, but not preserved. The nave was reroofed, internally a copy of the old one, but externally covered with slate rather than lead as previously. The cost of this work was £687 10s. The south porch was also restored, the windows and arch being renewed in Caen stone. Inside, the pews installed as recently as 1836 were replaced with benches and chairs, and the font was restored at the expense of the contractor, who was again W. Brown. A new stone pulpit supported on marble shafts was given by W.C. Smith, who also contributed a total of £465 for other parts of the restoration; it was designed by Thomas Jeckyll of Norwich and cost £45.[16] The chancel screen was restored. Sperling, writing in 1860, deplored the fact that the chancel still needed restoration; this did not

13   LPL, Incorporated Church Building Society, file 1696.
14   *VIT*, 103.
15   *Builder,* 16 (1858), 268; *Ecclesiologist,* 21 (1860), 16, 196. Sperling was vicar of Wicken Bonhunt.
16   *Chelmsford Chronicle,* 6 April 1860, 4; *Builder,* 18 (1860), 254. However, the pulpit is not mentioned in S. W. Soros and C. Arbuthnot (eds), *Thomas Jeckyll architect and designer* (London, 2003), and according to Sperling it was designed by S. S. Teulon (*Ecclesiologist* 21, 1860); *EAS,* 2 (1863), 157–63.

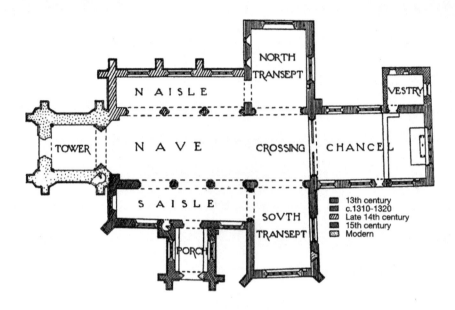

Figure 51 *Ground plan of St Mary's Church Newport.*

happen until 1911, and was paid for by Sir William Foot Mitchell of Quendon Hall, the lay rector.[17] Choir stalls were introduced in 1891, carved by Walter Holman of Newport.[18]

The church contains two monumental figure brasses. The first is to Thomas Brond (d. 1515), in civilian dress, with his wife Margery, two sons, and two daughters. The second, which is under the tower and not accessible, commemorates Katherine Nightingale (d. 1608) and her husband Geoffrey, also in civilian dress (see fig. 52). The inscription records that they had seven children. One of their sons, William (d. 1609), is commemorated by a separate brass inscription.[19] The chancel contains two mural monuments of note. The first is to Dame Grace Brograve (d. 1704) and her husband Giles Dent (d. 1711/12), the builder of Shortgrove Hall, and erected after his death. It is of white marble. The inscription is carved on *trompe l'oeil* drapery. On top of the tablet are shields of arms and an urn, below it a panel with two skulls. The other commemorates Joseph Smith of Shortgrove Hall (d. 1822) and is by Henry Westmacott. Above the long inscription is a draped urn. Joseph Smith is buried in a brick vault which was built on his orders below the north-west corner of the chancel in about 1795. The vault is entered by an external flight of steps, which is sealed over with stone slabs and further protected by iron railings that run between the vestry and the north transept.

---

17   *Ecclesiologist,* 21 (1860), 196; date on rainwater heads.
18   *VIT,* 103.
19   W. Lack, H.M. Stuchfield and P. Whittemore, *The Monumental Brasses of Essex* 2 (London, for the Monumental Brass Society, 2003), 512.

HERE LYETH BVRYED THE BODY OF KATHERINE NIGHTINGALE,
WIFE TO GEFFERYE NIGHTINGALE ESQVIRE, WHO HAD ISSVE
BETWENE THE 7 CHILDREN THOMAS, HENRY, WILLIAM, MARYE,
ANNE, IHONE AND ELIZABETH, SHE DEPARTED THIS LIFE Ŷ 9ᵀᴴ
OF NOVEMBER IN THE 54ᵀᴴ YEARE OF HER AGE, AND IN Ŷ YEA-
RE OF OVR LORD 1608. A GRAVE AND MODEST MATRON SHEE
WAS LOVEINGE & FAYTHFVLL TO HER HVSBANDE, CAREFVLL &
TENDER OVER HER CHILDREN, KINDE TO HER FREENDES, CVRTE-
OVS TO ALL, HELPEFVLL TO Ŷ POORE, HVRTFVLL TO NONE, HER
SORROWFVLL SVRVIVING HVSBANDE HATH CAVSED TO BE MADE
THIS DVRABLE MONVMENT AS A SADD MEMORIALL OF HIS GRE-
ATE LOSSE & HER WORTHE.

It contains also the coffins of his widow Margaret (d. 1847), son William (d. 1885) and William's widow Frances (d. 1898).[20]

There are fragments of 13th- and 14th-century stained glass collected in two lancet windows in the west wall of the north transept and arranged by Heaton, Butler & Bayne in 1894. It includes complete figures of St Katherine and St Michael.[21] The same firm also made the window in the north wall of the chancel, c.1909, and probably two windows at the west end of the south aisle and one in the north aisle, c.1887–91.[22] Three windows on the south side of the chancel were made by Lavers, Barraud & Westlake in the 1870s, and the window in the east wall of the south transept, commemorating R.M. Tamplin, son of the vicar, who died in the 'great fire' at Exeter in 1887, is by Clayton & Bell.

PARISH CHURCH PRE-REFORMATION

The discovery during restoration of the church in 2013 of a re-used Anglo-Saxon cross shaft fragment suggests that there may have been a church on this site from at least the late Anglo-Saxon period, though no documentary evidence survives.[23] Domesday Book does not mention the church as such, but it records a priest, Tascelin, as holding one hide in the hamlet of Birchanger 'in the king's alms'. Tascelin had other land in the bishop of London's manor of Little Warley in Essex.[24] One hide was a common endowment for a priest,[25] and Tascelin may have been the priest of the church at Newport; on the other hand, since his land in Newport came from the royal estate, he may have been a royal chaplain, who received the income and paid his own priest to perform the duties.

Sometime between 1107 and 1122, Henry I gave the church to the College of St Martin le Grand in London on the petition of their dean, Roger, who was also Bishop of Salisbury.[26] The College had been founded (or refounded) by Ingelric the priest in the reign of Edward the Confessor, and Ingelric endowed it with extensive lands in Essex and the churches of the royal manors of Witham and Maldon.[27] By the 12th century St Martin's had developed into a college of royal officials, and by the 13th century the dean was generally one of the clerks of the king's wardrobe.[28] This close connection with the crown enabled the dean and the canons to maintain their exemption from episcopal and archidiaconal supervision.[29] It also enabled them to assert their rights (not always successfully) to the chapel at Bonhunt and to appoint the Master of St Leonard's Hospital.

20   C.K. Probert described all the memorials visible in the church in 1856: BL, Add. Ms. 33520, pp. 22–9; J. Litten, 'Tombs fit for kings: some burial vaults of the English aristocracy and landed gentry of the period 1650–1850', *Church Monuments*, 14 (1999), 113.
21   *Building News*, 67 (1894), 132/xv; *Essex Review*, 3 (1894), 159–60.
22   S.M.B. Bayne, *Heaton, Butler and Bayne: a hundred years of the art of stained glass* (London, 1986), 123.
23   Secker, 'A re-used Anglo-Saxon cross shaft fragment', 222–3; above, p. 125.
24   DB, 971, 976.
25   John Blair, *The Church in Anglo-Saxon Society* (Oxford, 2005), 371–2.
26   WAM, 13167, nos cxxi, cxx, cl.
27   Ibid., Book 5, ff. 9b–10a; Pamela Taylor, 'Ingelric, Count Eustace and the Foundation of St Martin-le-Grand', *Anglo-Norman Studies*, XXIV (2001), 215–33; above, p. 37.
28   T.F. Tout, *Chapters in the Administrative History of Medieval England*, I (Manchester, 1920), 279.
29   WAM, 13167, nos. cxxxii, clii; ibid., 13247; ibid., Book 5 ff. 10a, 27a-b.

In 1291, the canons were granted a sum of 5s. per annum from Bonhunt chapel, and they were compensated at St Leonard's with a yearly payment of 3lb. of wax.[30]

During Stephen's reign the College temporarily lost control of the revenues of Newport church when Geoffrey de Mandeville seized its tithes and lands. He was subsequently forced to restore them, and in a letter to the bishop of London c.1144 he admitted that they had been taken unjustly.[31] The charter of restoration defined the College's rights as those given by Henry I, comprising the tithe of his demesne, or home farm, his demesne ploughlands and that of 'all men of the said vill in cattle, corn and all things titheable'. King Stephen also confirmed in two writs the right of the canons to hold the church of St Mary at Newport with chapels (possibly Bonhunt), tithes and lands and to carry away their corn as in the time of his uncle, Henry I.[32] Newport church was an important part of the College's endowment, and when the prebends of the College were established in 1158, Newport was assigned to the dean himself. The value was the fifth highest in the Archdeaconry of Colchester according to the assessment made in 1291–2.[33]

It is likely that Shortgrove had been added to the parish of Newport, rather than Widdington, by the end of the 12th century. The counts of Boulogne, patrons of the College, were also lords of the manor of Shortgrove. Between 1189 and 1198, William de Warenne, heir to the counts of Boulogne, ordered his sub-tenant, Geoffrey de Merc, to inform the bishop of London that he was rendering the tithes to St Martin's.[34] This had the effect of formally joining the two estates of Newport and Shortgrove within the one parish of Newport.[35]

Like several other early Essex churches which served royal centres, that at Newport is dedicated to St Mary the Virgin; in medieval times it also had the associated dedication to Our Lady of the Assumption.[36] The 15th-century house in the High Street known as Monk's Barn bears a fine carving on the front depicting the Virgin Mary crowned as Queen of Heaven, which may indicate a connection with the church, although the nature is uncertain (see fig. 53).[37]

After the appropriation of the church by St Martin le Grand, the advowson was in the hands of the dean, except during vacancies in that office, until 1503.[38] In that year the College and all its appurtenances, including the advowson of Newport, were appropriated to Westminster Abbey as part of the endowment of Henry VII's chapel.[39] At the Dissolution the advowson passed to the short-lived bishopric of Westminster,[40] and

30 Ibid., Book 5 ff. 93b-94a; R.C. Fowler, 'The Hospital of Newport', *EAS*, XI (1911), 269–70.

31 WAM, Book 5 ff. 28b–29a.

32 Ibid., 13167, no. cxxi.

33 Ibid., Book 5 ff. 18b–19a; ibid., 13247; *Tax. Eccl.*, 22–3.

34 WAM, 962 (transcript in ERO, T/A 172).

35 See above, p. 37.

36 WAM, Book 5 ff. 28a–29b, 109b–111a.

37 RCHM(E) *Essex* I, 204.

38 *Cal. Pat.* 1350–54, 529., where the vicarage of Newport is stated to be in the king's gift 'by reason of the late voidance' of the deanery of St Martin.

39 C. M. Barron and M. Davies (eds), *The Religious Houses of London and Middlesex* (London, for the VCH, 2007), 203–4; T. Tatton-Brown and R. Mortimer, *Westminster Abbey: The Lady Chapel of Henry VII* (Woodbridge, 2003), 61–2.

40 Newcourt, *Repertorium* II, 436–7.

Figure 53 *Carving below the oriel window on Monk's Barn, High Street, with figure of the Virgin and child flanked by angels playing musical instruments. Probably mid 15th century.*

then into the hands of the crown, where it remained until 1864–5. From then until the present day the right of presentation has belonged to the bishop.[41]

Little is known about the medieval vicars. An epitaph and brass to one of them, John Heynes *c.*1400, could be seen in the church in the early 18th century and was recorded by C.K. Probert in 1856.[42] Under the Act of 1402,[43] Newport was designated a 'perpetual vicarage' and therefore the benefice was to be held by a secular priest rather than a member of a religious order. In 1478, the vicar of Newport was described as a 'perpetual vicar' and was presumably therefore a secular priest as prescribed by the Act.[44] Newport was not a wealthy benefice: at the time of the valuation of ecclesiastical property in 1535, the annual income to Westminster Abbey from the rectory was assessed at £18 whereas that going to the vicar was higher at £22.[45] This suggests that the vicar depended for some of his income on fees and bequests for services such as saying masses for the dead as well as income from the lesser tithes.

Many of the bequests from pious laymen were for obits or masses to be said for their souls after death. Thomas Stordy in 1526 gave 20*d.* for the repair of the bells, and 10*s.* for a priest to sing a trental (30 successive daily masses for the dead) 'for my soule, my friends soules and all christian soules', and 10*s.* for another trental. Richard Wesley, John Wenham, Edmund Gosnall, Thomas Brond, Roger Couche and John Pratt left money

---

41   CCED, appointment of vicars from 1703; *White's Dir. Essex* (1863), 702–3; *Kelly's Dir. Essex* (1870), 155; *Crockford's Clerical Directory* (2011–12).

42   ERO, A12376; Newcourt, *Repertorium* II, 437; BL Add. Ms. 33520 p. 29r; ERO, D/DHt Z42, T/P 195/17/11.

43   4 Hen. IV, c.12.

44   WAM, Book 5 ff. 93b–94a.

45   *Val. Eccl.* I, 412, 440.

both for obits and for the poor, and four others left money for obits as well as for the poor, and four others left money for obits alone.[46]

Others made bequests for the church itself. John Heynes, the priest whose epitaph has already been noted, left land for its repair, and John Manningham, the master of St Leonard's Hospital in 1478, gave a property in Bridge End and an osier plot to pay for five candles in front of the crucifix. John Siprian gave land, a house and barn for repair of the church and one obit, while in 1539 William Long gave 20*d.* to the high altar to supplement his offerings and tithes, and 6*s.* 8*d.* to the repair of the church. Some made bequests in expiation of past sins, real or imaginary: in 1536, for example, Thomas Spurryer left 12*d.* to the high altar 'in oblacion for my tithes in tyme past negligently forgotten if any such be'.[47]

The most substantial gift associated with the church was that of Gace's Farm, with about 50 a. of land which was left to trustees in 1520 by John and Agnes Covill, and thus avoided seizure at the Reformation. After their decease, the trustees were to use the income to provide for requiem masses for the repose of their souls, to pay the lay subsidy on behalf of all the inhabitants of Newport, and to apply the residue for the benefit of the poor of the parish.[48]

Two religious fraternities or guilds existed in Newport. That dedicated to the Holy Cross or Rood was assessed for tax on £6 worth of moveable goods in 1524 but no other reference has been traced to it. The Corpus Christi guild was assessed on £3 6*s.* 8*d.* in 1524 and for the same amount in 1543, but it also had two properties near the church which were sold by the Crown in 1549 after the guilds and chantries had been dissolved.[49]

No evidence has been found for Lollardy in the parish, although main roads, such as that passing through Newport to Cambridge, have been identified as key to the flourishing of Lollard groups.[50]

PARISH CHURCH POST-REFORMATION

From Reformation to Restoration

After the Reformation supplementary sources of income such as for masses for the dead ceased: in 1548, for example, 15 grants of income or rents made by laymen and women for obits, lamps and candles were confiscated and sold to Thomas Goldyng of London and Walter Cely. Such losses exacerbated the poverty of the living and led to constant difficulties in finding a vicar. The parish was at times served by a minister removed from elsewhere in disgrace and, during long vacancies or non-residence by pluralists, it was served by a series of curates.[51]

---

46 ERO, D/P 15/25; TNA, PROB 11/22.
47 WAM, Wyks 287, 312; for Heynes see above, p. 132.
48 Ibid.; TNA, PROB 11/22; above, pp. 90–1.
49 TNA, E 179/108/155, E 179/108/171; above, p. 102.
50 Allan, *Chepyng Walden*, 156, 200–1, 206.
51 TNA, E 134/9, 10; LMA, Reg. Stokesley, f. 93; L&P Henry VIII IX, 661; Venn, *Alumni*; *VCH Essex* II, 110–15.

The vicar at the time of the Henrician reformation, Dr Robert Baryngton, was also abbot of Walden; on becoming abbot he let the tithes of Newport to 'one Dunham, a layman', who then appointed and funded a curate. Baryngton may have had Protestant leanings, for he was reported to Thomas Cromwell for having contracted 'a secret marriage'. His successor, Edward Kirkby (or Kirby), instituted in 1539, had been forcibly removed as abbot of Rievaulx for libelling Henry VIII, and he had also been accused of violence, extortion, and dissolute living while at Rievaulx. He did not change his ways after his appointment to Newport: in 1546 he was involved in a Star Chamber case over a will, and the defendants claimed he had forged the will and had authorised violence to maintain his case.[52]

After the death of Kirkby's successor, Thomas West (1546–57), the benefice was vacant for almost 20 years, and the parish was served by a series of curates each of whom stayed for no more than a year or two.[53] Even when a vicar, John Thorpe, was appointed in 1579 he stayed for only a year before moving to a more lucrative benefice in London.[54]

The difficulty in finding an incumbent who was prepared to remain in office probably encouraged the development of a lay piety that valued a style of preaching which could not necessarily be provided by the parish minister. This is perhaps indicated by the will of Thomas Martin, yeoman, who asked that at his burial 'there shall be some learned man to make a godly sermon to edify the people withal, if he may be conveniently had, and for his pains 6s. 8d.'.[55] Newport's location on a main route from London to Cambridge, the presence of well-to-do laymen with contacts in both places and a local economy less purely reliant on agriculture than surrounding parishes may also have played a part in the development of a puritan Protestantism in the parish.

John Lythall, vicar from 1581 to 1586–7, came from the Puritan wing of the Elizabethan Church of England. In 1566, as rector of St Christopher-le-Stocks, he had been one of the 37 London clergy suspended and their livings sequestered by Bishop Grindal in the 'Vestiarian Controversy' for refusing to subscribe to the official form of clerical vestments in the Church of England.[56] After this chequered career, Newport may have represented the best he could achieve. He died and was buried in Newport in January 1587.[57]

Lythall's successor, John Brawlerde (1587–1625), constantly struggled against poverty, disputing the right to tithes of hay from certain fields with the farmers of Parsonage Farm.[58] The living of Newport, estimated by witnesses in 1634 at only £13 to £20 a year without the tithes of hay, was inadequate to support a married clergyman with children. Parishioners recollected seeing Brawlerde bundling up hay and struggling with the farmer to take it away and one described him as 'a very poore man and wanted money to buy necessary sustenance for his self and his family and came to [my] house sundry times for a meales meate as having great need thereof for … he had not a bitt of bread in his house'.[59]

52   TNA, E 134/9, STAC 2/10; L & P Henry VIII, IX, 661; LMA, Reg. Bonner, f. 131; *VCH Yorkshire* III, 149–53.
53   CCED: Newport Parish Registers, *passim*.
54   Ibid; Venn, *Alumni*.
55   ERO, D/ABW 9/93.
56   LMA, Ms 9531/13; Reg. Parker, f. 873.
57   LMA, DL/C 358, f. 382r; NLHG, transcripts of Newport Parish Registers.
58   Ibid.; ERO, D/ABW: Newport wills.
59   TNA, E 134 9 & 10 Charles I, Hilary no. 15.

Around 1616 four Newport men were indicted at the Midsummer sessions in Chelmsford for circulating a libelous doggerel poem mocking the churchwardens, an (unlicensed) preacher, George Watson, and the 'Shepherde [who] should be an example in holiness of liffe' (presumably Brawlerde) for Puritan practices such as not making the sign of the cross, abandoning the surplice and allowing unlicensed preaching and communion to be received without kneeling.[60] This incident demonstrates not only that there was an openly Puritan style of worship in the church in Newport but also that there was resistance to it, or at least mockery, from some quarters among the laity. One of those accused was later indicted for entering the church and disturbing prayers there and 'Brayling upon the minister of your word, Constables & Churchwardens'.[61]

Tensions continued under Brawlerde's successor Robert Sparke[62] as Arminianism advanced in the diocese of London under bishops George Mountain (1621–8) and William Laud (1628–33).[63] Laud in particular made strenuous efforts to enforce traditional conformity in divine service and more decorous forms of church decoration and worship. Presentations to the Commissary Court in the 1620s and 1630s reveal disputes over the failure to provide a hood for the minister and a penance sheet and the church seating and railing of the altar.[64] The same records also show a steady level of presentations suggestive of social tension between a 'godly' element among parishioners and those they considered to be guilty of immoral behaviour such as failure to attend church, breaking the Sabbath by drinking and gaming, and sexual incontinence.[65]

Unlicensed preaching continued in the parish. Thomas Jefferey or Jephry, an unlicensed reader ('lector') and preacher ('concionator') who had been active in Newport alongside Brawlerde since at least 1622, was removed by the Commissary Court in July 1631 after the court heard that he refused to wear a surplice.[66] However, imposing conformity on Newport proved difficult. Peter Plumb, yeoman of Newport, was presented in 1635 for the typically Puritan practice of 'absenting himself from his parish church & gadding to other churches on severall Sundays in the afternoon since Christmas last'. His defence was boldly Puritan in tone, saying that he had to go to other churches in order to hear sermons.[67]

In 1634 Sparke attempted to improve the very poor income of the vicarage by pursuing a suit in the Exchequer Court over vicarial entitlement to the tithes of hay in certain fields against Sir George Willmott, knight, and Peter Wyke, respectively owner and farmer of the impropriate great tithes, valued, in contrast to the poverty of the benefice, at between £120 and £200 per annum. The case was decided against Sparke in 1636 and he seems to have abandoned active ministry in the parish shortly afterwards.[68]

60   ERO, Q/SR 214/27.
61   Ibid., D/ABA 1, ff. 83v, 100v, 149v.
62   TNA, E 134, 9 & 10 Charles I, Hilary no. 15; Venn, *Alumni*.
63   *ODNB* 39, 538–40; 32, 655–70.
64   ERO, D/ABA 1, ff. 124v, 78r, 81r, 168v; D/ABA, 8 ff. 10v, 133r, 199r.
65   Ibid., D/ABA series.
66   Ibid., D/ABA 2 ff. 52r, 93r; D/ABA 5 ff. 71v, 85r, 91r, 97v.
67   ERO, D/ABA 7, fo. 41v.
68   TNA, E 13/558, m. 56; LMA, Ms. 9531/15; BL, Add. Ms. 39534; Bodleian Library, Ms. Rawlinson B 373.

No permanent minister was appointed until 1703 and the cure of Newport was left to a series of curates.[69]

During the Commonwealth the vicarage and impropriate parsonage of Newport were sequestered.[70] However, the poverty of the living meant that there was no permanent minister. A survey of 1650 valued the vicarage at £18 a year, which was too little to persuade anyone to accept it.[71] There is limited evidence for the maintenance of surreptitious Anglican worship in the parish. In summer 1653 a warrant was issued against Robert Percivall, clerk, of Newport for 'great offences, misdemeanours and traitorous speeches'. Percivall had the support of some parishioners, who seem to have abetted his escape from custody before he could be conveyed to Colchester gaol.[72]

From the Restoration to the present day

After the Restoration of Charles II in 1660 and of the Anglican church between 1660 and 1662, the vicarage of Newport continued vacant for a further 43 years until 1703, presumably because of the poverty of the living. The parish was again served by a series of curates.[73] The last and longest-serving of these (1689–1703), Henry Rix, combined the curacy with the Masterships of Newport Free Grammar School, Saffron Walden Grammar School and additional curacies at Widdington and Stocking Pelham (Herts.), which together must have provided a reasonable income.[74]

Edmund Tatham, appointed as vicar in 1703, set about placing the income of the living on a sounder footing by cataloguing the tithes receivable and obtaining agreement for the commutation of tithes in kind to cash payment together with a 6*d*. in the £ rate.[75] The living was twice further augmented during his incumbency. The will of Giles Dent's son and successor Giles Dent the younger (d. 1712), provided £100 for the purchase of land for the maintenance of the vicar, and in 1720 the vicarage of Newport, valued at £20 a year, was augmented by £400 capital awarded under Queen Anne's Bounty. Some £200 of the bounty matched a private benefaction of £200 from Rebecca Dent, youngest daughter of Giles Dent senior and sister of Giles Dent junior. Tatham also drew rent from the vicarage house, which he had 'substantially' repaired; he himself lived elsewhere 'in the neighbourhood very near'.[76]

In 1710, during Tatham's incumbency, the Bray Trustees for Erecting Parochial Libraries established a parochial library at Newport.[77] The library was augmented in 1834, when 49 of the original volumes remained, and in 1879, when it had increased to 72 volumes, it was restored by the Smith family and 17 of the local clergy, and established

69   See below.
70   H. Smith, *The Ecclesiastical History of Essex under the Long Parliament and Commonwealth* (Colchester, 1932), 127, 292.
71   LPL, Comm. XIIa, vol. 8, ff. 453–4.
72   Smith, *Ecclesiastical History*.
73   Newport Parish Registers; *VIT*, 179; Venn, *Alumni*.
74   Venn, *Alumni*.
75   Notes dated 1704 on inside cover of parish register, ERO, D/P 15/1/2.
76   ERO, D/ABW 81/62; CERC, QAB/4/3/1, f. 25. QAB/2/1/2 ff. 167, 175–6; LMA, GL Ms. 25750/2.
77   Graham Best, 'Libraries in the Parish, 1640–1850', in *Cambridge History of Libraries in Britain and Ireland* II (1640–1850), ed. G. Mandelbrote and K.A. Manley (Cambridge, 2006), 324–44.

Figure 54 *Interior of St Mary's Church, Newport.*

in the room above the south porch.[78] It was again augmented in 1884, 1889 and 1896 under Revd Tamplin.[79] The surviving collection of some 800 volumes (of which around 100 are pre-1800, the balance being 19th-century theological works), in the original Bray cupboard with traces of the catalogue on the inside of the door, was still, in 2014, housed in the room over the south porch.[80]

However, despite these improvements, all the 18th-century vicars of Newport apart from John Rix, Benjamin Hughes and Thomas Bell were non-resident pluralists, and the parish continued to rely on a series of curates.[81] The clergy were not always sympathetic to their congregation, and their quality was not always high. William Cole implied that John Lane (1740–46), who was robbed and shot dead by a highwayman in Epping Forest in October 1746, had contributed to his end by his loud 'valiant' remarks while dining at Epping 'rather elevated with Drink'.[82] Benjamin Hughes (1780–96) was mentally unstable, described in the 1790 visitation return as 'a Lunatick' of whom the curate was afraid.

78 ERO, D/Q 25/25.

79 *Newport Parish Magazine,* June 1884; Bray Associates Records, *A Directory of the Parochial Libraries of the Church of England and the Church in Wales,* (London 2004), 299–301.

80 A. Archer, 'The Bray Library', *NN*, 37 (1992), 78.

81 Visitation records: LMA, GL Ms. 25750/2 (1723), 2573/2 (1738), 2574/3 (1741–2), 25755/2 (1747); LPL, FP Osbaldeston 6 ff. 174–5 (1763), FP Terrick 15 ff. 69–72 (1770), FP Lowth ff. 434–7 (1778), FP Porteous 29/5 (1790).

82 BL, Add. Ms. 5807 p. viii.

He and his wife and children were repeatedly referred between 1783 and 1788 to the Charity for the Relief of Poor Clergymen in the County of Essex for help on this basis and according to his successor Thomas Bell he died insolvent, leaving the vicarage house dilapidated and uninhabitable.[83]

Church attendance correspondingly fell. The 1770 return stated that there were 40 communicants in the parish, which consisted of c.130 houses. By 1778 the number of communicants had dropped to about 20, and by 1790 to 15. The parish therefore displayed several of the features of the Church of England considered problematic by members of the Anglican hierarchy concerned at the advances made nationally by dissent and Methodism and, in the final quarter of the century, by social and political unrest. By the end of the century visitation returns from Newport indicate that dissent, in the form of an Independent church, was making significant headway in the parish.[84]

Thomas Bell (1796–1828) held no other living and appears to have served the parish without a curate during most of his ministry.[85] However, many of the issues that had plagued the parish for three centuries continued: disrepair of the church and vicarage, and an income inadequate to support an Anglican clergyman and his family in a respectable style.[86] Bell was resident in the parish but not at the outset in the vicarage house which was seriously out of repair. In 1809 he began a lengthy correspondence with the Governors of Queen Anne's Bounty and the bishop of London seeking assistance with the estimated £170 needed to put the vicarage in good order.[87] In 1811 additional assistance came from Joseph Smith of Shortgrove and with a low-interest mortgage raised under the terms of the Clergy Residences Repair Act 1776, he was able to report by 1815 that the house was repaired and he was resident. By 1825 however, it was once again described as unfit for residence.[88]

Bell also faced deepening and embarrassing financial difficulties, despite the additional income received as Master of the Grammar School from 1793 and chaplain of the House of Correction from 1805. These were exacerbated by his difficult personality that had already caused problems at the Grammar School and now led to disputes with churchwardens and a leading parishioner, his landlord and magistrate George Pochin. He was rescued by financial assistance for his family from Elizabeth Cocks, a relative of Margaret Smith, wife of Joseph Smith of Shortgrove.[89]

Both women were actively involved in the Evangelical movement within the Church of England, and it is probably to Margaret Smith rather than Bell that any revival of Anglican worship in the parish at this period can be attributed, as Bell himself acknowledged. In addition to daily private worship at Shortgrove, the Smiths and their household regularly attended public worship in the church. They funded a Sunday school for 30 poor children in the parish and also supplied prayer books, Bibles and religious tracts to the poor.[90]

83   ERO, D/CZ 28/1/13; CERC, QAB/7/3/F3464.
84   LPL, FP Porteous 29/5. FP Randolph 11/48; below, pp. 145–7.
85   CCED; Newport Parish Burial Registers; Venn, *Alumni*.
86   LPL, FP Howley, 49/24.
87   CERC, QAB/7/3F3464; LPL, Randolph, ff. 68–71.
88   LMA, GL Ms. 10300/3.
89   Emory University (Atlanta GA), Pitts Theology Library, Prince Papers 1803–11, Ms. 209. The authors are grateful to the Librarian for permission to cite these papers.
90   LPL, FP Randolph 11/48.

A more active ministry was pursued by Bell's successor Edward Gould Monk, who was also Master of the Grammar School.[91] Monk also took private pupils and when in 1835 he was appointed chaplain to the House of Correction, the Bishop of London (Charles Blomfield) expressed concern at a workload which 'seemed scarcely possible to be done'.[92] In 1834–6 he oversaw the fundraising to repair the church building and increase the available seating. He also moved the pulpit, leading to objections from the lay rector, James Mounsey Cranmer of Quendon Hall, which were, however, not upheld by the Bishop whose reply indicated that the move was to the advantage of parishioners.[93]

In 1830 Monk's census of his parish recorded religious adherence.[94] A total of 648 inhabitants were recorded as members of the Church of England, a figure that included children, and so may make the category a 'default position'. However, of these only 36 took the sacrament and a mere four were described as 'regular'. Of the 36 communicants one quarter were men and three-quarters women, a gender imbalance that had been noted by Gould's predecessor Bell in 1810.[95] These active Anglicans represented what could be considered the village establishment: Revd William Bell, the son of the late vicar, and his wife, Mrs Birch the widow of the rector of Widdington, Mr Ward, gentleman, and his daughter, two schoolmistresses (Mrs Isabella Bailey, widow, and Mary Cox), and upper servants from Shortgrove. However, among the women communicants were four widows who were either paupers or in receipt of poor relief. Monk's readiness to minister to the less well-off is indicated by his scheme to provide a deacon to serve for the workmen's camp during the construction of the railway in 1844–5.[96] However, after a prolonged absence in North America on family business in 1848–50, Monk resigned to take up an appointment at Much Cowarne, Herefordshire.[97] The patron of this living was his uncle James Henry Monk, bishop of Gloucester. Once again, the relatively impoverished living of Newport could not compete when a richer opportunity presented itself: in 1859 Newport was valued at £143, to Much Cowarne's £280.[98]

Monk's successor was Revd John Chapman (1850–76) who married Elizabeth, the widowed sister of William Smith, son of Joseph Smith of Shortgrove. The Ecclesiastical Census of 1851 recorded church attendance on Sunday 30 March as 168 at morning service and 251 in the afternoon. There were apparently 530 seats available in the church, which was therefore roughly 30 to 40 per cent full.[99]

During his incumbency John Chapman was much preoccupied with the restoration of the church fabric, and some work continued under his successor, George Tamplin (1876–1909).[100] Tamplin and his family initially lived in the Old Vicarage in the High Street, but early in his ministry they moved to an early 19th-century house on Elephant Green, close to the church.[101] In 1882 Tamplin introduced a parish magazine. Its tone

91   Above, p. 104.
92   LPL, FP Blomfield 11, fo. 34.
93   Ibid., fo. 44, and above p. 51 for the Cranmers.
94   Monk, *Inhabitants*; ERO, T/B 581/1.
95   LPL, FP Randolph 11, f. 48.
96   LPL, Blomfield 44, f. 159.
97   ERO, D/Q 25/2.
98   *The Clergy List* (London, 1859).
99   TNA, HO 129/8/210.
100 Above, p. 127.
101 Roger Tamplin, 'The Tamplin Family', *NN*, 46 (1996), 6–8.

indicates a reforming and benevolent attitude by the upper echelons of parish society towards the behaviour of the working class, with a Penny Bank, Clothing and Coal Clubs and a Temperance Society. The attempt was not especially successful judging by the fortunes of the Temperance Society. Formed in 1883 with 66 members, by April 1884 Tamplin accused the middle and upper classes of 'holding themselves aloof' and in November 1887 it was described as almost defunct with many pledges broken.[102] Attendance at services was also dwindling and the sums collected at offertories poor. In April 1882, Tamplin reported that offertories had totalled £52 14s. 10¾d., and that there had been 100 communicants the previous year, which he thought 'satisfactory', although early services attracted an average of only 11 and the midday service 23. By February 1887, the number of regular communicants had dropped to 65.[103] In December 1903 the parish magazine was discontinued, though it was revived shortly after the outbreak of the First World War. It now adopted a more socially inclusive approach, covering the impact of the war on the parish, the sending of parcels to its 'boys' at the front, a positive approach to the building of new social housing after the war and concern for the village environment.[104]

Throughout the 20th century, finance, especially to repair the fabric of the church itself and Church House (the Grammar School building until 1878, then let to the church and bought by the vicar in 1910), remained a constant problem for a relatively small congregation (average adult attendance in 1993 was 95). In 1978 the stonework of the church windows required urgent work estimated to cost £75,000 and in 1989 running costs were £15,000 but income only £12,800 for example.[105] In response to these issues, Newport became a joint benefice with Widdington in August 1984.[106] The 19th-century vicarage was in its turn sold in 1998 and a more cost-efficient house built in the 1970s purchased for £190,000.[107] However, there has been significant change in the extent to which the Anglican parish looks outwards both locally and as part of the international Anglican Communion and in the active involvement of a wider section of the lay congregation. The average attendance at the main 10.00 am service in 2011 was 65, 30 per cent of whom came from outside the parish; attendance reached 100 at festivals and over 150 at Remembrance Sunday and the rota of Readers totalled 40 persons.[108] One of the most notable changes has been in the roles adopted by women.[109] In June 1990 Elizabeth Dixon was appointed churchwarden and in 1994 Joy Pugh was licensed as a Reader. When Revd Scott Sanderson resigned in 1998, the PCC unanimously resolved that one of their criteria for selecting a new incumbent was 'not to oppose the appointment of a woman vicar'. Although the next incumbent was a man, Revd Robert Griffiths, his successor in 2007 was a woman, Revd Dr Barbara Sherlock. Revd Neil McLeod succeeded her in 2011, and a further programme of restoration and renovation

102 *Newport Parish Magazine*, 1882–7.
103 Ibid., 1887.
104 Ibid., 1903, 1914–15.
105 Ibid., 1978, 1989, 1994. For Church House, see above, pp. 105–6.
106 Information from Diocese of Chelmsford.
107 No. 5 Meadowford, Newport: information from Land Registry.
108 *Parish Profile* (Newport PCC, 2011): http://www.chelmsford.anglican.org/assets/files/parish_profiles/2011, p. 12.
109 Ibid., pp. 10–12.

Figure 55 *Hospital Farm, built on the site of St Leonard's Hospital, probably 16th or 17th century, demolished 1907. Oil painting either by Luther Mitchell (head teacher of the primary school 1881–1919) or his wife.*

began in 2013. In 2013 Quendon and Rickling were united with the benefice of Newport and Widdington.

St Leonard's Hospital

The medieval hospital known as St Leonard's was dedicated to St Mary (the patron saint of the parish church) and St Leonard, and the post-dissolution farm known as Hospital Farm, stood by the east side of Cambridge Road in the northern part of the village. Moulded stonework, probably from a chapel, can still be seen in the wall of St Leonard's Close and the adjacent boundary wall. The stone pieces are of high quality; they bear traces of red paint and have been dated to the early 13th century. Some burials have been found nearby from the former cemetery.[110]

The origins of the hospital are unclear. In the reign of King John (1199–1216) Richard de Newporte declared that he had founded a hospital in honour of St Mary and St Leonard, and had appointed a chaplain, Peter, as master. He granted lands and rents to

---

110 D. Andrews and B. Nurse, 'The Hospital of St Leonard's at Newport', *EAH*, 20 (1989), 84–91; *VCH Essex* II (1907), 190–1.

sustain the brethren, priests and laymen, and said that the brethren would be able freely to elect a master when there was a vacancy. In 1218, Richard de Newporte confirmed their election of a new master on the death of Peter.[111] However, it may have been established earlier, for almost every year from 1156/7 until 1220 the king gave a small gift of 2s. to the infirm of Newport. Whilst the amount would hardly have maintained a hospital, it could have been an endowment made to an institution which had other resources.[112] John Flambard, a donor who granted property to the hospital in 1340, stated that the hospital had been founded by the king; [113] and in 1227 Henry III made a more significant grant of the right to hold a fair once a year around the feast of St Leonard (6 Nov.).[114] This was the origin of the Newport Colt Fair, which continued until the 19th century.[115]

Since the 1860s St Leonard's has occasionally been described as a leper hospital.[116] The large boulder nearby, formerly called the 'great stone', has acquired the name of the 'leper stone', from the popular belief that lepers left money in a hollow in the stone in exchange for food. Nevertheless, the only reference to a sufferer in Newport is to 'Thomas le leper', a burgess with property in the town in 1299.[117] The hospital is more likely to have been originally intended for the poor, sick and infirm generally, although like many others, it gradually changed into a college of priests. Grants of property by John Flambard in 1340 and by John Quintyn in 1346 were both to help support a chaplain to celebrate divine service in St Helen's, Bonhunt, and the hospital respectively.[118]

By 1344 and probably earlier, the hospital was recognized as being subject to the jurisdiction of the dean of St Martin le Grand, who had been assigned the church of St Mary Newport in 1158. It was the custom of the priests and brethren, however, to elect one of their number to be master and warden and present him to the dean for admission.[119] From at least 1289, the choice of master was a common cause of dispute, and in the 1340s the issue reached the king's chancellor and the lawcourts. Edward III eventually confirmed the choice of the brethren, and in return the brethren agreed to give St Martin's 3lb. of wax every Martinmas.[120] Robert, 'son of the master of the hospital', held two acres of land at Shortgrove in 1306, which suggests a layman as master then.[121] The institution of a cleric as master appointed by the dean of St Martin's had been established by 1478 when the dean authorised the exchange of John Bedford, master, with John Mannyngham, rector of Stanwick (Northants).[122]

111 Andrews and Nurse, ibid.; VCH Essex II p. 190; WAM, 977.
112 Andrews and Nurse, 'Hospital of St Leonard's', 84; VCH Essex II, 190–1; R.M. Clay, The Medieval Hospitals of England (London, 1909), 178–9.
113 ERO, A12376 Box 17, Newport (2); TNA, C 143/253/5.
114 Cal. Chart. 1226–57, 62.
115 Above pp. 60–61.
116 J.H. Sperling, 'On the churches of north-west Essex', EAS, 2 (1901), 161; I.C. Gould, 'The Hospital, Newport', ibid., 10 (1909), 264.
117 ERO, T/B 3/73.
118 Cal. Pat. 1338–40, 523; 1345–8, 209.
119 Ibid., 1343–5, 329.
120 Ibid., 346; Cal. Close 1343–6, 424; Year Books of the Reign of King Edward III, 20(i), ed. L.O. Pike (London, Rolls Series, reprinted ed. 1971), no. 58, pp. 378–83; WAM, 5, f. 103d.
121 Webb, 432.
122 WAM, 5, f. 94v.

Evidence of the hospital's burial ground has been discovered on several occasions. The skeleton of a large man was found in 1907 when the farmhouse which had been established on the site after the dissolution was demolished, and further bones were unearthed when foundation trenches were being dug in 1985 for houses in St Leonard's Close. These are the only bones to have been thoroughly analysed. Although only six graves were noted, the fragmented remains of between eight and 15 individuals were found. They suffered from a variety of complaints, but no signs of leprosy were found. The only measurable bone was a right shin bone belonging to a woman of between 25 and 30 years of age and 5 ft 6¼ in. tall. She had on her ankle an upward extension of the joint known as the squatting facet, which is generally thought to have been caused by an individual adopting a squatting posture when at rest.[123]

In 1535, the master was receiving an income of £11 10s. 8d., and enough was left to support two fellows at £6 a year, but no more for charitable purposes.[124] A chaplain was allotted 6s. in the year 1542–3 for celebrating mass in the hospital and 2s. 7d. was spent on wine, wax, bread and other necessities. The premises were sufficiently extensive at this time to require 24s. 5d. to be spent on the repair of the houses, barns and stables. The hospital derived most of its income from rents and the profits of the annual Colt Fair, which in 1542–3 were let to Henry Denham for £5 a year. Denham also occupied 'houses, buildings, dovecotes, gardens, orchards, lands and grounds within the site, fence and circuit of the said hospital' for £3 a year, so the area would appear to have included a farm. The hospital was dissolved on 15 April 1543, and a pension of £6 was granted to Philip Fawdon, one of the fellows. By c.1550 it had passed into the hands of Sir Ralph Warren, lord of the manor of Newport Pond.[125] Archaeological excavations failed to reveal the location of these buildings or any associated with the hospital, but the farm was probably incorporated in what was later known as Hospital Farm, demolished in 1907 (see fig. 55).[126]

POST-REFORMATION CATHOLICISM

There is little evidence for Catholic recusancy after 1558 apart from the will of Geoffrey Nightingale (1619) in which his son Henry was disinherited because he was a papist, and the presentation of John Harvey at the Commissary Court as a recusant in 1640.[127] Replies to 18th-century visitation articles all give a nil return for actual or reputed Roman Catholics except for a single instance of a 'Foreigner & man cook' who 'resides here not often, & only as he waits on his Master' in 1767.[128] No Catholics were recorded by Edward Monk in his parish censuses of 1830, for example, and the parish had no landowning families who adhered to Catholicism.

123 Andrews and Nurse, 'Hospital of St Leonard's', 87; B. Hooper, 'Human bones – report', NN, 26 (1986), 19–20.
124 Val. Eccl. I, 440.
125 TNA, SC12/5/74; above, pp. 49–50.
126 Andrews and Nurse, 'Hospital of St Leonard's', 87; Gould, 'Hospital, Newport', 264.
127 TNA, PROB 11/135; ERO, D/ABA 9, f. 256r.
128 LPL, FP Terrick 22, f. 169; the Newport entry in 1676 Compton census does not survive.

In December 1850, however, in apparent response to the restoration of the Roman Catholic hierarchy to England earlier in the year, two Newport residents, H. Ratcliffe and J. Clarke, organised an anti-papal demonstration through the village culminating in a firework display on the Common, in which 2,500 people are said to have participated, and the pope was burned in effigy. Many houses in the village carried anti-papal and anti-Puseyite (High Anglican) posters.[129] There is no evidence that the organisers were reacting to any influx of Catholics to the parish, and the demonstration may have been part of a wider campaign against both the restoration of the Catholic hierarchy and the spread of Puseyite (High Anglican) practices in the Church of England.

PROTESTANT DISSENT

Baptists

By 1653 there was a group of Baptists in the parish with connections to Henry Denne's Church of Christ at Fenstanton (Cambs.),[130] but it does not appear to have been an organised or well-established congregation. Denne visited Newport with Christopher Marriatt on 8 September 1653 'intending to enquire after the state of those persons who had formerly walked in the fellowship of the gospel'. In the evening they called at the home of Thomas Fordham, a tanner, who provided them with supper and made a declaration of his belief that 'the soul and spirit of man is God'. After a lengthy theological dispute, Denne and Marriatt expressed disappointment at the lack of 'prayerful progress and assembly' in the parish and left, staying overnight elsewhere before leaving the next day.[131] There was never an organised Baptist assembly in Newport, and no Baptists were recorded in Monk's census in 1830.

Independents/Congregationalists

From the late 17th century Independents, or Congregationalists, were the main Protestant dissenting group in Newport. Between 1682 and 1778 Newport Independents were among the members of meetings of dissenters from several neighbouring parishes based first in Arkesden (Wood Hall) and later at meeting houses in Clavering and Great Wenden. Their Church Book shows that the meeting also occasionally circulated around other parishes including Newport. The church had a large female membership. Of 86 members in 1692 listed in the back of the Church Book, some 53 were women (35 'sisters' and 18 wives of male members). They operated on a relatively democratic basis, although with some restriction by gender: the sisters were never deacons, for example. Democracy led to a high level of disputes and the book records arguments over the selection and sacking of ministers, allegations about fellow members, and admissions and expulsions. Standards were high. In February 1739 a married woman from Newport (Mrs Moulle) applied to join and made the usual public declaration of her

129 *Essex Standard*, 20 Dec. 1850.
130 *ODNB* 15, 804–5.
131 E.B. Underhill, *Records of the Churches of Christ, gathered at Fenstanton, Warboys and Hexham, 1644–1720* (London, 1854), 77–80.

Figure 56 *The Old Manse, High Street. A Georgian house provided by Benjamin Cleaver as a residence for the Congregational Minister, 1780.*

conversion experience, but was judged 'lacking to the whole church' and made to wait until March before being 'taken into fellowship'. In April 1768 Thomas Living of Newport was declared no longer a member 'haveing by the Church been often reproved and admonished against his Excessive drinking but haveing no visabel & desiered suckses uppon him but acted seemingly more hardned'.[132]

By the 1770s, the meeting at Wenden was poorly attended and the building dilapidated beyond economic repair. In February 1778, the minister Mr Harrison and some of the Newport members proposed moving the Wenden meeting house to Newport. The proposal was controversial: 'meaney of our frends did not approve of & made meany of them unesey'. Nevertheless, the construction of a meeting house at Newport on land (on the High Street to the north of the junction with Frambury Lane) given by Henry Cranmer of Quendon Hall, went ahead. On Whit Sunday 1779, the first sermon was preached there to a full congregation. In 1780 Benjamin Cleaver provided

132 ERO, D/NC 35/1; *The Story of Newport (Essex) Congregational Church compiled by Rev. Arthur Ince and published in connection with the Jubilee celebrations, June 1929* (1929), in SWTL and ERO, D/NC 69/6/3.

the house now known as the Old Manse, High Street, for use as a home for the minister, originally vested in Trustees (see fig. 56).[133] The meeting house had cost a total of £386 8s. 6¼d. of which £146 0s. 2d. was met by subscription and the balance borrowed.[134]

Relations among the Newport Independents and with their ministers were characterised by disagreements.[135] In October 1780 there appears to have been a breach between Mr Harrison and the Newport congregation. He resigned without giving reasons, and so as to 'preserve peace and unanimity' he was asked not to deliver a farewell sermon. He was also refused letters of dismission (leave to depart) on the grounds that he had separated himself from them. By 1784 Harrison's successor, John Bailey, was in dispute with church members over his view that infant baptism should be reserved for those who had at least one parent 'walking in all the Ordinances of Christ, and a member of the visible Church'. Several members left the church over the issue and in 1785 Bailey was forced out of Newport (though his supporters retained the chapel at Clavering) and was replaced by Revd Edward Bryant.[136]

Bryant remained minister for 29 years until his retirement in January 1814. He died in June of the same year. For 20 of those years, however, the congregation underwent a serious schism. In 1794 five members formed a new meeting originally in a building belonging to Benjamin Cleaver behind the Old Manse but in 1805 they purchased the Old Manse from him for the nominal sum of 10s. for use as the meeting house.[137] This breakaway group became known as the 'Little Meeting' (Bryant's congregation being the 'Old Meeting'). In 1795 the Little Meeting appointed a pastor, Mr Dobson, but he left in 1796. His successors lacked full support, and dissatisfaction with their level of commitment to the meeting meant that their ministries were usually short-lived. Little Meeting members were equally harsh towards one another and the church book records suspensions and excommunications for non-attendance, disorderly and drunken behaviour, and fornication. On the retirement of Bryant from the Old Meeting, the schism was healed. The two meetings signed a written agreement of union which was unanimously agreed by each congregation and on 6 February the first united meeting was held in the Old Meeting House with James Hopkins as minister. He continued to serve until September 1850.[138]

Despite the schism, the meeting appears to have prospered in this period. In 1829 there was an Independent congregation of approximately 300, although this may have included members from other parishes.[139] In response to questions from the Anglican hierarchy about numbers and activities of dissenters, the Independents were said in 1770 to amount to five or six families and were using a barn for worship. In 1778 the reply was similar.[140] By 1790 there were many Independents or Congregationalists, and their

133 ERO, D/NC 35/1, 69/2/2.
134 Ibid., D/NC 69/2/1.
135 Ibid., D/NC 35/2.
136 Ibid.
137 Ibid., 69/2/13.
138 Ibid., D/NC 69/1/1.
139 Ibid., Q/CR 3/2/79.
140 LPL, FP Terrick 15, ff. 69–72; FP Lowth 5, ff. 434–7.

number was claimed to have increased since the building of the chapel around 12 years previously.[141]

In his return of 1810, Revd Bell assessed dissenters as accounting for about one quarter of the population of Newport, 177 persons, with two teachers, two meeting houses (following the schism) and a recently established Sunday school for some 20 children. Although he felt that the numbers had neither grown nor shrunk over the 16 years he had been in the parish, he added at the end his own view 'that Dissenters of every Denomination are extremely active & leave no means unattempted to gain proselytes'.[142] By 1830 Revd Monk counted 93 families of Independents in his census. Some were labourers, but they were drawn largely from the middling sort, especially shopkeepers (the Gurson, Cato and Wakefield families), and the skilled artisan classes (a shoemaker, carpenter, watchmaker and carrier, for example).[143] A list of 'Members Living' in 1851 with new entries to 1863 at the back of the Church Book contains 135 entries and the national Ecclesiastical Census of 1851 indicates an attendance at services of 208 in the morning, 246 in the afternoon and 217 in the evening with a total of 390 seats available.[144] Discipline among members continued to be strict. The most serious case was probably the charge of unspecified improper and indecent conduct of Henry Pavitt in October 1862, which appeared to involve allegations made against him by young boys and resulted in his name being erased from the church.[145]

By the mid 19th century the increase in numbers necessitated the construction of galleries on each side of the meeting house. This work was completed in 1856 at a cost of £125 met entirely by funds raised. Activities by the 1860s included revival meetings 'of a highly interesting and profitable nature' and a Meeting for Young People under Revd George Coster. In July 1861 a school room (between the Old Maltings and the Old Manse in the High Street, also known as the Congregational Hall) was opened at a cost of £246 0s. 10d.[146] The money again came from a fundraising effort the previous summer. A two-day bazaar in Bull Field with a band and photographic tent contributed £112 1s. 6d. and 'sacred' concerts a further sum, leaving less than £30 debt by the opening day.[147]

The extended chapel building did not prove adequate for long. A new minister, Revd John Hutchin, had arrived in January 1878 and in the same year it was reported that the building was in 'greatly in need of repair' with foundations inadequate for rebuilding. A new chapel building, 'a neat and substantial Edifice in the Romanesque style' of red brickwork relieved with white bricks and stone work under a slate roof, galleried and with pitch pine fittings was designed by Charles Pertwee of Chelmsford. Donations totalled £818 including £300 from W. Perry of Widdington Hall, and his nephew Isaac of Chelmsford also contributed to the cost.[148] The chapel was officially opened on 18 June 1879 with a special service and a public tea at 1s. per ticket.[149] It seated 450 and was

---

141 Ibid., Porteous 29/5.
142 Ibid., FP Randolph 11/48.
143 Monk, *Inhabitants*; ERO, T/B 58/8/1.
144 ERO, D/NC 69/1/1; TNA, HO 129/8/210.
145 ERO, D/NC 69/1/1.
146 Ibid., 69/1/1, 69/2/7.
147 Ibid., D/NC 69/1/1.
148 Ibid., D/NC 69/2/10.
149 Ibid., D/NC 69/6/1.

Figure 57
*Congregational Chapel,
High Street. Built
1878–9 and demolished
1978.*

built at a cost of £1,307 4s. 9d., almost all of which had been raised by subscription and collections from a congregation, many of whom were poor (see fig. 57).[150]

Church membership remained relatively healthy throughout the later 19th century, with 115 names on the roll in both 1888 and 1900 and some 200 to 300 attending the farewell presentation to Revd Hutchin in 1888. During the remainder of the 19th and 20th centuries the church continued to run a Sunday school, a choir and various clubs and societies, raised funds through a Ladies' Working Society and distributed charity as cash and in the form of a clothing club. However, there was pressure from other evangelical groups – the Primitive Methodists and Salvation Army – and from economic circumstances which led to emigration both to the colonies and elsewhere in Britain. By 1903 the roll had dropped to 78 names and by 1928 to 67. At the golden jubilee of the new chapel in 1929, Revd Ince commented that 'There is a continual exodus of young life to the towns, and only the tiniest inflow of people from the outside…meanwhile the stalwarts and faithful diminish in numbers because they grow old'. He also blamed increased mobility, due to the rise of the car, and a fall in family attendance.[151] The slide continued, and in 1945 only four people attended the annual meeting. The ministry was subsequently shared with Clavering (to 1964) and then Saffron Walden. Following the merger of the Congregational and Presbyterian churches in 1972 to form the United Reformed Church, the chapel was demolished in 1978. The Church later bought 55

150 Ince, *Newport Congregational Church*; ERO, D/NC 69/1/3.
151 Ince, *Newport Congregational Church*, 31–3; ERO, D/NC 69/1/3. 69/6/1.

Wicken Road, which became a United Reformed Chapel, while the Old Manse became a private house with additional housing developed in the grounds of the old church.[152]

Methodists

Methodism did not make early strides in Newport or the surrounding district in the 18th century (when it was a reform group within the Church of England), although George Whitefield preached on Saffron Walden Common to a crowd of some 2,000 as early as June 1739.[153] In 1770 and 1778 there were apparently no Methodists or Moravians in the parish.

Methodism first appears in Newport during its 'sober years of ascending respectability and social status…from the early 1820s to 1849'.[154] In 1821, a genteel Methodist preacher, Charlotte Steigen-Berger, moved from London to Saffron Walden and began a preaching mission in the town and surrounding villages. Initially based at a licensed barn on Castle Street in Saffron Walden, by the end of 1821 there were licensed preaching rooms in several villages, including Newport.[155] In 1827 a meeting house or chapel in the parish of Newport was certified by Thomas Ludham, Minister, as intended to be used for public worship by Wesleyan Methodists.[156] Two years later there was a Wesleyan Methodist congregation in Newport of 150–200 persons.[157] There is no record of the location or nature of this Wesleyan meeting house, but in 1830 Revd Monk noted that Wesleyans met 'at a barn in the parish regularly'. He identified 40 parishioners from 21 households as attending these meetings, but their attachment does not seem to have been exclusive as 29 also attended the Independent church and three the Church of England.[158] The Wesleyans were equally divided between men and women, and were predominantly labourers and their families, although they also included two families in service with the St Aubyn family at Shortgrove. They were of slightly lower social status than the Congregationalists, although, there was some considerable overlap. The appeal of Methodism was broadly similar to that of the independent churches – a challenge to the paternalism and hierarchy of the Church of England, the opportunity for lay participation in both addresses and singing and a greater number of roles for women. It tended to profit from 'the erosion of old structures and the weaknesses of established denominations', conditions which arguably applied to the Anglican parish of Newport.[159]

In 1839 a circuit of the breakaway evangelical and revivalist Primitive Methodist Connexion was established in the district by a mission from the meeting of Upwell (Norfolk). Primitive worship was distinguished by large-scale open-air prayer, or camp, meetings and the use of travelling preachers. Membership grew rapidly during the

152 J. Brooks, 'Newport Free Church', *NN*, 11 (1979), 74–9; L. Rapkin, 'Newport United Reformed Church', *NN*, 26 (1981), 45; below, p. 158.
153 Cooper, *Well-Ordered Town*, 225; ERO, T/A 778/19.
154 E. P. Thompson, *The Making of the English Working Class* (2nd edn, London,1968), 920.
155 J. Holland-Brown, *Memoir of Charlotte Sophia Steigen Berger of Saffron Walden* (London, 1879), 51–2
156 ERO, Q/SBb 489/9.
157 Ibid., Q/CR 3/2/78.
158 Ibid., T/B 58/1/1.
159 D. Hempton, *The Religion of the People. Methodism and Popular Religion, 1750–1900* (London, 1996), 2, 7, 10.

1840s and the movement was especially strong among poorer sections of society.[160] In 1841 there were 11 members in Newport, rising in 1850 to 19 and a further two on trial.[161] By 1849 they were meeting in a cottage with a capacity of 80 and certified as a dissenters' meeting house by the bishop of Rochester in 1850.[162] This was possibly Distaff Cottage, Belmont Hill, the home of Charles Norman, tailor, a leading member of the congregation, serving as Lecturer by 1852, Secretary by 1853 and President in 1860.[163] The Primitive Connexion seems to have displaced the Wesleyans; in 1851 there was only a Primitive Methodist congregation in Newport, of 25 in the morning, 50 in the afternoon and 64 in the evening.[164]

However, in the 1850s and 1860s membership numbers began to wane in both the district (from a peak of over 800 to 450–500 by 1853) and Newport. By 1855 Newport had disappeared from the list of places recorded in the Circuit Minutes,[165] though at least some of the Newport members, including Charles Norman, continued their membership at Clavering, which had a chapel from 1844. On 16 June 1862 these Newport members were split by a bitter dispute when at a Quarterly Circuit Meeting held in Saffron Walden Norman presented charges made against George Barker by 'certain females of Newport'. The meeting eventually found that the charges were 'a vile fabrication' by 'very wicked women'. Barker and Norman were effectively separated – Barker being appointed assistant leader at Clavering and Norman allowed to meet in class at Littlebury or Stansted. Norman, however, continued to agitate by going from house to house in Stansted with the women's accusations. He and William Bird of Newport submitted letters of resignation which were discussed at an adjourned Quarterly Meeting in Linton on 25 June when both men were separated from the Connexion.[166]

There were sporadic efforts to re-establish Newport within the Primitive 'Plan' in 1869, when Bird seems to have been reconciled, and again in the 1880s. There were two Sabbath preaching services from 1882 and summer camp meetings in 1884 and 1885. J. Searle was appointed 'exhorter' in 1884 and the Congregational minutes for 1888 record some defections to the Primitive Methodists, but Methodism never became a significant force in the parish probably due to the lack of a chapel building (although the minutes for 1885 refer to a tenanted 'Newport Cottage property') and the presence of a large and active Congregational church.[167] In the 1880s enthusiasm for revivalist religion was also met by the Salvation Army.

The Salvation Army

The Salvation Army, founded in 1865 by former Methodist minister William Booth, sent a 'victory cavalry fort or caravan' to Newport in the summer of 1886.[168] The Army

160 J. Cooper, 'A fine field for usefulness: Primitive Methodism in the Saffron Walden Circuit, 1839–1900', *Family and Community History,* 5:1 (2002), 45–57.
161 ERO, D/NM 3/2/1.
162 TNA, HO 129/8/210.
163 J. Cooper, 'Methodism in Newport', *NN,* 43 (1995), 18; ERO, D/NM 3/3/1, 3/3/9, 3/5/1.
164 TNA, HO 129/8/210.
165 ERO, D/NM 3/2/1, 3/3/1, 3/3/9, 3/5/1.
166 Ibid., D/NM 3/1/1.
167 Ibid., D/NM 3/1/1, 3/1/2; D/NC 69/1/3.
168 *The War Cry,* 5 June 1886; *ODNB* 6, 635–7.

was apparently already active in the parish and appears to have proved immediately attractive, particularly to a section of the labouring population at a time of agricultural depression. It may also have drawn support from the other Nonconformist groups in the parish. In September 1885 the minutes of the Primitive Methodists recorded that 'Bro. Searle be seen respecting his position among us, & that his name come off the plan if he has joined the Army'.[169] At his retirement in 1888, Revd Hutchin of the Congregationalists noted that other members of his church had also 'self-excluded' by joining the Army.[170]

The Army's presence, made more permanent by the opening in spring 1887 of a Temple in Newport (sometimes also referred to as a barracks), was viewed with outright hostility by some inhabitants.[171] On 9 October 1886 the Saffron Walden County Petty Sessions heard that during an Army procession on 30 September, Cecil Rand, labourer, had assaulted Mary Ann Hanchet, a Salvationist, with a pail, pushing her in the chest, and abusing her 'shamefully'. Rand was a member of Newport's 'Skeleton Army', which followed the Salvationists, taunting them and attempting to break up their parades. From 1881 *ad hoc* Skeleton Armies were organised throughout England to oppose Army marches, sometimes at the instigation of publicans who objected to the Army's message on alcohol. Newport appears to have been the exception in this part of Essex, however, as there were no press reports of similar incidents elsewhere.[172] On this occasion, according to Salvationist witness Caroline Law, wife of a Newport pensioner, 'they were all round them, and pushing the Salvation Army about'. It seems that Rand had been using the pail as an improvised drum to provide rough music. Letters, on both sides of the argument, were sent to the *Hertfordshire and Essex Observer*, which reported the case, but did not publish the correspondence. The case was dismissed on payment of half the expenses.[173] A further scene which also indicates why the Army's methods were sometimes unpopular, was reported the following month when the Army, 'with drum and band' and again pursued by the Skeletons, was passing the offices of a tradesman, who ordered them to stop as 'he would have none of it'. The Salvationists, to the great amusement of the wider audience, gathered round him and asked 'Brother, are you saved?' and concluded with prayers.[174]

Opposition to the Salvation Army also came from the 'parish establishment'. In May 1890, chimney sweep Joseph Searle (possibly the same J. Searle who had left the Methodists in 1885), sent a suspiciously well-crafted letter to the *Hertfordshire and Essex Observer* in which he suggested that Gace's charity had passed him over while distributing funds to less deserving cases (he had been born in the parish in 1829, always paid his parish dues and reared a large family) as 'the Committee do not like me because I am a Salvationist'. The following week a letter along the same lines from 'An Inhabitant' was not printed on grounds of lack of space.[175] In 1891 a more dramatic storm blew up. The vicar, Revd Tamplin, apparently remonstrated with parents of those

169 ERO, D/NM 3/1/2.
170 Ibid., D/NC 69/1/3.
171 *Herts and Essex Observer*, 28 Feb. 1891, 8; the exact location is unknown.
172 http://www.salvationarmy.org/uk/uki/Heritage Archives (accessed 16 Nov. 2013).
173 *Herts and Essex Observer*, 16 Oct. 1886, 2.
174 Ibid., 6 Nov. 1886, 3.
175 Ibid., 3 May 1890, 5; 10 May 1890, 8.

Sunday school children who once the school had finished, moved on to attend the Salvation Army meeting, threatening to strike them off the roll. However, on 7 March a free tea to celebrate the fourth anniversary of the Army's Temple, proved irresistible. Some 105 children, 59 of whom were from the Sunday school, dressed in their Sunday best and clutching their own mugs were lured by a cart and drum passing around the village and the prospect of plum cake. Tamplin '*wuz* angry like' and at Sunday school asked those who had attended to stand up and then promptly expelled them. He was dragged through the mud in several newspapers as 'An Unchristian vicar'. Tamplin alleged that many in the parish were on his side against proselytizing by the Army, that there had been no permanent exclusions from Sunday school, and that numbers had in any case been exaggerated. Some damage had been done though. An editorial in the paper criticised him for making 'a grave mistake', though understandable under trying circumstances, for which he should have apologised, and a letter from an Anglican churchman of Newport, 'Tolerant', protested at the 'consummate intolerable want of tact in dealing with other religious bodies'.[176]

Despite, or perhaps because of, this opposition, the Army remained in the village and seems to have prospered. Sergeant Major A. Nixon reported in April 1890 that 'On Sunday we had blessed times. Three surrendered to God'. The 1891 census recorded two Army officers, Frederick W. Carpenter and his assistant Charles Whiteham living in Station Road, which may therefore have been the location of the Temple. In 1900 the Corps was 'still alive, and had three souls here, all good cases, last Sunday'.[177] The 1901 census recorded Laurence Rubic as the Army officer at Station Road. The Corps was originally part of the London and East Essex division, but in 1895 when the British Territory was divided into provinces, it came under the Cambridge Division of the Eastern Province. By 1905 it formed a 'Circle Corps' with Clavering, with officers based in Newport holding meetings in surrounding villages.[178] Named officers appointed in November 1905 were a Mr Parr as Commanding Officer and Mr Fearn, Lieutenant.[179] No subsequent evidence, however, has been found for the Salvation Army presence or activity in the parish.

The Religious Society of Friends (Quakers)

The Society of Friends never had a significant presence in Newport. There was no meeting house and they were represented by only one or two families at any given time. From the mid 17th century meetings were held in private houses in Wenden and Saffron Walden. In June 1669 Matthew Day, a grocer of Newport, was taken from the house of John Churchman at Wenden, together with Anthony Penniston and Churchman himself, and fined the large sum of £23 5s. probably for non-payment of tithes.[180] Later, Day was involved in the establishment of a meeting house in Saffron Walden, selling a weaver's cottage on the High Street (the site of the current Meeting House) to the Friends for

---

176 Ibid., 21 March 1891; R. Sandall, A.R. Wiggins and F.L. Coutts, *The History of the Salvation Army* (London, 1947), IV, 380.

177 *The War Cry*, 26 April 1890, 27 Jan. 1900.

178 Information from Steven Spencer, Assistant Archivist, The Salvation Army Heritage Centre, London SE5 8BQ.

179 *The Field Officer*, Dec. 1905, 479.

180 *A Collection of the Sufferings of the People called Quakers* (London, 1753), I, 203.

£20. A large back room which had housed the loom became the first meeting room and was licensed in 1693.[181] Day was a member of the Thaxted meeting, although he was buried in the Saffron Walden burial ground (behind the Meeting House) in May 1701.[182] Other Newport families who were members of Friends' meetings at this period were the Bashams/Bassams/Bassums and Bennits or Bennetts. The Friends' registers have entries for the marriage of Frances Bassum, spinster of Newport Pond to George Gilbey of Widdington in March 1683 and the burials in Saffron Walden of Sarah, daughter of William and Sarah Bennit in December 1685 and her widowed mother, also Sarah, in June 1707. During the 1680s Matthew Day, Samuel Basham and George Gilbey were all repeatedly presented at the county Assizes at Chelmsford for non-attendance at the parish church.[183] In 1699 the parish register records the baptism of William Munsey 'a poor man…when he was above 20 years old, being formerly a Quaker'. William Muncey of Newport Pond, buried in the Friends' ground at Saffron Walden in 1690, was probably his father.[184]

In the 1715 parliamentary by-election for an Essex county member, John Wyatt of Newport affirmed rather than take the oath, usually an indication that the voter was a Friend. The burial of an infant surnamed Wyatt is recorded in the Friends' register for 1718 and in 1740 the Friends' minutes recorded that Hannah Wyatt of Newport, daughter of Rebecca, had breached meeting discipline, by an 'Irregular proceeding… in going to the Priest for a Husband'.[185] In 1770 Revd John Rix stated that there was 'one family only of Quakers', and in 1778 that there was one Quaker. He was presumably referring to the Nottage family. James Nottage, a surgeon, had transferred to the Thaxted meeting from Baldock and Royston in 1740.[186] He and his wife Elizabeth were both active in the meeting. They were appointed by standing order as receivers of applications 'of those who may want Servants or of Servants who may want Places'. James became a trustee of the Stansted meeting house and burial ground in 1752 and both regularly attended the respective men's and women's monthly meetings which, in addition to promoting religious self-examination, were responsible for discipline, arranged charitable collections and disbursements, liaised with Friends elsewhere in Britain in person and by letter and corresponded with Friends in America. James was buried in the Saffron Walden burial ground in May 1773 and Elizabeth in May 1789.[187]

Revd Monk's religious census of 1830 listed one 'Quakeress', Mary Wilson aged 75, wife of Thomas Wilson, for whom no religious affiliation was given. Thomas in fact had died in June 1830 and was buried at the Friends' ground in Saffron Walden, the Friends' register noting that he was 'N.M.' (non-member). After the Wilson family, no further references to Newport Quakers have come to light.

181 J.M. Whittington, *The Early History of the Thaxted Meeting* (York, 1995), 2.
182 Saffron Walden Meeting House: transcript of registers, now ERO, A13685.
183 ERO, T/A 418/191/52 194/33, 34, 196–7.
184 Ibid., A13685.
185 ERO, LIB/POL 1/3; Whittington, *Early History*, 77.
186 ERO, A13685; LPL, FP Terrick 15, ff. 69–72, Lowth 5, ff. 434–7.
187 ERO, A13685.

POST-WAR DEVELOPMENT

The Town and Country Planning Act 1947 ended the right of a landowner to develop his land at will, and required planning permission for all land development to be obtained from the local authority.[1] In the case of Newport this was the Saffron Walden Rural District Council until 1974, and then Uttlesford District Council. The Act also required local authorities to draw up policies and proposals for land development within their districts. The Essex county development plan, 1957,[2] envisaged that development in Newport would be allowed only if it was of a character and on a scale that suited the locality. The plan was reviewed in 1964, and again residential development was to be limited to what was consistent with the planned growth in population within the Rural District – about 5,000 from 1961 to 1981.[3] Between 1951 and 1971 the population of the village grew, well within the range of the plan, from 1,090 to 1,262.[4] This increase was accommodated in part by social housing, particularly along Frambury Lane adjacent to the pre-war council houses, and partly by small-scale development and in-filling, for example on London Road.[5] Both the parish council and the rural district council objected to proposals for house building outside the area designated for development, such as along the western end of Wicken Road, saying that it would not like to see ribbon development along a narrow village road.[6]

In 1969, however, the rural district council designated Newport as a 'Category A' village, which meant that residential development, including some estate development, would be permitted provided that it was suitable in character, siting, materials and design. In 1970 the county council produced a village study intended initially to be a consultation document. This study defined the village development limits for the first time. On the east side of the village the limit was determined by the river, railway, and rising ground while at the north and the south ends of the village development was to be restricted to the fringes of the A11 (London Road, High Street, Belmont Hill and Cambridge Road). The striking feature of the proposed limits, however, was that although development was to be permitted along Frambury Lane and to the south of Wicken Road, an area in the centre of this site lay outside the designated area. Within a few years this was proved contentious.[7]

1   10 & 11 Geo, VI c.51.
2   NPC, Planning Files, 1975 development.
3   Ibid.
4   http://www.visionofbritain.org.uk; above, p. 5.
5   NPC, Minute Book 1961–71, *passim*.
6   Ibid., 25 May 1965.
7   NLHG Collections, ECC, Newport Village Study 1970.

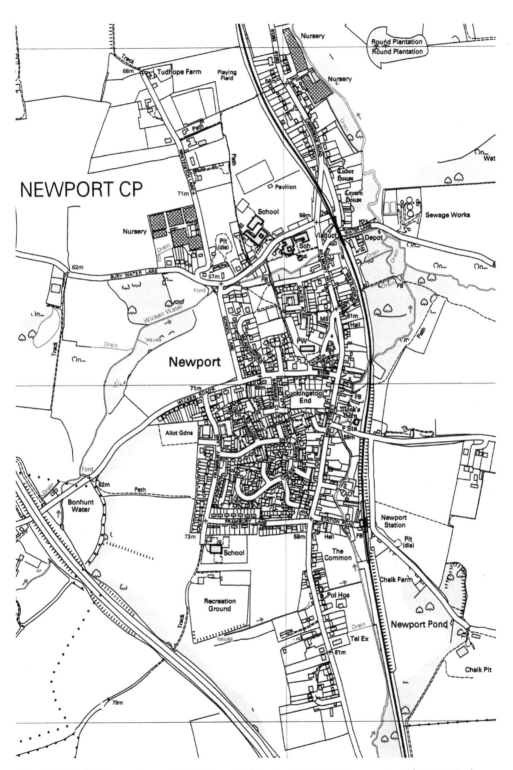

Map 5: *Part of Ordnance Survey 1:10 000 map of Newport, 2005. © Crown copyright 2005. Ordnance Survey Licence No. 100056080.*

The 1970 study was revised in 1972 as the Village Policy Plan.[8] By then development of part of Barnard Close was complete, and planning permission had been granted for a very extensive residential development by Federated Design and Building Group consisting of 121 houses, of which 46 were to be semi-detached and 75 terraced houses. The spine for the development was a new road running east from Frambury Lane, named Cherry Garden Lane,[9] and there was to be a hard surface footpath running north to south through the development. The name Cherry Garden Lane was suggested by the Primary school children,[10] but it preserved the memory of a cherry garden which at one time had occupied part of the site. In layout and design this estate conformed to the principles that were gathered together and published in 1973 as the *Essex Design Guide*, and part of the development was illustrated in the Guide.[11] Some of the houses fronted Cherry Garden Lane itself, but others were grouped round small greens linked by footpaths with vehicular access only at the rear of the houses, and the intention was to give a 'villagey' feel to the development.

Two other sites were designated for housing development in the 1972 plan, Gace's Acre and land close to the corner of Wicken Road and School Lane.[12] In the 1920s two pairs of cottages known formally as Croft Cottages, but informally as 'Dutch houses' (because they were built with stepped gables in the Dutch style) had been built on Gace's Acre, and after the war some prefabs were built there. During the 1960s, however, Jack Reynolds, a resident of Newport and a member of the Saffron Walden Rural District Council, suggested that sheltered accommodation, mainly for elderly people in the village, should be built on the site. In 1962 much of the land came on the market, and the council bought it; in 1969 the council bought two other small plots adjacent to the main plot, and almost with its dying breath in March 1974, it agreed to build sheltered accommodation on the site. There were 30 flats for the elderly, ten bungalows and ten three-bedroom houses. The flats were built in a block called Reynold's Court, after the man who had worked so hard to bring the scheme to fruition.[13] At the corner of Wicken Road and School Lane the council granted permission in 1971 for 13 houses with garages later developed as Meadowford.[14] After the new primary school in Frambury Lane was opened in 1974 the head teacher's house on the old site became a private residence, but the conversion of the school itself into three cottages was delayed until about 1986 because the original conveyance had specified that if the building ceased to be a school the land should revert to the Smith family of Shortgrove.[15]

The 1972 plan also designated two other substantial areas in the village which might be developed. One was the area bounded by School Lane to the west and Bury Water Lane to the north. This was developed as Tenterfields *c.*1986. The other was the land which lay outside the village development area under the 1970 proposals, even though it was surrounded by land which had been or was being developed for housing: the

8   Ibid., Newport Village Policy Plan 1972.
9   SWRDC, Minute Book, 5 Feb. 1970; above, pp. 33–4.
10   NCPS, Head Teacher's Log Book 1965–83.
11   ECC, *A Design Guide for Residential Areas* (Chelmsford 1973).
12   Village Policy Plan 1972, drawing no. 3.
13   SWRDC, Minutes 25 March 1969 and thereafter; H.J. Reynolds, 'Gace's Acre', *NN*, 4 (1975), 17–20.
14   SWRDC, Minute Book, 11 Nov. 1971.
15   Above, pp. 98–9.

1971–3 estate along Cherry Garden Lane, and the pre- and post-war social housing along Frambury Lane. The development of this land, amounting to 10.7 a., was to prove contentious.

Under the 1972 plan this area was not due for development until after 1981, so as to allow for the measured integration of newcomers into the village.[16] Even so, in 1974 Fairview Homes applied for planning permission to erect 141 houses on this site, which extended to the High Street frontage.[17] Public policy in the early 1970s favoured the rapid release of substantial amounts of land for residential development, especially in south-east England,[18] and the developers planned affordable housing, which could be built quickly.[19] The parish council objected to the proposal, partly on the grounds that the development would be premature and too fast. It was not widely supported in the village and planning permission was refused.[20] The developers reduced the number of houses to 131, abandoned plans to develop the High Street frontage, and successfully appealed. The development went ahead between 1975 and 1979.[21] It is a dense development, without some of the features suggested in the *Essex Design Guide*; but the provision of a substantial quantity of affordable housing enabled the village to retain a balanced population of generations and incomes, and thus a steady demand for facilities such as schools and medical services.

The development of these large estates increased the population by over 50 per cent between 1971 and 1981: from 1,262 to 1,994.[22] Over the next 20 years, however, population growth slowed markedly, reaching 2,208 in 2001 and 2,352 in 2011.[23] A number of smaller-scale housing developments went ahead in the late 1970s and onwards, some on former farmyards in the centre of the village.[24] When the Quendon estate sold Pallett's Farm in 1976, for example, the new owner of the freehold proposed a small development of shops in the farmyard. This was turned down, but the adjacent barn fronting the High Street was eventually developed as business premises.[25] Between 1984 and 1986 the farmyard of Pond Cross Farm was also developed, but this time the farmyard barns were converted into dwelling houses, alongside a group of newly-built houses.[26] In 1987 14 houses were built on the site of Parsonage Farm. This development was named Gilbey Green, after Ted Gilbey who had looked after the clock in the church tower for over half a century.[27] The houses were larger than those on the Cherry Garden Lane estate: most of them had four or five bedrooms, and all of them had double garages.

Other commercial and industrial premises in the village closed in these years and were developed for housing. Ginger's Timber Yard, which had been a major presence

16   Village Policy Plan, 1972: paragraph 1.3 and drawing no. 3.
17   ERO, D/J 52/2/2; NPC, Minutes 1974–6; Planning Files, 1975.
18   Department of the Environment, Circulars 102/72, 122/73.
19   NPC, Planning Files, 1975 development.
20   ERO, D/J 52/2/2; NPC, Minute Book, 2 Feb. 1976.
21   ERO, D/J 52/2/2; NPC, Planning Files 1975, Minute Book, 2 Feb. 1976.
22   Census returns 1971, 1981.
23   Ibid., 1981–2011.
24   Above, p. 71.
25   ERO, D/J 52/2/2, SALE/B7877; NPC Minute Book, 26 Jul. 1977
26   P. Davies, 'Living in a Barn', NN, 26 (1986), 83.
27   'The End of Parsonage Farm', ibid., 28 (1987), 91.

behind the houses on the west side of the High Street and an important source of employment from the 1920s onwards, closed in the 1960s, and in the 1970s Bullfields and part of the Cherry Garden Lane estate were built on its site.[28] In the late 1980s a group of houses called St Leonard's Close, after the medieval hospital, was built on part of the Carnation Nurseries site, where the parish and district councils had opposed development for some years; and after the county council depot on Bury Water Lane closed in the early 21st century a small housing development replaced it.[29] From the late 1970s, therefore, instead of large-scale estate development new housing in the village generally consisted of small closes, usually cul-de-sacs leading off the main roads, such as Chestnut Court on the west side of the High Street.

One site which was particularly sensitive was the land either side of the Congregational church on the west side of the High Street, which lay within the Newport Conservation Area designated in 1968. The church had fallen into such disrepair that its demolition had been proposed as early as 1971, but in 1975 the district council refused planning permission for a new church on the site.[30] The church was demolished in 1978,[31] but before then Fairview Homes had bought most of the site and planned to build houses on it. They were refused planning permission, however, on the grounds that the designs did not conform to the village plan, and that the proposed density was too great. Fairview then sold the land, and it was eventually developed as low-density housing, which the local authority believed was in keeping with the character of the High Street.[32]

In 1979 the parish council reflected on the developments over the past ten years.[33] The effect, they thought, had been to produce an imbalance of smaller starter homes, and this had led to a rapid turnover in the population as growing families left the village in search of larger houses. Such houses should therefore be included in any further development, as indeed they were at Meadowford and Gilbey Green. The council also thought that no further development on the scale of the 1970s should be contemplated at least until 1991, and none after that unless population growth justified it.

Accordingly, the 1991 Village Development Plan envisaged no further development within the village 'envelope', but subsequent public policy favoured substantial residential development in north-west Essex.[34] The rapid increase in house prices in the region, and changes in the structure of the family, renewed demand for low cost or 'affordable' housing, particularly for local people who might otherwise be priced out of the market. In 1989 the chairman of the parish council told the annual parish assembly that 'we urgently need low cost building for local people', and in 1991 the parish council proposed that some affordable housing should be built specifically for local people.[35] This was discussed from time to time over the next 12 years, and in 2003 the Inchcape Family

28   J. Bines, 'Ginger's Timber Yard', ibid., 77 (2012), 28–9.
29   ERO, D/J 52/2/1; NPC, Minute Book, 12 Nov. 1973.
30   ERO, D/J 52/2/1, 52/2/2; NPC, Parish Assembly Minute Book, 22 Mar. 1971, 13 Sept. 1976; Parish Council Minute Book, 11 Mar. 1975.
31   Above, p. 148.
32   ERO, D/J 52/2/2; NPC, Minute Book, 1974–7.
33   ERO, D/J 52/2/2; NPC, Minute Book, 26 Feb. 1979.
34   Uttlesford District Council, 1991 Development Plan.
35   ERO, D/J 52/1/1; NPC, Parish Assembly Minutes, 25 Apr. 1989.

Trust, which owned part of the Quendon Hall estate, made a piece of land on the east side of London Road available for development by the Rural Housing Trust. The development was named Bowker Close, after Bill Bowker, a district and parish councillor and a strong supporter of the scheme who had recently died. To some extent it met the need for affordable housing: some of the houses were intended for shared ownership purchase; others were for rent; and there were seven small flats.[36] The pressure for larger-scale residential development remained strong, however, and in 2011 the district council, as part of its dispersed housing plan for the district, proposed the construction of a minimum of 370 new houses to be sited mainly at the north end of the village on land bounded by Whiteditch Lane, Bury Water Lane and the railway.[37]

In the late 1970s the parish council was also concerned that the increase in the housing stock had not been accompanied by a commensurate increase in the availability of employment in the village.[38] The developments of these years had served to enhance still further the village's character as a dormitory or commuting village, with most adults being employed outside the village. A survey of the residents of Newport in 2010 showed that only 28.3 per cent of those who replied were employed in the village. Some 31.5 per cent travelled over 30 miles to work (London is 40 miles by train from Newport), and of the 18 per cent who travelled to work by train many were no doubt London commuters. Two respondents, however, said that they travelled to work by aeroplane, probably from Stansted Airport. A similar pattern is discernible in the 2011 census.[39]

As early as the 1960s the parish council had said that it was not opposed to the development of some light industry in the village. One site proposed in 1963 for such development was off Debden Road, but nothing came of it, perhaps because access was difficult.[40] Other areas that were considered for small-scale industrial development were Station Road and the site of the district council depot at Bridge End.[41] Nothing came of either proposal. In the later 20th century a number of small businesses were established in the village. After the closure of the maltings in Station Road, for example, the premises were converted into industrial units. The conversion took place in two stages, in 1982 and 1989, and there were eventually 23 units and three office suites in the building.[42] In 2010 planning permission was granted to convert part of the premises into residential accommodation, with the attraction that they were next to the railway station, and some of the former business tenants had to move elsewhere.[43]

Retail development was not commensurate with population growth in the village; indeed the number of shops declined in the later 20th century when the population – and car ownership – were increasing rapidly. The 2010 survey showed that 93.1 per cent of those who replied shopped for food outside Newport, almost invariably by car, though 45.4 per cent said that they also used the Village Stores.[44] Compared with other villages

36   J. Rose, 'Bringing a Little More to Newport', *NN*, 68 (2007), 14–15.
37   *NN*, 77 (2012), 5; 78 (2012), 4.
38   ERO, D/J 52/2/2; NPC, Minute Book, 19 May 1977.
39   Newport Village Survey, 2010; www.neighbourhood.statistics.gov.uk.
40   NPC, Minute Book, 22 Apr. 1963.
41   SWRDC, Minute Book, 26 Feb. 1971.
42   *VIT*, 170.
43   Pers. obs.
44   Newport Village Survey, 2010.

Figure 58 *The procession of the Olympic Torch through Newport in July 2012.*

in the district, however, Newport was well served for shops. By 2014 it still had a village store (incorporating the post office), a baker, hairdressers and beauty salon, a petrol station and a pharmacy, along with two car repair businesses and a cycle repair business. It also had an Indian restaurant, two pubs, and a garden centre. Although in the early 21st century Newport was perhaps less self-contained and self-sufficient than at any time in its history, the rapid growth in its population after 1970 had enabled it to remain a more balanced and varied community, with a wider range of services, than many rural communities in south-east England.

LIST OF ABBREVIATIONS

BL	British Library
Cal. Chart.	*Calendar of the Charter Rolls preserved in the Public Record Office* (HMSO, 1903–27)
Cal. Close	*Calendar of Close Rolls* (HMSO, 1892–1963)
Cal. Inq. p.m.	*Calendar of Inquisitions Post Mortem* (HMSO, 1904 onwards)
Cal. Pat.	*Calendar of Patent Rolls* (HMSO, 1906–86)
CBA	Council for British Archaeology
CCED	Clergy of the Church of England Database
Census returns	Census returns 1861–1911, TNA, RG 9/1120,10/1707, 11/1816, 12/1431,13/1733, 14/10471. Photocopies 1861–1901 in NLHG Collections
CERC	Church of England Records Centre
Close Rolls Henry III	Close Rolls, Henry III (HMSO, 1902–75)
CRO	Cambridgeshire Record Office
CRR	*Curia Regis Rolls* (HMSO, 1923–79)
DB	Domesday Book, Alecto edn, ed. A. Williams and G.H. Martin, (London, Penguin Classics, 2003)
EAH	*Essex Archaeology and History*
EAS	*Essex Archaeology and History* (formerly *The Transactions of the Essex Archaeological Society*)
ECC	Essex County Council
ERA	*Journal of the Eastern Region of the Royal Institute of British Architects*
ERO	Essex Record Office
Essex Wills	*Essex Wills*, abstracted by F.G. Emmison, 12 volumes (Chelmsford, 1982 onwards)
FFE	*Feet of Fines for Essex*, ed. F.G. Emmison, Marc Fitch and others, 6 vols (Colchester, 1899–1993)
GEC	*The Complete Peerage*, ed. GE. Cockayne, 2nd ed, revised by Vicary Gibbs, 13 volumes (London, 1910–59)
Hist. Parl.	*History of Parliament* (various editors), 10 vols, (London, for the History of Parliament Trust, 1964 onwards)
HRO	Hertfordshire Record Office

IPM	Inquisition *post mortem*
L&P	Letters and Papers of Henry VIII (HMSO, 1864–1932)
LMA	London Metropolitan Archives
LPL	Lambeth Palace Library
Meyer Letters	Rothschild Archive, London: copies of correspondence of Carl Meyer
MHLG	Ministry of Housing and Local Government
Ministers' Accounts	*Ministers' Accounts of the Earldom of Cornwall* 1296–1297, ed. Margaret Midgley (Camden 3rd series, LXVI), 2 volumes, 1942
MISM	Memorial Inscriptions, St Mary's Church, Newport, Essex, Recorded by Newport Local History Group (Newport, Essex, 1983)
Morant	Philip Morant, *History and Antiquities of the County of Essex,* 2 volumes (London, 1768)
NCPS	Newport County Primary School.
NLHG	Newport Local History Group
NMR	National Monuments Record (Swindon)
NN	*Newport News* (The Village Magazine)
NPC	Newport Parish Council
NRO	Northamptonshire Record Office
ODNB	*Oxford Dictionary of National Biography*, ed. H.C.G. Matthew and Brian Harrison, 61 volumes (Oxford, 2004)
OS	Ordnance Survey
Patent Rolls	Patent Rolls, Henry III (vols I & II, 1901–3)
PCC	Parochial Church Council
PHA	Petworth House Archives
Pipe R.	*Pipe Rolls* (London, for the Pipe Roll Society)
PROME	*Parliament Rolls of Medieval England*, ed. C. Given-Wilson, 16 volumes (Woodbridge and London, 2005)
RCHM(E)	Royal Commission on Historical Monuments (England)
Rot. Chart.	*Calendarium Rotulorum Chartarum* (London, Record Commission, 1803)
Rot. Litt. Claus.	*Rotuli Litterarum Clausarum*, ed. T.D. Hardy, 2 volumes (London, 1833 and 1844)
SPAB	The Society for the Protection of Ancient Buildings
SWRDC	Saffron Walden Rural District Couinl
SWTL	Saffron Walden Town Library
TNA	The National Archives
VCH	*Victoria County History*

Venn, *Alumni*	J. Venn, *Alumni Cantabrigienses*, 10 volumes (Cambridge, 1922–54)
VIT	B. Nurse, J. Pugh and I. Mollet, *A Village in Time: the History of Newport, Essex* (Newport, Essex, 1995)
WAM	Westminster Abbey Muniments
WSRO	West Sussex Record Office

NOTE ON SOURCES

This history of Newport is largely based on primary source material, both printed and manuscript, and it is the manuscript sources which are discussed here. The list is best used in conjunction with the footnotes to each section and the List of Abbreviations, where full references are given to printed primary and secondary sources.

The two principal archives used for this history are The National Archives and the Essex Record Office. Others are listed in alphabetical order.

The National Archives (TNA) at Kew (formerly The Public Record Office) is the main repository in England for the records of national government from the late 12th century onwards, with some earlier material. For the medieval and early modern periods, calendars (brief abstracts) of some administrative records have been published. Details are given in the footnotes and in the List of Abbreviations.

The classes of manuscript documents used in this history are:

ASSI 35/11/72: Records of Assize courts
BT 31: Board of Trade, files of dissolved companies
C 2: Court of Chancery proceedings
C 3, C 10: Court of Chancery pleadings
C 132: Inquisitions *post mortem*, Henry III
C 142: Inquisitions *post mortem*, 1485–1649
C 143: Inquisitions *ad quod damnum*
C 54: Chancery, Close Rolls.
C 211/5: Chancery, Commissions of Lunacy
CHAR 6/2/3: Records of the Charity Commission, Minute Books
CP 25/2: Court of Common Pleas, Feet of Fines
CP 43: Court of Common Pleas, Recovery Rolls
E 13: Exchequer, Plea Rolls
E 134/9: Exchequer, Rentals and Surveys
E 179: Exchequer, Lay Subsidy returns
E 210: Exchequer, Ancient Deeds
E 371: Exchequer, Court of Augmentations records
ED 2: Board of Education, parish files
ED 35: Board of Education, secondary school files
ED 103: Board of Education, building grant applications
EXT 6/143: Account of expenses of Richard de Anstey
HO 38/15: Home Office, Warrant Books
HO 45: Home Office, Registered papers
HO 129/8: Home Office, Ecclesiastical Census returns

IR 18: Tithe Commission, Tithe files
IR 29: Tithe Apportionment records
IR 30: Tithe maps
JUST 1/229: Rolls of Justices in Eyre, Essex Eyre Roll 1227
MAF 32: Ministry of Food, National Farm Survey, individual farm records
MAF 68: Ministry of Agriculture, parish summaries of agricultural returns
MH 12: Records of the Local Government Board
MT 120: Ministry of Transport, Highways: general planning files
PROB 11: Register of Wills in the Prerogative Court of Canterbury
RAIL 186: Eastern Counties Railway, minutes, reports, accounts
RAIL 541: Northern & Eastern Railway, minutes, plans, etc.
RAIL 981: Eastern Counties Railway, timetables
RAIL 1111: Railway Companies' reports and accounts
RAIL 1075: Railway Companies' prospectuses
SC 6: Special Collections, Ministers' and Receivers' accounts
SC 12: Special Collections, Rentals and Surveys

Essex Record Office (ERO): The Record Office holds records of the county administration, archidiaconal records, and records of the diocese of Chelmsford (but not bishops' registers and other material relating to the Diocese of London: see below). It also holds numerous parish records, private records, and transcripts of records held elsewhere, including many manorial court rolls and records of educational institutions.

The classes of documents used in this history are:

A9193: Records of Newport Free Grammar School, 1925–49
A10550: Reports etc. relating to the building of the M11 Motorway
A12122: Papers concerning Gace's Charity
A12376: Working papers for Victoria County History of Essex
A13685: Records of the Society of Friends, Thaxted monthly meeting
C/DB 3/4: Records of Essex Fire and Rescue Service
C/DO 10/3: Reports of School Medical Officers
C/12/61: Second World War Air Raid Precautions reports
D/ABA: Diocese of London, Archdeaconry records: commissary acts
D/ABR: Diocese of London, Archdeaconry records, register of Essex wills
D/ABW: Diocese of London, Archdeaconry records
D/B 2/OFF2/65: Annual reports of Medical Officer for Saffron Walden RDC
D/B 2PAR5: Records of Saffron Walden Borough Council
D/CT/252: Newport Tithe apportionment and map
D/CT/398: Widdington Tithe apportionment and map
D/CZ 28: Diocese of Chelmsford, Records of Charity for Relief of Poor Clergymen
D/DBI T46 and SALE: Sale catalogues relating to Shortgrove estate
D/DH: Miscellaneous Essex records
D/DK M113: Court Rolls of manor of Newport Pond
D/DKW O4: Records of the Turnour Family, poll list
D/DP M1164: Records of Petre estate, Clavering estates
D/DP 15/25/33: Newport Charity records, deeds relating to Gace's Charity
D/DU 775: Records relating to the Shortgrove estate, including conveyances

D/DU 205/19: Map of Shortgrove estate and manor of Newport Pond, 1786

D/DQ 14: Court rolls of Shortgrove manor

D/DYV and D/F 35/12/25: Records of the Cranmer-Byng family

D/DU 205: Rentals etc. of Essex and Suffolk manors

D/DU 1122: Architects' drawings of Shortgrove stables, 1975–6

D/F 8: Records of Messrs. Chancellor, architects, Chelmsford

D/J 52/2/2: Newport Parish Council, minute book 1974–81

D/NC: Congregational Church records

D/P 15/8/2: Newport parish registers (Transcript in NLHG Collections)

D/P 15/8/5: Newport parish book

D/P 15/25/55: Newport deeds

D/Q 25: Records of Newport Free Grammar School

E/MM/353/1: Newport Primary School, managers' reports

LIB/POL: Poll Books

Q/RDC/53: Newport Enclosure award and map

Q/RPL: Land Tax assessments

Q/RUA 28: Northern and Eastern Railway, accounts

Q/SBB, Q/SO, Q/SR: Quarter Sessions records

SALE/A1055: Particulars for sale of Shortgrove estate, 1894

SALE/B1493: Particulars for sale of Shortgrove estate, 1924

SALE/B1574: Particulars for sale of Shortgrove estate, 1889

T/A 168: Microfilms of court rolls

T/A 169/1: Microfilms of Hearth Tax returns

T/A 778: Microfilms of replies to visitation articles of the bishop of London

T/B 3: Transcript of Register Book of Tilty Abbey, which includes the 1299 extent of the manor of Newport

T/M 142/7: Microfilms of Newport manorial court records

T/M 298: 1727 Map of Newport and survey of estates of Henry O'Brien earl of Thomond

T/P 195/17/11: William Holman's Ms History of Essex, Uttlesford Hundred, *c*.1720.

British Library (BL)

Add. Mss. 33520–5: Monumental Records and Arms Collected from Churches and Mansions in Essex by C.K. Probert, 1846–87

Add. Ms. 39534: Abstracts of dispensation rolls in the Public Record Office, 1594–1634

Microfilm M2470: Microfilms of estate records of the Duchy of Cornwall

Cambridgeshire Record Office (CRO)

51R 51/29/2B: Court Book for manors of Priory, Hovells, etc. in Ickleton, Cambs, 1770–1850

296B190: Note of dilapidations at Shortgrove Hall, 1835

588/E111, 112: Sale catalogues of furniture, wine, and part of the library at Shortgrove, 1883, 1889

588/E115: Cutting from local paper about sale of library at Shortgrove, 1889

588/E117: Sale catalogue of paintings and other contents at Shortgrove, 1892

Hertfordshire Record Office (HRO): T/P 3: Records of the Hockerill (Essex & Herts) Turnpike Trust

Lambeth Palace Library and Church of England Record Centre (LPL & CERC): The Library and the Centre hold the central records of the Church of England. The Library also holds material relating to the diocese of London, including visitation records 1763–1900, and the Fulham Papers (FP), the official papers of many of the bishops of London. The following records have been consulted for this history:

FP, Registers of bishops Osbaldeston (1762–4), Terrick (1764–77), Lowth (1777–87), Porteous (1789–1809), Randolph (1809–13), Howley (1813–28), and Blomfield (1828–56)
Incorporated Church Building Society files
Liber Cleri, dispensation rolls
National Society Records, Newport file
QAB: Records of Queen Anne's Bounty

London Metropolitan Archives (LMA): Much material relating to the diocese of London which is not held at LPL is held by the London Metropolitan Archives. The records consulted for this history include:

Registers of bishops John Stokesley (1530–9), Edmund Bonner (1540–9) and   Edmund Grindal (1559–70)
Wills proved in the Consistory Court of the diocese.

Newport County Primary School (NCPS): The Head Teachers' Log Books are held at the school, and have been consulted by kind permission of the Head Teacher

Newport Local History Group (NLHG): The Local History Group holds a collection of documents, photographs and memorabilia relating to Newport. The collection was originally assembled by Terry Searle.

Newport Parish Council (NPC)
Some records relating to Newport Parish Council are in the Essex Record Office, but most are held at the Council's office in Newport, and the following have been used for this history:

Fire Brigade file
Highways Agency files
Parish Boundaries file
Parish Council Minute Books (Minute Book for 1974–81 is in ERO)
Parish Assembly Minute Books
Planning files

Northamptonshire Record Office (NRO)

E(GB)18: Copy of will of Henry O'Brien earl of Thomond, 1738
E(GB)22: Final settlement of estates of Henry O'Brien: deed of assignment

Saffron Walden Town Library (SWTL) holds some of the Minute Books of Saffron Walden Rural District Council (which included the parish of Newport); others are in the ERO.

Westminster Abbey (WAM): The Library and Muniment Room holds the records of the College of St Martin le Grand in London, whose possessions included the parish church of Newport. The records used for this history are:

962: Essex deeds of St Martin le Grand

13167: Cartulary roll of St Martin le Grand, 14th Century

13247: Deeds of the College of St Martin le Grand

Book 5: Cartulary of St Martin le Grand, late 15th century

Peculiar Court of Westminster, Wills, Wyks 5: now transferred to City of Westminster
    Archive Centre

West Sussex Record Office (WSRO): The Petworth House Archives (PHA) can be consulted at the Record Office, and the following documents have been used in this history:

PHA 1139, 10957: Papers relating to the administration of the estates of Henry O'Brien
    earl of Thomond

PHA 1605: Copy of will and codicil of Henry O'Brien earl of Thomond, 1738

PHA 6280: Inventory of contents of Shortgrove Hall, 1774

PHA 7428: Estimates and accounts for alterations at Shortgrove Park, mid 18th century

PHA 7874, 7875: Papers relating to the administration of the estates of Percy Wyndham
    O'Brien, earl of Thomond

PHA K 5/9: Correspondence about Shortgrove Estate, 18th century

PHA K 5/X16: Deed of transfer of Shortgrove Estate from earl of Egremont to Percy
    Charles Wyndham, 1782

Note on Websites

All the websites cited in the footnotes were accessed between 2011 and 2014.

INDEX

CPSIA information can be obtained
at www.ICGtesting.com
Printed in the USA
JSHW010029010421
13027JS00008B/47